The WTO and its Development Obligation

The WTO and its Development Obligation

Prospects for Global Trade

Elimma C. Ezeani

ANTHEM PRESS
LONDON · NEW YORK · DELHI

Anthem Press
An imprint of Wimbledon Publishing Company
www.anthempress.com

This edition first published in UK and USA 2011
by ANTHEM PRESS
75-76 Blackfriars Road, London SE1 8HA, UK
or PO Box 9779, London SW19 7ZG, UK
and
244 Madison Ave. #116, New York, NY 10016, USA

British Library Cataloguing-in-Publication Data
A catalogue record for this book is available from the British Library.

Library of Congress Cataloging-in-Publication Data
The Library of Congress has cataloged the hardcover edition as follows:
Ezeani, Elimma C.
The WTO and its development obligation : prospects for global trade /
Elimma C. Ezeani.
p. cm.
Includes bibliographical references and index.
ISBN-13: 978-1-84331-849-1 (hardcover : alk. paper)
ISBN-13: 978-0-85728-950-6 (ebook : alk. paper)
ISBN-10: 1-84331-849-0 (hbk)
1. World Trade Organization. 2. Developing countries–Commercial
policy. 3. International trade. I. Title.
HF1385.E943 2010
382'.92–dc22
2010011710

ISBN-13: 978 0 85728 406 8 (Pbk)
ISBN-10: 0 85728 406 1 (Pbk)

This title is also available as an eBook.

TABLE OF CONTENTS

Chapter Three: Developing Country Integration   55

PREFACE

My appreciation of the impact of trade liberalisation and the organisation of the global trading system under the World Trade Organisation was limited to a vague acknowledgement of the fact that things seemed to have changed dramatically in my country, Nigeria, in the early 1990s. Apart from the strained living conditions imposed by continuous military rule, there were no real connections made between the declining rates of product manufacture and food availability and the country's attempts to abide by the single undertaking requirements of the WTO. Knowledge of trade liberalisation, of the impact of the WTO Agreements on the domestic economic system was at best academic. Developing countries' criticism of the rules-based system was mainly directed to the perceived highhandedness of the more developed countries and not to what it should have been – on the capability of the system to sufficiently address the development needs and concerns of its Members. It was not until the Seattle protests that widespread criticism of the WTO began in the public and in the mass media.

Sitting amongst a group of well-read practicing barristers one day, the issue of the Seattle protests came up. As I listened intently, I tried to understand the reasons for the protests. But it was difficult. The difficulty was caused by the fact that even those who had a better understanding of the global market finally admitted that the work and relevance of the WTO was not easy to explain. There were too many issues to consider. What was most glaring, however, was that the Organisation's less-developed countries were not faring any better in the global trading system in spite of the promises of Membership of the rules-based system.

What promises? What benefits? What exactly was the WTO all about and why do developing countries seem to fare worse under a system that claims it exists for the good of every Member? What was the basis of organised global trade in the first place? Were there practical and honest attempts to address the constraints of market integration on developing countries? These and many other questions were examined, but even at the end of the informal discussion, we dispersed unconvinced of our own arguments for and against the WTO.

Years later, I was excited at the thought of finally being able to study in depth the rules-based system and the development considerations arising under the WTO which formed the background to this work. In light of the protracted deadlock of the Doha Round, the nagging question was this: why are developing countries part of the WTO? If it was a 'rich club' or an organisation solely for the developed countries – why is the idea of accession sold to developing countries? Furthermore, what special benefit is the WTO supposed to bring to countries considering that its original reasons for existence under the GATT had been more or less satisfied?

The answer to both questions is that the foundational objective of the WTO from the time of the GATT envisioned an efficient organisation of global cross-border trade (and economic endeavour) for the purposes of improving dismal economic and social conditions in the aftermath of the Second World War and the Great Depression. The recession of the modern era arising from the collapse of financial and banking structures across the globe in the last quarter of 2008 – even as the Doha Round of Trade Talks continues without a clear end in sight – again renews the urgent need for the world to respond to the socio-economic crisis threatened by this new period of recession. Working in the realm of global trade, WTO rules exist to help producers of goods and services, exporters and importers conduct their business, while allowing governments to meet imperative social and environmental objectives, of which development is paramount.

However, the focus of the WTO is no longer development, but has 'wrongly' become the promotion of the free trade theory as regulated by the respective WTO Agreements. This is the unseen problem, with the deadlock in the current Round that may well persist beyond the Round. This work therefore attempts to outline the predominant issues as they relate to the pursuit of development considerations under the WTO namely:

1. What is the WTO obligation to development?
2. What is the central aim and focus of an international organisation for global trade?
3. Do the economic theories which guide the WTO support this obligation to development in the modern world?
4. How has the issue of development been considered within the rules-based system? Do the rules sufficiently reflect this development objective?
5. How does the compulsory judicial mechanism at the DSB review development considerations? Is there room for such considerations at all?
6. What about the domestic responsibility of Members who are in greater need for consideration of their development status?

7. What is the appropriate response to developing country integration and to the need for the WTO to assume a stronger and more efficacious role in development?

The conclusion from my findings argues that being an organisation with the central aim of socio-economic development, the WTO must embrace a holistic concept of development. It must visibly adopt a development-driven approach to trade.

Why is it important for these issues to be addressed? While other organisations such as the IMF and the World Bank receive steady criticism and suggestions to improve their impact in the developing world, the WTO gets away with claiming that it is not a development organisation. While this allows the Organisation freedom from intense public scrutiny, the disregard for the basis of the free trade ideology is detrimental to any efforts the WTO makes in addressing the needs and concerns of its developing country Membership at present. It further limits whatever assistance the Organisation can make towards global development efforts in general. In addition, it does not address the reality that most of the peoples in its Majority membership (i.e. developing countries) are not making the gains they should from global trade – the gains of socio-economic advancement in their domestic environment. While their countries may belong to an international organisation, the persons who actually engage in trade do not enjoy the benefits.

Furthermore, the main problems of developing countries, which are a limited production capacity and an inability to access the wider global market, merit greater consideration than is currently given. While it is good to talk about enabling market access for developing countries, the core issue of seeing how to assist developing countries in their efforts at producing domestic and globally competitive goods for the international market must be taken into consideration.

Most of the research which is relevant to this area has been conducted on a singular basis – an examination of economic trends; a review of world trade statistics; a legal analysis of certain provisions; a review of dispute settlement decisions; and development reviews. This work goes a step further by consolidating the various angles of the problem into a broader perspective by reviewing the WTO, the rules, and the development question for a better understanding of the problems and possible solutions. It also questions the efficiency of the economic theory of comparative advantage; undertakes an assessment of the meaning of development; identifies the disparity in production capability across the WTO membership; and considers the development needs of developing countries and the slow economic progress of these countries who have access to the same rules as their developed country counterparts.

This review of the WTO as an organisation for development through trade can only be properly pursued by considering the intrinsic character of the WTO as a development body, the impact of development provisions on the rules, the potential of current development activity including the AFT and the DDA, the judicial review of the development question at the DSB, the study of developing country needs, and the importance of domestic efforts from both developed and developing countries themselves, in order to address the challenges faced by the latter. These are considerations which offer a broader dimension to the question of how membership of the WTO can assist in the alleviation of poverty, in raising standards of living, in increasing opportunities for the individual, in increasing employment and for general socio-economic advancement.

To satisfy the need for practical proposals as a way forward, this work organises the various perspectives considered in a way which integrates them and drives the work towards a logical, coherent and practicable conclusion. It is necessary and indeed essential that academic research should analyse, evaluate and synthesise available and relevant information in order to arrive at well reasoned and pragmatic solutions. I have tried to do this, maintaining the objectivity of legal analysis while incorporating the various issues which determine that the WTO must re-orient itself towards this development objective particularly for the benefit of the majority of its Membership and their citizens. My conclusion is thus: that the WTO *is* a development organisation and can make real contributions to the lives of the millions who engage in trade activity, hence the 'development through trade' obligation that this work projects.

LIST OF CASES

GATT / WTO Disputes

Argentina-Safeguard Measure on Imports of Footwear *WT/DS121/AB/R*

Argentina-Hides and Leather *WT/DS155/R*

Australian Ammonium Sulphate *GATT BISD Vol 11*

Australia-Measures Affecting Importation of Salmon *WT/DS18/AB/R*

Brazil-Measures Affecting Patent Protection *WT/DS199*

Brazil-Measures on Minimum Import Prices Complaint by US, *WT/DS197*

Brazil-Aircraft *WT/D46/AB/R*

Canada-Patent Protection of Pharmaceutical Products (Canada – Pharmaceutical Patents) *WT/DS114/R*

Canada-Aircraft *WT/DS70/AB/R*

EC-Approval and Marketing of Bio-Tech Products *WT/DS91*(US), *WT/DS92*(Canada), *WT/DS93*(Argentina)

EC-Imposition of Anti-Dumping Duties on Cotton Yarn from Brazil *ADP/137*

EC-Bed Linen *WT/DS141/R*

EC-Customs Classification of Certain Computer Equipment *WT/DS62/AB/R, WT/DS67/AB/R, WT/DS68/AB/R*

EC-Measures Affecting the Importation of Certain Poultry Products *WT/DS69/AB/R*

EC-Measures Affecting Meat and Meat Products (EC-Hormones) *WT/DS26/AB/R, WT/DS48/AB/R*

EC-Refunds on Exports of Sugar (GATT) BISD 26S/290

Permanent Court of Justice (PCIJ)

International Court of Justice

LIST OF STATUTES AND
INTERNATIONAL AGREEMENTS

International

Agreement Establishing the World Trade Organisation 1994

Africa Growth and Opportunity (AGOA) Act

EC Treaty

New Partnership for African Development (NEPAD) Framework Document

Paris Declaration of Aid Effectiveness 2 March 2005

North American Free Trade Agreement (NAFTA)

United Nations Charter 1945

Vienna Convention on the Law of Treaties 1961

Japan

Japanese Customs and Tariff Law-Kanzei Teiritsu Ho (Customs and Tariff Law)
Law No. 54, 1910 (as amended)

United States of America

Buy America Act 1988

Tariff Act 1930 (Title VII – as amended by the CDSOA adding a new
section 754)

Trade Act 1974 (Super 301)

Telecommunications Trade Law 1988

Trade and Development Act 2000

Federal Republic of Nigeria

Copyright Decree Nigeria Decree No. 48 1992

Copyright Decree Nigeria Decree No. 42 1999

Copyright Act Nigeria Vol. V Cap 68 LFN 1990

Customs, Excise, Tariff etc (Consolidation) Act Vol. VI Cap 88 LFN 1990

Export Prohibition Act Vol. VIII Cap 121 LFN 1990

Economic and Financial Crimes Commission Establishment (EFCC) Act 2004

Import Prohibition Act Vol. X Cap 171 LFN 1990

National Office of Industrial Property Act Vol. XVII Cap 268 LFN 1990

Nigeria Customs Duties (Dumped and Subsidised Goods) Act Vol. V Cap 87 LFN 1990

Nigerian Export Prohibitions List in the Customs, Excise Tariff etc. (Consolidation Decree No. 4 1995)

Nigerian Investment Promotion Commissions (NIPC) Decree No. 32 1998

Nigerian Investment Promotion Commissions (NIPC) (Amendment) Decree No.16 1995

Nigerian Public Enterprises (Privatisation and Commercialisation) Decree No. 28 1999

Nigeria Foreign Exchange (Monitoring and Miscellaneous) Provisions (FEMMP) Decree No.17 1995

Patents and Design Act Nigeria Vol. XIX Cap 344 LFN 1990

Pre-Shipment of Exports Decree No. 10 LFN 1996

Pre-Shipment of Imports Decree No. 11 LFN 1996

Trade Marks Act Nigeria Cap 436 LFN 1990

Trade (EEC Preferences Under the Lome Convention) Act Vol. XXIII Cap 434 LFN 1990

Trade (Generalised System of Preferences) Act Vol. XXIII Cap 435 LFN 1990

ABBREVIATIONS

AB: Appellate Body (WTO)

AGOA: Africa Growth and Opportunity Act

DC: Developing Country

DDA: Doha Development Agenda

DSB: Dispute Settlement Body (WTO)

DSU: Dispute Settlement Understanding

EC: European Community

ECOWAS: Economic Community of West African States

EU: European Union

FTA: Free Trade Area

GSP: Global System of Preferences

LDCs: Least Developed Countries

LFN: Laws of the Federal Republic of Nigeria

NAFTA: North American Free Trade Agreement

NEPAD: New Partnership on African Development

PTA: Preferential Tariff Arrangement [Agreement]

RTA: Regional Trade Agreement

SMEs: Small and Medium Scale Enterprises

WTO: World Trade Organisation

ACKNOWLEDGEMENTS

This work is based on research carried out during my doctoral programme at King's College London and I must first thank my family whose support ensured I stayed the course of my studies. To my parents, the Hon Justice A. O. N. Ezeani and His Worship Chief Magistrate Mrs D. C. Ezeani, my brothers and sisters, Rudi, Emeka, Chiamaka, Funnie and Chika, I owe the deepest gratitude for their love and encouragement, so also to my precious nephew Chikelundu. My extended family were also extremely supportive; in particular, I am grateful to my aunt, Chief Mrs May Akonobi who early on advised me that it was better to get the work done while I still could!

I thank my friends, many of whom took an active interest in my research, in particular, Dr Mohammed Akanbi, Barrister Rolake Omolodun and, Dr Jude Ezeanokwasa (Rev Fr); and my former colleagues at King's for their continued friendship and goodwill. My thanks also to the many professionals working in the trade and development field who gave freely of their time and thoughts during my research including: Prof Asif Qureshi (University of Manchester), Julian Morris (IPN); Elizabeth Guerk (UNCTAD), Franklin Cudjoe (Centre for Humane Education, Imani Ghana); Ximena Escobar Nogales (Centre for Applied Studies in Negotiations, CASIN, Switzerland); Francis Cheneval (University of Zurich) and Dr Paul Arnell, (RGU, Aberdeen). I am also indebted to the continued support of my Professor Piet Eeckhout, my erstwhile supervisor at King's. Finally I thank the team at Anthem Press for their interest in the publication of this work.

While there have been many whose ideas have helped to consolidate my arguments, any errors herein are entirely mine.

INTRODUCTION

1. Background

Since its creation out of the prior General Agreement on Tariffs and Trade (GATT) in 1995, the World Trade Organisation (WTO) has attracted the interests of many. Individuals, corporations, governments, policy makers, NGOs, and academics are drawn to study this international organisation which has in such a short time made significant impact on the lives of all people in our global community.

With over 20,000 pages of legal documents comprising WTO negotiated agreements over trade and other trade related issues and a plethora of decisions reached under the various dispute settlement cases brought before the Dispute Settlement Body of the Organisation, the legal framework of the WTO presents a formidable mass of scholarly material. Research into the activities of the organisation has been remarkable and varied. It has ranged from analyses of the general practicability of a rules-based approach to trade regulation, to recurrent arguments over the potential gains of participation in a rules-based system for less developed country members of the Organisation.

This latter scope of research activity has occupied the interests of scholars in both developing and developed countries. Most of the work done in this area has been preoccupied with identifying the importance of global market integration for developing countries. The literature has centred on particular aspects of developing country participation – agriculture and the need for greater access to developed country markets; the restrictions of the agreement on Intellectual Property which confront those countries which have not evolved a strong intellectual property framework prior to their accession to the WTO; the challenges of assuming further obligations on new proposals in trade negotiations without a sufficient capacity for entering into trade negotiations in the first place. This work in contrast, presents a holistic view: the view that what is important is to identify the nature and potential of the WTO as an organisation which can contribute to the socio-economic well-being of individuals and societies across the world as they engage in global economic endeavour.

The research here is at a more fundamental level, and offers concrete reviews of WTO action in line with the Organisation's development obligations. Much has been made of developing countries and the problems they confront with implementing the obligations in accordance with the 'single undertaking' requirement of accepting all the agreements under the WTO as binding. Yet in the course of judicial dispute settlement proceedings, the question as to how much influence a developing country's obligations under the WTO has on the latter's potential for economic advancement is still extant.

In the Doha Round of trade negotiations, the prevalent issues have revolved around development and the commitment of the WTO to this concept for the benefit of its developing country membership. A *quid pro quo* stance has been taken up by developing and developed countries on either side of the debate. The divide is on the one hand, on the concessions to be made in respect of tariffs applicable to imports of agricultural goods and on the other hand, on the level of liberalisation over Non Agricultural Market Access (NAMA) which developed countries insist developing countries have to concede. While this 'eyeballing' continues as it probably will even beyond the Doha Round, the crucial need to rationalise the question of development and how it fits into the WTO paradigm is overlooked to the detriment of the individuals and communities in developing countries.

The basic demand of the research is for the adoption of a holistic development perspective in the sphere of global trade. The approach involves focusing on the essential underpinnings of the primary goal of the international trading system, that of development. We consider this concept in depth: what it really means; how it is a character of the rules-based system, and the obligations of the WTO to this effect. We consider how international action can facilitate a sovereign nation to trade its way out of poverty and aid reliance, in essence, through development-oriented action at the WTO.

Presently, the greater majority of WTO membership is constituted of developing countries. This is not the only reason why this research ought to be of significance to the Organisation. The reality is that conditions of reduced socio-economic standards are not stagnant. They may not continue only in the poorer countries of today. Wars, famine, economic recessions, stock market failures and other natural and man-made disasters can draw a country backwards as the Great Depression of the 1930s and the Second World War have shown. The more recent global recession arising in late 2008, is even more reason to seek for ways to address the socio-economic fluctuations which many of the world's poorest peoples are not equipped to overcome. It is instructive that the first two events mentioned were in actual fact the motivations for the Allied Forces led by the United States and Britain post World War II, to embark on strategic reconstruction to boost their ailing economies in the aftermath of these events.

Socio-economic downturns are a constant threat to any country in the modern world. Economic growth and reconstruction towards development by the process of improved and well-modelled legal framework for cross border trade in goods and services is a real guarantee for countries in such need. But economic development and advances in trade activity can only be assured when the rules have factored in from the outset the importance of development and how this ought to be incorporated into the world trading system.

Our view is that the WTO has development obligations which are steadily being eroded by the emphasis on facilitating the open trade mechanism without a concurrent emphasis on the impact of the mechanism on the lives and social well being of individuals in developing countries. The objective of the WTO ought not to rest solely on facilitating the participation of the less developed countries of the world in global trade. It must keep in mind the obligation to facilitate the human and socio-economic progress of citizens across its Membership as this work points out.

2. Conclusion

The focus of the research is to stress the importance of maintaining a proper approach to the development question in the WTO. To continually assert that the WTO is not a development organisation and yet promise developing countries that they stand to gain by participating effectively in a development-oriented rules-based system impacts negatively on the credibility of the WTO. The Organisation cannot expect to move forward in its objective of bringing the global trading environment closer to both rich and poor alike without considering ways to improve the development-oriented nature of the Organisation. The WTO by adopting this attitude does not live up to its commitments to its majority participants: the developing countries.

It cannot be denied that trade offers the vast majority of peoples in poor and rich countries alike – an opportunity for self fulfilment, and a means of providing the basic living necessities for themselves and their families. The income from trade is also a source for communal provision of the social and welfare needs such as electricity, pipe borne water, education, social security, and increased opportunities for personal achievement, which are the hallmarks of every developed nation.

What this research does is to reiterate the original objective behind the adoption of a trade liberalisation strategy in the international trade environment. This objective was for a peculiar and much needed form of development: to ameliorate the financial burdens and adverse socio-economic conditions faced by countries during the Great Depression of the 1930s and in the aftermath of World War II. This is why the Preambles of the GATT and the WTO Agreement and also, of the various WTO Agreements pay heed to the goal of economic development in setting out the legal framework of the multilateral trading system.

Today, assessing the current developmental stages across the WTO membership, several questions remain. Can it be that the needs and concerns of the millions of peoples in developing countries have become overwhelming for the international community and in particular for the global market? Does the free trade theory still have the capacity to resolve the economic concerns of what to produce and to whom to sell, given the increased market area of the global economy? Has the implementation of the free trade mechanism facilitated or hindered the fundamental objective of the WTO which is to work for economic development of the peoples in its Member States? What is development and what hope does WTO action in this respect hold for the less developed Member States of the Organisation?

These questions remind us that the continued relevance of the WTO rests significantly on its ability to assist and sustain *the lives* behind its Membership towards a closely integrated global market economy. For the sake of the millions of people living in the developing countries of the world who are able and willing to engage in trade and other economic endeavour as a means of sustenance, development is a goal, the pursuit of which the WTO must not depart from as it continues its task of regulating the global trade liberalisation process.

Chapter One

THE WTO AND THE RULES-BASED SYSTEM

1.1. Understanding the WTO

The WTO is an umbrella organisation established after the Uruguay Round of multilateral trade negotiations. The *WTO Agreement* states that the Organisation is meant to provide the common institutional frame works for the implementation of those agreements.[1] The basic functions of the WTO are:

(a) to implement, administer, and carry out the WTO Agreement and its Annexes,[2]
(b) to act as a forum for ongoing multilateral trade negotiations,[3]
(c) to serve as a tribunal for resolving disputes,[4] and
(d) to review the trade policies and practices of member states.[5]

The package of agreements is annexed to the *WTO Agreement* and is binding on all members of the organisation as a single body of law.[6] Under Article II (2) of the WTO, the Multilateral Trade Agreements under Annex 1, 2, 3 are binding on all the members. Pursuant to Article II (3) however, Annex 4 on the Plurilateral Trade Agreements is binding only on members who have accepted it. These Agreements are geared towards the provision of a common institutional framework for the conduct of trade relations among Members of the WTO in matters related to the agreements and associated legal instruments included in the Annexes to the Agreement.[7]

The reference to the WTO as a 'rules-based' system is due to the sophisticated structure of international trade regulation based on various trade agreements and also, by the compulsory dispute settlement system which includes a judicial-style review mechanism.

The Agreements under the WTO are as follows:

1. The Final Act
2. Agreement Establishing the WTO
   Annex 1A: Agreement on Trade in Goods

    1. General Agreement on Tariffs and Trade (1994)
    2. Uruguay Round Protocol to the General Agreement on Tariffs and Trade
    3. Agreement on Agriculture
    4. Agreement on Sanitary and Phytosanitary measures
    5. Agreement on Textiles and Clothing
    6. Agreement on Technical Barriers to Trade
    7. Agreement on Trade-Related Investment Measures
    8. Agreement on Implementation of Article VI (on antidumping)
    9. Agreement on Implementation of Article VI (on customs valuation)
    10. Agreement on Preshipment Inspection
    11. Agreement on Rules of Origin
    12. Agreement on Import Licensing Procedures
    13. Agreement on Subsidies and Countervailing Measures
    14. Agreement on Safeguards

Annex 1B: General Agreement on Trade in Services
Annex 1C: Agreement on Trade-Related Aspects of Intellectual Property Rights
Annex 2: Understanding of Rules and Procedures Governing the Settlement of Disputes
Annex 3: Trade Policy Review Mechanism
Annex 4: Plurilateral Trade Agreements
    4(a): Agreement on Trade in Civil Aviation
    4(b): Agreement on Government Procurement
    4(c): International Dairy Agreement[8]
    4(d): International Bovine Meat Agreement[9]
3. Ministerial Decisions and Declarations

To enable it administer these Agreements the WTO has five main organs:

a. The Ministerial Conference.
b. A General Council which functions as the WTO Dispute Settlement Body and Trade Policy Review Body.
c. A Council on Trade in Goods.
d. A Council for Trade in Services.
e. A Council for Trade Related Aspects of Intellectual Property Rights.[10]

The Ministerial Conference and the General Council are made up of representatives from all the Member states.[11]

    The Ministerial Conference is the highest authority of the WTO. It may take decisions on all matters under any of the multilateral trade agreements. The Conference is required to meet every two years.[12] Five standing committees deal with trade and development; balance-of-payments restrictions; budget, finance and administration; trade and the environment; and regional agreements.[13]

The General Council handles the day to day functions of the Organisation in between Ministerial Conferences.[14] It names the members of the other main organs.[15] It also convenes "as appropriate", as the WTO Dispute Settlement Body and as the WTO Trade Policy Review Body.[16] Article IV (5) of the WTO Agreement provides that the three councils (Council for Trade in Goods, Council for Trade in Services, and the Council for Trade-Related Aspects of Intellectual Property Rights) working under the guidance of the General Council shall oversee the implementation and administration of the three main WTO Agreements.[17]

A Trade Negotiations Committee (TNC) was set up by the Doha Declaration at the WTO Ministerial Conference in Doha, Qatar. This Committee also operates under the authority of the General Council.[18] Under Article V (1; 2), the General Council is also responsible for 'co-operation' with other organisations (both inter-governmental organisations and non-governmental organisations in responsibilities and matters 'related to those of the WTO'.

The workings of the WTO are overseen by the WTO Secretariat.[19] This administrative office is located in Geneva and is headed by a Director General. Since decisions are taken only by WTO Members themselves, the Secretariat actually has no decision making powers. Its various divisions either come directly under the director-general or one of his deputies.[20] The main duties of the Secretariat are:

- to provide administrative support to the various councils and committees;
- to provide administrative support under the dispute settlement system;
- to provide technical assistance to developing countries;
- to monitor and analyse developments in world trade;
- to provide information to public and media; and
- to organise ministerial conferences.

1.2. Decision Making and Policy Review in the WTO

Article IX (1) of the *WTO Agreement* states that, 'the WTO shall continue the practice of decision-making by consensus followed under GATT 1947'. The explanatory note to this Article explains that 'the body concerned shall be deemed to have decided by consensus on a matter submitted for its consideration, if no Member, present at the meeting when the decision is taken, formally objects to the proposed decision'.[21] A consensus is also required for a decision to grant a waiver in respect of any obligation subject to a transition period or a period for staged implementation that the requesting Member has not performed by the end of the relevant period.[22]

Where a consensus cannot be reached, the WTO can make a decision by a vote.[23] At meetings of the Ministerial Conference and the General Council, each WTO member state has one vote with the European Union having a number of votes equal to (but not more than) the number of its member states that are members of the WTO. Where a vote is required, the decision will be made by simple majority unless it has been provided otherwise under the WTO Agreement or the other Multilateral Trade Agreements.[24] The significance of the vote and its influence on the decision making process can be accounted for under the increasing number of WTO Member States. Under GATT 1947, there were fewer countries and less controversial concessions to be made.[25] This was because the GATT 1947 had only 23 signatories. More than a hundred countries signed the Uruguay Round accords in Marrakesh in April 1994 (with others still adopting the observer status in the GATT).[26] Currently, the Organisation boasts of over a hundred and fifty Members[27] including Least-Developed Countries (LDCs) designated as such by the United Nations.[28]

It is important to bear in mind that the WTO Agreement is a single undertaking binding all its members with the exception of the plurilateral Agreements.[29] As such, countries must comply with the obligations under the Agreement. They cannot elect trade policies contrary to their obligations, an obligation drastically reducing the power of States to determine their economic policies. Thus, in addition to an expanding Membership, the increased interest of various diverse protest groups including media scrutiny in the negotiations of the WTO means there are more interests to pacify. In the early days of the Organisation, Jeffery J Schott commented that:

> [...] The WTO will likely suffer from slow and cumbersome policy-making and management — an organization with more than 120 member countries cannot be run by a 'committee of the whole'. Mass management simply does not lend itself to operational efficiency or serious policy discussion [...][30]

Generally speaking, unless there is a well co-ordinated opposition to decisions which adversely affect the weaker Members of any organisation, the interests of stronger factions will almost always prevail.[31] Fears that countries would lose a hold on their policies and will have their interests and concerns ignored in the face of the ever-expanding free-trade Organisation have been present right from the inception of the WTO. However, some scholars five years after the WTO was established noted that:

> The reciprocal influence of the processes taking place in the context of the WTO, in particular encouragement for the multilateral negotiation and

development of internationally agreed standards and for practices of dialogue and consultation before the adoption of trade-restrictive action, may provide some (albeit slight) cause for optimism in the face of fears about the growth of a free trade leviathan which increasingly restricts the policy choices not only of individual states, but also of the European Union itself.[32]

The WTO seems to have anticipated the interests of a Member State who considers that it may not be able to carry out the obligations imposed by the Agreement. Article IX:(3) provides that in exceptional circumstances, the Ministerial Conference may decide to waive an obligation imposed on a Member by this Agreement or any of the Multilateral Trade Agreements, provided that any such decision shall be taken by three fourths[33] of the Members.[34] Article IX:4 provides that 'a decision by the Ministerial Conference granting a waiver shall state the exceptional circumstances justifying the decision, the terms and conditions governing the application of the waiver, and the date on which the waiver shall terminate'.[35]

A Member State applying for a waiver must describe the measures it proposes to take, specify the policy objectives it seeks to obtain, and explain why it cannot achieve those objectives without violating its objectives under GATT 1994.[36] In other words, a waiver of obligations under the WTO Agreements must be specific.[37] The measures to be taken in respect to the waiver must be clearly stated making this exception necessarily strict in order to preserve the uniformity of the general obligations undertaken by of all WTO Member States.[38] In *EC-Bananas III*, the EC (under the Lomé waiver) sought to extend the scope of the waiver granted under *GATT* Article 1(Most-Favoured-Nation Treatment) to Article XIII (Non-Discriminatory Administration of Quantitative Restrictions). Overruling the Panel's acceptance that the scope of Article 1 was identical to that of Article XIII, the AB noted:

> Although the WTO Agreement does not provide any specific rules on the interpretation of waivers, Article IX of the WTO Agreement and the Understanding in Respect of Waivers of Obligations under the General Agreement on Tariffs and Trade 1994, which provide requirements for granting and renewing waivers, stress the exceptional nature of waivers and subject waivers to strict disciplines. Thus, waivers should be interpreted with great care.[39]

The WTO maintains a list of waivers in three categories: Waivers concerning the Harmonised System; Waivers concerning Regional Trade Agreements; and Other Waivers which concern certain provisions under respective Agreements.[40]

1.3. Dispute Settlement Under the GATT/WTO

At the time the ITO Charter was drafted, there were no elaborate provisions on dispute settlement.[41] Provisions on dispute settlement were incorporated into GATT Articles XXII and XXIII[42] although these provisions were not extensive. 'Consultation' was encouraged between contracting parties[43] and Article XXII provided that there should be a 'sympathetic consideration' to any desires for a consultation by any contracting parties in matters regarding the operation of the GATT. Article XXIII on the other hand, provided for circumstances where any contracting party considered that its benefits under the Agreement were being nullified or impaired due to the failure of another party to carry out its obligations, by the application of any measures, or by the existence of any situation. The provisions did not impose any sanctions but counselled the party complained against to give 'sympathetic consideration to the representations or proposals made to it'.

After the initial consultation, Article XXIII (2) gave the CONTRACTING PARTIES power to investigate and recommend action and to give a ruling on the complaint. It also gave the CONTRACTING PARTIES power to authorise in serious cases the suspension of GATT obligations to other contracting parties.[44]

In *Australian Ammonium Sulphate*[45] an early case under GATT 1947, 'nullification or impairment' was defined as including actions by a contracting party which harmed the trade of another, and which "could not reasonably have been anticipated" by the other at the time it was negotiated for a concession. Subsequently, the Panel in the dispute – *Uruguayan Recourse to Article XXIII*[46] while considering the provisions on 'nullification or impairment', was of the view that where measures applied by a contracting party were in conflict with the provisions of the GATT, a *prima facie* case of nullification or impairment had arisen. It went further to state that while it is not precluded that a *prima facie* case could arise even where there has been no infringement of the GATT, it was incumbent on the complaining country invoking Article XXIII to give detailed submissions of its grounds or reasons for invoking Article XXIII.[47] The burden of proof then shifted to the accused country asserting that it had not breached Nullification or Impairment provisions.[48]

It is important to note that significant advancements have been made in this area of dispute settlement in international trade relations. At first, diplomatic negotiations were the sole means of dealing with controversies. Then working parties composed of country representatives were established to investigate and formulate recommendations. In 1995, the GATT Contracting Parties began referring disputes to 'Panels', *ad hoc* groups of experts acting in a neutral capacity. However Panel decisions had no official or binding effect but were referred to the GATT Council which could make the 'appropriate recommendations'.[49]

Apart from a number of shortcomings including the sparse provisions on the dispute settlement process, delays in the formation of panels, the blocking of an unacceptable decision[50] and delays in the implementation of Council recommendations, the dispute settlement process under the GATT was relatively successful.[51] A series of agreements and understandings on dispute settlement were created over the years to formalise the panel procedures.[52] To make the dispute settlement process even better, a more comprehensive mechanism was adopted by the WTO in the *Understanding on the Rules and Procedures Governing the Settlement of Disputes.*[53] Article 3 (1) of the DSU affirms the continued application of Articles XXII and XXIII of GATT 1947.[54]

The primary aim of the WTO dispute settlement mechanism is 'to secure a positive solution to a dispute'.[55] The DSU provides for a variety of dispute settlement mechanisms: Consultations; Good offices, Conciliation and Mediation, Ruling/Recommendation of established Panels, Review by Appellate Body, and Arbitration.[56]

1.3.1. Consultations

Each covered agreement incorporates its provisions on consultations.[57] A Member's request for consultation under a covered agreement, shall unless mutually agreed be replied to within 10 days after its receipt and consultations entered into within 30 days of receipt of the request. If these terms are not met, the Member requesting consultations may proceed directly to the establishment of a panel.[58] In cases of urgency, including those concerning perishable goods, Members shall enter into consultation within a period of no more than 10 days after receipt of the request. If after 20 days from the date of receipt of the request, the dispute is not settled, the complaining party may request the establishment of a panel.[59] Requests for consultation are notified to the DSB and the relevant Councils and Committees by the requesting Member.[60] Consultations are confidential and without prejudice to the rights of Members in any future proceedings.[61]

1.3.2. Good Offices, Conciliation and Mediation[62]

The Director-General may, acting in an *ex-officio* capacity, offer any of these means with a view to assisting Members to settle a dispute.[63] The procedures are voluntary, confidential and without prejudice to the rights of either party in any further proceedings under the DSU. They may be requested or terminated at any time. Once terminated, a complaining party may request the establishment of a panel. They may also continue during the course of a panel proceeding.

1.3.3. Panels[64]

A Panel is established at the request of a complaining party at the latest, at a DSB meeting following that wherein the request was first made unless the DSB reaches a consensus not to establish. The terms of reference for a Panel are:

> To examine, in the light of the relevant provisions in (name of the covered agreement(s) cited by the parties to the dispute), the matter referred to the DSB by (name of party) in document … and to make such findings as will assist the DSB in making the recommendations or in giving the rulings provided for in that/those agreement(s).[65]

Panel members are selected with a view to ensure their independence, diversity of background, and wide experience.[66] A single panel may be established to handle multiple complaints and if more than one panel is established, the same persons shall serve as panellists on each of the separate panels to the greatest extent possible.[67] Third parties having substantial interest in a matter may notify its interests to the DSB and make written submissions to the panel. The submissions shall be reflected in the Panel Report.[68]

A Panel has a right to seek information and technical advice from any individual or body, or from any relevant source.[69] It may also consult experts on scientific or technical matters and request advisory opinion from them pursuant to Appendix 4 DSU on the rules for the establishment of such a group. There is also a provision for the interim review of panel proceedings under Article 15 DSU. Here, the panel issues sections of its draft report to the disputing parties who may submit any comments in writing. The findings of the final Panel Report will also include the arguments made at the interim stage.

A Panel is composed of three, or if the parties agree within 10 days of the establishment of the panel, five panellists[70] who serve in their individual capacities.[71] Panels follow the Working Procedures in Appendix 3 to the DSU.[72] A panel should issue its report within 6 months, or 3 months in the case of urgency. The period from establishment to circulation of a panel's report must not exceed 9 months.[73]

1.3.4. Appellate Review[74]

A standing Appellate Body is established by the DSB. It is composed of 7 persons, 3 of whom serve on any case in rotation according to the working procedures of the Appellate Body.[75] The Appellate Body is comprised of recognised authorities in law, international trade and the subject matter of the covered agreements, unaffiliated with any government but representative of WTO membership.

The proceedings for Appeals are limited to 60 days from the date a party formally notifies the DSB of its decision to appeal to the date the Appellate Body circulates its report. An extension of no more than 90 days is provided where the initial 60 days will not suffice.[76] The proceedings are confidential and opinions expressed are anonymous.[77] An appeal is limited to issues of law covered in the panel report and legal interpretations developed by the panel.[78] The Appellate Body may uphold, modify or reverse the legal findings and conclusions of the panel.[79] Only parties to the dispute may appeal a panel report.[80]

The total period for DSB decisions should be no longer than 12 months including appeals.[81]

1.3.5. Arbitration

This is an alternative means of dispute settlement provided for under the DSU.[82] Resort to arbitration is subject to mutual agreement of the parties who shall agree on the procedures to be followed. Third parties can only be party to an arbitration proceeding on the agreement of the parties to arbitration. Arbitration awards shall be notified to the DSB and the Council or Committee of the relevant agreement.[83] The provisions on implementation of recommendations and rulings and on compensation and suspension of concessions under Articles 21 and 22 DSU apply *mutatis mutandis* with respect to arbitrations.[84]

1.3.6. Adoption of Reports

Panel Reports are adopted unless there is a consensus in the DSB against their adoption or a party formally notifies the DSB of its decision to appeal.[85] If there is an appeal, the DSB will not consider the report until the appeal is completed.[86] The report of the Appellate body is adopted by the DSB and unconditionally accepted by the parties unless the DSB decides by consensus not to adopt the report within 30 days following its circulation.[87]

1.3.7. Recommendations/Rulings[88]

The DSU provides for a 'reasonable period of time' for compliance with the decisions of the DSB.[89] This period may however not exceed 15 months or in exceptional circumstances, 18 months.[90] Here, the DSB pays particular attention to matters affecting the interests of developing country members.[91]

1.3.8. *Compensation and Suspension of Concessions*

These are temporary measures available in the event that recommendations and rulings are not implemented within a reasonable period of time.[92] Compensation is voluntary and must be consistent with the covered agreement. If no satisfactory compensation has been agreed within 20 days after the date of expiry of the reasonable period of time, any party having invoked the dispute settlement procedures may request authorization from the DSB to suspend the application to the Member concerned of concessions or other obligations under the covered agreements.[93] Article 22(3) provides principles and procedures to be followed by a complaining party in considering what concessions or other obligations to suspend.

1.4. Legal Interpretation Under the Dispute Settlement Understanding

Article 3(2) of the DSU states that the purpose and function of the DSB is to provide security and predictability to the multilateral trading system, secure a positive solution to disputes, preserve the rights and obligations of Members under the covered agreements and, clarify the existing provisions of those agreements in accordance with customary rules of interpretation of public international law.[94] Thus, the DSB undertakes its assignment by application of laws and legal principles. From the reference to customary rules of interpretation of public international law by the DSB and the nature of the Rules and Agreements under the WTO, it is clear that the legal regime of the Organisation falls within the domain of public international law.

Legal study of the WTO has identified this area as falling under the nascent International Economic Law (IEL) scholarship. John H. Jackson refers to IEL as 'embracing the law of economic transactions; government regulation of economic matters; and related legal relations including litigation and international institutions for economic relations'.[95] He suggests that '90% of international law is in reality international economic law in some form'.[96] Although it does not have 'the glamour and visibility of nation-state relations (use of force, human rights, intervention etc) it involves many questions of international law and particularly treaty law'.[97] In a recent work, he examines the link between the WTO and international law stating that 'the WTO, as surely the most intricate and profound legal component of international economic law, is linked in profound ways to general international law'.[98]

The incorporation of public international law principles invariably underscores the adjudication process in the DSB.[99] Principal are, Articles 31 and 32 of the *Vienna Convention on the Law of Treaties 1969* on the interpretation of International Treaties. Under Article 31, the 'good faith principle' provides for the interpretation of a treaty 'in good faith in accordance with the ordinary meaning to be given to the terms of the treaty in their context and in the light of its object and purpose'.[100]

The ordinary meaning of a word can be found in the dictionary and the DSB refers to the ordinary meaning of words in almost all cases where the interpretation of a particular word or term has been disputed.[101] Rules of international law applicable in the relation between the parties are also to be taken into account.[102] Pauwelyn notes that this includes reference to rules of general international law binding on all States examples of which include rules other than those on treaty interpretation (such as the non-retroactivity of treaties), rules on state responsibility (such as those on countermeasures), or general principles such as due process or good faith.[103]

This is not to mean that WTO rules can be overridden or that the common agreements of WTO member states can be overruled. Article 3(2) DSU sends a note of warning to the DSB stating that 'recommendations and rulings of the DSB cannot add to or diminish the rights and obligations provided in the covered agreements'. To do otherwise would mean to act contrary to the common agreement of *all* WTO Members as expressed in the WTO agreements.

Bilateral agreements will also be considered by the DSB where applicable. In the *European Communities-Measures Affecting the Importation of Certain Poultry Products*,[104] Brazil argued that a bilateral agreement between itself and the European Communities (EC) was applicable to the dispute. The Panel noted that the agreement had been negotiated within the framework of GATT Article XXVIII and therefore decided to consider the agreement to the extent relevant to the determination of the EC's obligations under the WTO agreements vis-à-vis Brazil. The Appellate Body affirming the Panel's decision stated that it found no reversible error in the Panel's treatment of this bilateral agreement.[105]

Some scholars argue that WTO adjudication should be limited to the WTO Law alone.[106] As has been pointed out however, 'the law within the scope of WTO agreements is not broad enough to meet the needs of the Panels in dealing with particular disputes; therefore, it appears inevitable to extend the scope of law applicable to the Panels'.[107] In addition, the texts of several of the Uruguay Round Agreements explicitly refer to other international agreements which serve as direct sources of law in WTO dispute settlement proceedings. An example is the *Agreement on Trade-Related Aspects of Intellectual Property Rights* (TRIPS) which refers to several of the major international intellectual property conventions including the *Paris Convention, the Berne Convention, the Rome Convention,* and *the Treaty on Intellectual Property in Respect of Integrated Circuits.*[108]

Given that the WTO Rules have not excluded the application of rules of general international law, the DSB has also considered certain issues pertinent in a dispute in the light of customary international law. The Panel in *Korea-Measures Affecting Government Procurement*[109] was moved to make these considerations. In that case, the US had argued against certain procurement practices of the Korean Airport Construction Authority (KOACA) and other authorities responsible for airport procurement. At Panel level, it asserted that it had acted erroneously in the belief that the International Airport Project being constructed in the Republic of Korea was covered by Korea's accession to the *Agreement on Government Procurement.* The Panel in considering this issue of 'error' stated:

> Error in respect of a treaty is a concept that has been developed in customary international law through the case law of the Permanent Court of International Justice and the International Court of Justice... The elements developed by the case law mentioned above have been codified by the International Law Commission in what became the Vienna Convention on the Law of Treaties 1969.[110]

The Panel went on to cite Article 48 of the Convention which provided for the circumstances under which a State may invoke an error in a treaty as invalidating its consent to be bound by that treaty. It then concluded that since this Article had been derived largely from case law of the relevant jurisdiction the PCIJ and the ICJ, there was little doubt that it represented customary international law and was therefore applicable to the case.[111]

This decision has been severely criticised as extending the powers of the Panel to legislation, and to obliging states to comply by regulations which they had not expressed an intention to be bound by.[112] It is of course an argument with merit. Parties ought to be bound only by their expressed intentions to be so bound. However, one cannot agree that the application of general principles of international law must be expressly provided for in a treaty (such as the WTO Agreement) before it is considered in the settlement of disputes arising in the context of general international law. By its very nature the WTO Agreements cannot contemplate all the general principles of international law. Where rules of international law offer relevant interpretation it is invaluable that they be considered unless there is an explicit intention to exclude these rules.[113]

Chapter Two

DEVELOPMENT AND THE WTO APPROACH

2.1. Trade, the WTO and Development – An Introduction

The dictionary definition of *trade* is: 'the buying and selling of goods and services; a commercial activity of a particular kind'.[1] *Development* signifies a progress from a less sophisticated phase to a more advanced stage. It is defined as 'a new stage in a changing situation; a new product or idea'.[2] Synonyms include: advance; betterment; change; enlargement; growth; progress.[3]

In the past, 'development' remained within the realm of discourse on economic and social rights of individuals and societies around the world. As such, development work is largely credited to the activities of international agencies such as the World Bank and the International Monetary Fund (IMF) and alliances between nations under which some financial assistance is offered to the less developed countries of the world, such as the *G8*. The World Trade Organisation (WTO) with its rules-based system, its compulsory dispute settlement mechanism and its promotion of the free trade ideology, has not hitherto been counted as an international development agency. Therefore, it could be argued that ascribing a development character to this trade organisation may well be beyond its circle of influence. It is important to assess the validity of both sides of the argument.

Trade and development, the two concepts which form the basis of this study, must necessarily be assessed in the context of their relationship within the WTO. The starting point is to appreciate the WTO: what it stands for, how it came into being, and how it functions in the trading environment. The understanding, both of the WTO and of most trade practitioners, is that the Organisation is principally, a trade negotiating body.[4] The trade negotiation role of the WTO in the multilateral trade arena is not in doubt. Part of the appeal of a regulated system for multilateral trade even under the umbrella of the 1947 General Agreement on Tariffs and Trade (GATT) was and still is the accessibility it affords its membership to negotiate on a wide range of trade and economic related issues.

International trade has grown in the past century largely because the world's nations have expressed a joint interest in eliminating protectionist domestic legislation and in promoting the free trade mechanism for trade in goods (and services).[5] The historical foundations of the modern multilateral trade regime after the Second World War in the aftermath of the Great Depression of the 1930s have been well documented.[6] The onset of the Great Depression brought severe hardship on the people. Millions were without work and the financial institutions were crippled from lack of funds. There was very little industrial activity and the products manufactured were in turn threatened by imports from other countries. [7]

One of the critical policy agenda embarked upon by the major trading nations to address this socio-economic malaise was the enactment of protective trade legislation to safeguard their domestic industries and businesses from imports. In 1930, the US enacted the *Hawley-Smoot Tariff Act* (1930). Other major trading countries such as the UK retaliated with preferential tariff treatment for goods originating in the British Imperial Empire as agreed at a Conference in Ottawa Canada in 1932.[8] In spite of the protectionist measures, the global depression worsened. In 1933, an attempt at a *World Monetary and Economic Conference* to address the tariff structures for purposes of multilateral trade failed because participants believing that to do so would bring financial disaster on their domestic industries, refused to relax their trading restrictions.[9] By 1934, the US had begun bilateral trade negotiations with its major trading partners to reduce tariffs on a reciprocal rather than a unilateral basis.

In the aftermath of the war and in the economic crisis that ensued across the Allied territories, the idea of tariff regulation with a view to the promotion of easier movement of goods across borders was suggested in the 1941 *Atlantic Charter*. Therein the governments of the United States and Great Britain promised to endeavour to 'further the enjoyment by all States, great or small, victor or vanquished, of access, on equal terms, to the trade and to the raw materials of the world which are needed for their economic prosperity'.[10] This idea was echoed in the *Summary of Agreements* reached after a United Nations Monetary and Financial Conference in Bretton Woods, Hampshire, USA (the Bretton Woods Conference) in 1944.[11]

From the Bretton Woods Conference two international organisations evolved: the IMF[12] and the International Bank for Reconstruction and Development (IBRD or World Bank).[13] A third agency, plans of which were later aborted was to be the International Trade Organisation (ITO).[14] The ITO was meant to administer a comprehensive code governing the conduct of world trade. Owing to a subsequent lack of government support under President Harry Truman in 1948,[15] efforts to establish the ITO were abandoned. The failure of the proposed ITO to foster and coordinate a regulated trade body resulted in the adoption of what was at the time considered a temporary arrangement, the GATT.[16] However, it was the GATT which would evolve from an original twenty three members in 1947, to the modern international trading system known as the WTO, in 1994.

In essence, while the mechanics of alleviating the economic recession of the 1930s focused on the creation of an international institution to oversee cross border trade activity, the objective was to redress the socio-economic problems of the period. The Preamble to the 1947 Agreement of the old GATT indicates this vision clearly. The document stated unequivocally that the representatives of the governments at the GATT recognised *inter* alia, that 'their relations in the field of trade and economic endeavour should be conducted with a view to raising standards of living [and] ensuring full employment'.[17] The subsequent *Agreement Establishing the World Trade Organisation* (*WTO Agreement*) in its Preamble also recognised these aims of the GATT. It states that there is a 'need for positive efforts designed to ensure that developing countries, and especially the least developed among them, secure a share in the growth in international trade commensurate with the needs of their economic development'.[18]

These objectives were agreed by the 'Parties' who entered into the *WTO Agreement* as the following passage establishes:

> *Recognizing* that their relations in the field of trade and economic endeavour should be conducted with a view to raising standards of living, ensuring full employment and a large and steadily growing volume of real income and effective demand, and expanding the production of and trade in goods and services, while allowing for the optimal use of the world's resources in accordance with the objective of sustainable development, seeking both to protect and preserve the environment and to enhance the means for doing so in a manner consistent with their respective needs and concerns at different levels of economic development,
>
> *Recognizing* further that there is need for positive efforts designed to ensure that developing countries, and especially the least developed among them, secure a share in the growth in international trade commensurate with the needs of their economic development.[19]

There can be no doubt that goals such as "raising standards of living" and "ensuring full employment" for the benefits of the peoples in WTO Member States allude to a development objective by the Organisation. If as the WTO preamble provides, developing countries are expected to gain a share of growth in international trade and international trade is conducted with a view to raising standards of living, then it is only reasonable to expect that the WTO owes the achievement of these objectives as an obligation to its developing country Members.

Yet in spite of this obligation which has been adopted by the Organisation or perhaps because of it, some scholars have been keen to point out repeatedly that 'the WTO is not a development organisation'.[20] There have also been arguments against the perception of the trade liberalisation process under the WTO as the 'panacea for all the challenges of development'.[21] Director General of the WTO, Pascal Lamy, while reiterating this view however points out that the WTO has a role in engineering development. He said:

> Even though perceptions differ as to what is really meant by 'development' and what should be the means to achieve the end goals of 'development', trade and development are increasingly perceived as being inextricably linked to each other...Obviously, and this goes without saying, trade cannot be the only engine of growth...many other pieces will have to fall into place if the developmental objectives are to be achieved...but there can be little argument over the fact that trade will be an integral part of any such strategy...and even though [the] WTO is not a developmental organisation, by implication, as the body which facilitates multilateral trade rules, it has an important role to play in engineering growth and development.[22]

The crucial issue is that whereas well-known development agencies work directly in areas where aid is needed 'the WTO is a government to government organisation'.[23] The interconnectedness between trade and development especially in the context of the WTO becomes less obscure when we appreciate that the Organisation is in actual fact, a *trade organisation with a development obligation*. This interconnectedness is illuminated in our subsequent discourse on development.

2.2. Development and the Developing Country

There is neither a WTO Agreement on Development nor any one source of 'International Development Law'[24] to which the DSB may refer to in any disputes which have 'development' as a central matter. What then is development and how does it relate to the work of the WTO?

Stiglitz offers an apposite explanation of what development means:

> Development is not about helping a few people get rich or creating a handful of pointless protected industries that only benefit the country's elite; it is not about bringing in Prada and Benetton, Ralph Lauren or Louis Vuitton, for the urban rich and leaving the rural poor in their misery [...]

Development is about transforming societies, improving the lives of the poor, enabling everyone to have a chance at success and access to health care and education.[25]

The UN Declaration on the Right to Development also notes that 'the human person is the central subject of development and should be the active participant and beneficiary of the right to development'.[26]

The approach to trade and development in the WTO is slightly less visionary than that of the UN. Ismail observes that:

The debate about development in the WTO is often assumed to be about increasing the effectiveness of special and differential treatment for developing countries in the WTO. This perception relegates the debate about development to the margin of the WTO. Development is thus regarded as an afterthought, as a "nice to do" or at most an "optional extra".

This perception of the development dimension is misconceived. It is argued [...] that developing countries have fundamental interests in the WTO that are at the core of the trading system and its functioning.[27]

In his work, *Development as Freedom*, Sen posits that 'development can be seen... as a process of expanding the real freedoms that people enjoy'.[28] He notes that:

Development requires the removal of major sources of unfreedom: poverty as well as tyranny, poor economic opportunities as well as systematic social deprivation, neglect of public facilities as well as intolerance or overactivity of repressive states [...][29]

[...] the lack of substantive freedoms relates directly to economic poverty, which robs people of the freedom to satisfy hunger, or to achieve sufficient nutrition, or to obtain remedies for treatable illnesses, or the opportunity to be adequately clothed or sheltered, or to enjoy clean water or sanitary facilities. In other cases, the unfreedom links closely to the lack of public facilities and social care, such as the absence of epidemiological programmes, or of organised arrangements for health care or educational facilities, or of effective institutions for the maintenance of local peace and order. In still other cases, the violation of freedom results directly from a denial of political and civil liberties by authoritarian regimes and from imposed restrictions on the freedom to participate in the social, political and economic life of the community.[30]

In order to identify the development needs and concerns of developing countries, an overview of what identifies a country as a *developing country* is imperative.

A critical feature of the countries which are adjudged to be of 'developing' status is the predominantly agriculture-oriented enterprise. These countries lack the technological innovations and industrialisation processes which enable their developed counterparts in diversifying income earning factors from basic agricultural processes to processes such as manufacturing and provision of highly skilled technical services. Still, 'agriculture is very important for developing countries in terms of their economic growth, poverty alleviation, food security, and environmental sustainability'.[31]

The dictionary defines a developing country as a 'poor agricultural country that is seeking to become more advanced'.[32] As this definition portrays, most developing countries rely on the most basic forms of low skilled, mechanical agricultural processes. Although the influence of the sector is not huge in terms of financial benefit to developing countries considering the comparatively negligible impact of agriculture on their national earnings or income, it is the basic means of livelihood and sustenance to a greater number of the population in these economies.[33]

If these countries are to become advanced in the fast paced modern global economy, it is clear that mere engagement in basic forms of agricultural enterprise will never be enough. Skilled labour, improved and sophisticated farming systems involving R&D, and support from the government of a well regulated economy are needed. Presently, the agricultural endeavours in these countries are very modest, predominantly for individual or family sustenance and found mainly in rural settings. Farming, fishing, and such other activities are done without the highly-skilled and industrialised methods utilised in more advanced economies. There is very little external and institutional financial support.[34]

Possible gains from agriculture are further limited by the inability to access world agricultural markets owing to the subsidies and protectionist measures adopted by richer developed countries.[35] This makes competition with the agricultural products of highly industrialised nations almost an impossible task. Although developing countries have been expanding their share of world markets, in the area of agriculture where as the dictionary definition suggests, developing countries will necessarily be at a greater advantage, the richer industrial countries still maintain a greater market share.[36] For instance, the United States, a leading figure in the developed economies is one of the world's largest producer, exporter and importer of agricultural products with huge financial contributions from its government.[37] It has also been acknowledged that 'agriculture's wider contribution to the EU's prosperity is considerable'.[38]

It must be pointed out that continued dependency on agriculture may not be in the long term interests of developing countries if they expect to make significant gains in the current trading environment. The share of agriculture in the value of world trade has been in steady decline with trade in high technology (such as electronics and computer equipment); medium technology (such as automobile and machine parts) products; and trade in commercial services, on a fast increase.[39] Also, new technologies and advances in food production mean that subsistence-level agriculture will be no match for the quicker, faster and better ways of food production. Without efficient technological systems to convert raw produce into processed goods, developing countries cannot but lose market share in the face of stronger competition. Moreover, internal policies on food safety, public health and, environmental protection restrict exports which do not meet the standards set by importing countries; production and processing standards which most developing countries struggle to satisfy.

In any event, the form of engagement in agricultural enterprise is not the determinant factor used by international agencies in categorising countries according to their development status. It is therefore necessary to assess what, according to international standards, makes a country a 'developing country'.

2.2.1. Developing Country – Classifications

The origins of designating some countries as developing countries in modern policy-making may be traced to a statement by the US President, Harry Truman (1945–1953) who in his inauguration speech before the US Congress, drew attention to the poor conditions in poorer countries referring to these as "underdeveloped" areas.[40] Those 'poor conditions' are still relevant in the present times and include that:

> [...]These nations generally have low levels of technology, basic living standards and little in the way of an industrial base. Their economies are mainly agricultural and are characterised by cheap, unskilled labour and a scarcity of investment capital [...]
>
> [...] Around 70% of the world's population lie in the developing countries almost all of which are in Africa, Asia, Oceania and Latin America. Many countries, outside the margin towns, are poverty stricken and hunger, disease and illiteracy are still common place.[41]

Some developed countries, territories, and independent organisations have adopted their own methods of development classification for purposes of aid assistance programmes.[42] However, the *United Nations Statistics Division Code 491* states:

> There is no established convention for the designation of developed and developing countries or areas in the United Nations system. In common

practice, Japan in Asia, Canada and the United States in northern America, Australia and New Zealand in Oceania and Europe are considered developed regions or areas. In international trade statistics, the Southern African Customs Union is also treated as developed region and Israel as a developed country; countries emerging from the former Yugoslavia are treated as developing countries; and countries of eastern Europe and the former USSR countries in Europe are not included under either developed or developing regions.[43]

Bulajic notes that:

> Criteria for determining which countries are "developing countries" have political, economic and legal aspects and may be viewed from a number of different angles. Consequently, there are serious difficulties in reaching a consensus on what exactly constitutes a "developing country".[44]

We may however consider the criterion of international bodies whose work is relevant in the development agenda.

A. The World Bank

The World Bank is incorporated in the World Bank Group.[45] Its two main organs, the International Bank for Reconstruction and Development (IBRD) focusing on middle income and credit worthy poor countries, and the International Development Association (IDA) which deals with the poorest countries of the world, together offer financial and technical assistance to developing countries.[46] The World Bank classifies countries[47] in line with its main criterion which is GNI (Gross National Income[48]) per capita. Previously referred to as the Gross Domestic Product, financial data analysed in this criteria include the total value of goods and services produced in a country together with income received from earnings overseas.[49]

According to the organisation, every economy is classified as '[...] low income, middle income (subdivided into lower middle and upper middle), or high income. Low- and middle-income economies are sometimes referred to as developing economies'.[50] There is however no explicit definition of the term 'developing country'. Rather, in its guide to its *World Development Indicators 2005* the World Bank explains its rationale for using the term 'developing economies':

> The use of the term is convenient; it is not intended to imply that all economies in the group are experiencing similar development or that other economies have reached a preferred or final stage of development.

Note that classification by income does not necessarily reflect development status.[51]

B. The Organisation for Economic Co-operation and Development (OECD)

Originally created as an economic counterpart to the North Atlantic Treaty Organisation (NATO), the OECD comprises about thirty of some of the world's rich countries.[52] Amongst other objectives, it provides in its words, 'one of the world's largest and most reliable sources of comparable statistical, economic and social data'.[53] In its list of Official Development Assistance (ODA) recipients,[54] it classifies 'developing countries' into more extensive categories[55]:

1. Least Developed Countries.
2. Other Low Income Countries with per capita GNI less than $825 in 2004.
3. Lower Middle Income Countries and Territories with per capita GNI $826–$3255 in 2004.
4. Upper Middle Income Countries and Territories with per capita GNI $3256–$10,065, in 2004.

C. The United Nations Committee on Trade and Development (UNCTAD)

UNCTAD came into being in the early part of the 1960's as concerns about the benefits to developing countries of international trade increased.[56] The Organisation 'promotes the integration of developing countries into the world economy' in its three-fold functions as a forum for intergovernmental discourses; research and analysis; and technical assistance for developing countries especially LDCs and economies in transition.[57]

UNCTAD adopts the reasoning of the World Bank cited earlier with regards to the terms 'developing' and 'countries'.[58] It states that 'the designations "developed" and "developing" are intended for statistical convenience and do not necessarily express a judgement about the stage reached by a particular country or area in the development process'.[59]

After a preliminary grouping in three categories: Developed Economies; South-East Europe; and Commonwealth of Independent States (CIS); further open-ended categorisation identifies developing economies as 'all other countries and territories in Africa, America, Asia and Oceania not specified above'.[60] It goes on to classify these economies on an income-earning basis as high-income countries (per capita GDP above $4500), middle-income countries (per capita GDP $1000–$4500), and low income countries (per capita GDP below $1000).[61]

D. The United Nations (UN)/Committee for Development Policy (CDP)

The UN has its historic beginnings in the agreement for international co-operation by the Allied Forces to foster peace and ensure world security in the aftermath of the Second World War. Today, its key mandate is 'the promotion of higher standards of living, full employment and conditions of economic and social progress and development' a goal to which it dedicates 70% of its work.[62] In line with these purposes, the organisation sets international development objectives, including the Millennium Development Goals adopted in September 2000. In *The World Economic Survey 2005*,[63] the UN adopts similar statistical analysis of developing countries as UNCTAD above.

A subsidiary Committee to the United Nations Economic and Social Council (ECOSOC), the CPD[64] is more closely concerned with issues affecting developing countries. It provides inputs and independent advice to ECOSOC[65] on emerging cross sectional development issues and on international cooperation for development focusing on medium and long term aspects.[66] The Committee pays special attention to an analysis of Least Developed Countries and advises the United Nations Economic and Social Council on the countries which ought to be added to the List of LDCs and which countries ought to be graduated from the List, presumably to the group of developing countries. It makes this review every three years.[67]

The Committee considers three criteria in determining a country's state of development[68]:

1. Income level, assessed on Gross National Income (GNI) per capita.
2. Stock of human assets measured on a Human Assets Index (HAI).
3. Economic Vulnerability measured by an Economic Vulnerability Index (EVI).

E. The International Monetary Fund (IMF)

The IMF's activities are largely in conjunction with developing countries to which it lends financial assistance for economic programmes and projects designed to revamp ailing economies. Its purposes include promoting international monetary cooperation, exchange stability, and orderly exchange arrangements; to foster economic growth and high levels of employment, and to provide temporary financial assistance to countries to help ease balance of payments adjustment.[69] It has now extended its services to surveillance of economic development, lending, and technical assistance.[70] It bases its categorisation on national economic factors including real GDP, unemployment rates, source of export earnings, source of external finances; debt-servicing. It has three principal classifications: advanced countries; developing countries; and countries in transition.[71]

F. The Group of 8 Industrialised Nations (The G8)

Recognition of a country as a 'developing country' by groups such as the G8[72] is of interest to poor countries that rely on the promises of aid assistance or trade relief from industrialised nations. The G8 is an informal, exclusive group of eight representatives, comprising the world's leading industrialised nations – the United Kingdom, United States of America, France, Germany, Italy, Canada, Japan, Russia. The Group has no Head Quarters, budget or permanent staff, and its annual meetings are hosted by whichever country has the leadership of the body for the material year. Each country is represented by its leader who voluntarily agrees to comply with the policies and objectives agreed at the Group's meetings.[73]

G. The World Trade Organisation (WTO)

Although the WTO makes reference to the 'needs and concerns' of its developing country membership, makes specific special provisions for developed country members in respective WTO Agreements, and has even adopted a special focus on development in the Doha Round of trade talks, it offers no definition of a developing country neither does it on its own initiative categorise an accession country as a developing country. It is entirely an *ad hoc* self selection process which sees a country acquiring a 'developed country' status after agreement with other Member States.[74]

Nevertheless, it must be pointed out that there is a reference to 'those contracting parties the economies of which can only support low standards of living and are in the early stages of development', in the GATT.[75] Also, beneficiary countries which are in a preferential scheme such as the *Generalised System of Preferences* (GSP) operative under the *Enabling Clause*, are also referred to and acknowledged as developing countries by their benefactors. However, LDCs which are countries designated as such by the United Nations[76] are expressly mentioned in the *WTO Agreement*. The Agreement provides that LDCs 'will only be required to undertake commitments and concessions to the extent consistent with their individual development, financial and trade needs or their administrative and institutional capabilities'.[77]

As at July 2008, there were about thirty two least developed countries. In all, over three-quarters of WTO Members have successfully acceded to the WTO either as developing countries, or as least developed countries.[78]

2.3. Developing Country Participation in Organised Global Trade

Developing country participation in international trade began well before the establishment of the GATT or of the WTO. The periods of colonialism were not solely about imperial powers seeking out new territories to rule. They were also ventures into trade, the newly discovered colonies seen both as sources of raw materials, and as outlets for manufactured goods.[79] Trebilock and Howse[80] noted that throughout the nineteenth century, the European powers had pursued colonial acquisitions as a means of exploiting the gains from free trade. With the onset of the Depression and the collapse of the free trade treaties in the late 1870's, this policy was pursued with vengeance.[81]

An inquiry into how the developed countries of the modern world achieved the economic gains shows that their achievements are not entirely owed to open trade practices.[82] In considering the profitable means of socio-economic advancement open to them, the conclusions of such an inquiry are important as developing countries will benefit from the knowledge of how their developed counterparts charted the path to development. Thus it would not be presumptuous for developing countries to ask: Was there a link between early trade policies and practices of our developed country counterparts and their subsequent advances in development? On what measures were these policies and practices based?

Ha-Joon Chang in his widely acclaimed study of developed country ascendancy in the international trade environment notes that:

> As is well known, there have been heated debates on whether these policies and institutions are suitable to the developing countries. The curious thing is that even those who are sceptical of their suitability rarely question whether these are the policies and the institutions that the developed countries actually used in order to become rich. However, the historical fact is that the rich countries did not develop on the basis of the policies and the institutions that they now recommend to, and often force upon, the developing countries.
>
> Almost all of today's rich countries used tariff protection and subsidies to develop their industries in the earlier stage of their development. It is particularly important to note that Britain and the USA, the two countries that are supposed to have reached the summit of the world economy through free-market, free-trade policy, are actually the ones that most aggressively used protection and subsidies.[83]

An examination of the current development successes of East Asian countries such as Japan, China, India, Malaysia, and Singapore rebuts the argument that a country can only achieve development through trade based solely on the standards and practices laid out in approved international institutions like the IMF and World Bank. It further refutes the claim that success in the global market is predominantly reliant on trade liberalisation policies carried out without government intervention. Citing the Asian experience, Stiglitz and Charlton observe that:

> In many countries trade policy in particular did not follow the orthodox free trade prescriptions. The governments of many Asian countries pursued a two-track policy of protectionism for industries not ready to compete internationally and promotion for export-ready industries. For example, governments intervened in many industries by providing credit through banks supported in one way or the other by government, restricting competition from imports, constraining new domestic competitors, and developing export marketing institutions.[84]

They note that the examples of China and India are demonstrative:

> Both have successfully integrated into the world trading system, and both have benefited greatly from international trade, yet neither allowed orthodox trade and industrial policies. China has been particularly careful to ensure that its economic development strategy is gradually implemented and carefully sequenced [...]
>
> China began to grow rapidly in the late 1970s but trade liberalisation did not start until the late 1980s, and only took off in the 1990s after economic growth had increased markedly. The Indian story is similar: growth increased in the early 1980s while tariffs were actually going up in some areas and did not come down significantly until the major reforms of 1991–3.[85]

Commenting further on developed country success in this sphere, the authors state that:

> None of today's rich countries developed by simply opening themselves to foreign trade [...] All the developed countries used a wide range of trade policy instruments which should make their WTO ambassadors blush when they sit down to negotiate with today's developing countries.[86]

In our view, allowance ought to be given to the growth of indigenous acceptable trade policies if indeed a progress is to be made within the diverse regions which remain underdeveloped. As has been noted:

> There can [also] be no doubt that the successful cases of development over the last fifty years have pursued inventive and idiosyncratic economic policies. To date, not one successful developing country has pursued a purely free market approach to development.
>
>   In this context it is inappropriate for the world trading system to be implementing rules which circumscribe the ability of developing countries to use both trade and industry policies to promote industrialisation. The current trend to force a narrow straitjacket of policy harmonisation on developing countries is simply not justified by the available evidence.[87]

The points made above are altogether more compelling when it is recalled that the present world trade system came into existence almost fifty years after the original attempts at a unified trading system. The fact is that the rules available under, and proclaimed by, the WTO, have not always existed in the history of trade. Rather, the various agreements which comprise the trade rules established by the WTO are the politically motivated compromises agreed as solutions; *solutions* which have emerged in the bid to find the means to *sanction* those considerations presumed to be instrumental in maintaining the open trade philosophy of the modern trading system.

Efforts at developing country integration must therefore take note of the peculiarities of these societies. Most developing countries are less economically viable, face a myriad of internal constraints, and will necessarily require a gradual introduction to the flavours of trade liberalisation. Stiglitz points out that:

> Trade liberalisation conducted in the wrong way, too fast, in the absence of adequate safety nets, with insufficient reciprocity and assistance on the part of developed countries, can contribute to an increase in poverty [...]
>
>   Complete openness can expose a country to greater risks from external shocks. Poor countries may find it particularly hard to buffer these shocks and to bear the costs they incur, and they typically have weak safety nets, or none at all to protect the poor [...][88]

At the moment, the solution sought in the trade and development debate is on how to maintain participation in world trade for developing countries and at the same time, indeed as a prime goal, to ensure the development both economic and social, of the developing world. As we consider below, this has for long been a concern for the international trading system.

2.3.1. Development as an Emerging Issue in International Trade

The earlier attempts at creating an international trade body via the *Havana Charter of 1948* were abandoned because of criticism particularly in the United States, regarding Chapter Three in the proposed Charter on Economic Development and Reconstruction. The Chapter had addressed the participation of developing countries which made up even at those early stages, the majority of the countries involved in talks to establish ITO.[89]

This resistance against the inclusion of special provisions for developing countries however did not forestall further attempts. In the GATT Ministerial Declaration of 29 Nov 1957, the Ministers saw as a major problem, 'the failure of the trade of less developed countries to develop as rapidly as that of industrialised countries'.[90] It was thought that a Panel should be established to assess this slow progress of the developing country membership. A Panel of Experts was appointed with a renowned economist, Gottfried Haberler as chairman. The resulting document, the Haberler Report,[91] examined the growth of the domestic industries of developing economies *vis a vis* their potential of becoming equal competitors in a global trading environment. The Report considered the genuine difficulties faced by these financially constrained and technologically challenged countries. It recognised that the less developed countries whose production capacity did not extend beyond primary products needed 'special promotion during the first stages of industrialisation when the process of learning industrial techniques is in its early stages'.[92]

The Report pointed out that poorer countries were more likely to face balance-of-payments difficulties than their richer counterparts, justifying the need for the former to control the influx of imports into their domestic markets. Arguing for 'special considerations' for these 'under-developed primary producing countries', the Report stated that 'insofar as import restrictions can turn the international terms of trade in favour of the restricting country, it can be argued that poorer countries should have a somewhat greater freedom in their use than richer countries'.[93]

The findings of the Haberler Report were not implemented although it made a strong case for the argument that more freedom from constraining trade rules were required by developing countries if they were to grow a competitive advantage building on their early stages of industrialisation. However without any further action on the considerations raised, the Report only added a 'moral force to the arguments of the increasing number of developing countries'.[94]

The failure of the adoption of the Report did not in any event put an end to concerns as to how developing countries could benefit from the multilateral trading system. Further efforts have resulted in the inclusion of development-oriented provisions in the trade rules, and in a number of activities undertaken at the WTO. These efforts include: GATT Article XXIII (Nullification and Impairment); GATT Article XVIII (Governmental Assistance to Economic Development); GATT Part IV (Trade and Development); The Enabling Clause (a waiver of the Most Favoured Nation-MFN rule); Special assistance to LDCs; Special and Differential Treatment (SDT) provisions across the WTO Agreements; the creation of a Committee on Trade and Development; the trade related technical assistance and training activities of the Secretariat; the technical co-operation efforts with other international agencies; and the recent Aid for Trade (AfT) Initiative.

A. GATT Article XXIII – Nullification and Impairment Provisions

This provision was at the centre of the dispute in the aforementioned case, *Uruguayan Recourse to Article XXIII*.[95] Uruguay had brought a complaint against fifteen developed country Members.[96] The complaint referred to the general difficulties created by the restrictive measures affecting Uruguayan exports to the territories of the developed countries. These restrictive measures applied to imports of certain products which Uruguay in its submission claimed comprised of a considerable number of Uruguayan exports.[97] The measures included import permit requirements, import charges, and state trading (requiring some of the developed countries to ascertain the quantity and value of indigenous goods thereby imposing import restrictions on exports from other countries). Uruguay also complained of discriminatory practices in the form of import permit requirements which were not extended to non-OECD countries such as Uruguay.

The Panel was faced with considering whether these restrictions had in fact so adversely affected Uruguayan exports that they could be said to have nullified or impaired Uruguay's benefits under the GATT. To do this, it had to determine the 'resulting inequality in the terms on which temperate zone primary producers participate in world trade'.[98] The Panel did not find for Uruguay in its claim on Nullification and Impairment in a number of cases[99] and where it was of the view that there had been a *prima facie* case of nullification or impairment of benefits accruing to Uruguay under the GATT, it only made recommendations in respect of the redress sought against the developed countries on a respective basis.[100]

The Panel explained its reluctance to find wholly on behalf of Uruguay in three respects:[101](a) Contentions of the developed country representatives that the measures complained against *were* in line with the Agreement or with other 'existing legislation' were not challenged or contradicted by Uruguay and the Panel was of the view that in the circumstances it was beyond its competence to examine the justification of the contention; (b) the status of variable import levies or charges raised had been previously considered by a Session of the Contracting Parties without a resolution and the Panel did not consider it appropriate to examine the consistency or otherwise of the measures under the Agreement; and (c) the possibility of adverse effect on Uruguay's cereal trade by the EEC's introduction of a new Regulation on Cereals under its Common Agricultural Policy (CAP) which Uruguay had hitherto not considered in its original submission. The last reason is rather an obvious predicament considering the Regulation was introduced *after* the Uruguayan Complaint. As such, this question was not addressed by the Panel as the Contracting Parties including Uruguay were at the time still considering the Regulation's consistency with the General Agreement.

It is noted that Uruguay's complaints save for that against the applications of discriminatory import permit requirements, were concerned with the general application of Article XXIII and did not raise issues on whether the restrictions were adverse to Uruguay particularly because of the country's status as a developing country. Moreover, the discriminatory import permit requirements were more of a complaint against the general preferential treatment granted by OECD countries to their counterparts in the organisation, than a claim against the lack of development considerations for a developing country.

In assessing this dispute's contribution to the development dimension in international trade, it could be argued that the Uruguayan Complaint and the resulting decision by the Panel did not achieve much. However with the Uruguayan complaint, it was evident that developing countries were becoming bolder in expressing their concerns in the trading environment including in the recourse to the dispute settlement process.

B. GATT Article XVIII – Governmental Assistance to Economic Development

In 1955, a revised Article XVIII was included in the GATT. The Article's provisions recognised that for the less economically prosperous Member States to be able to implement programmes and policies for the purposes of economic development, it was necessary to incorporate certain flexibilities in the GATT Agreements. Paragraph 2 of the Article identified the aim of the provisions which was to 'raise the general standard of living' and 'to take protective or other measures affecting imports' which aims were 'justified in so far as they facilitate the attainment of the provisions' of the GATT. The Article survived in the GATT of 1994 under the new WTO.

The impact of Article XVIII was in two key areas. The first was for the protection of vulnerable industries for which the article provided that contracting parties could be allowed to 'maintain sufficient flexibility in their tariff structure to be able to grant the tariff protection required for the establishment of a particular industry'.[102] The second was that governments of developing countries were allowed to apply quantitative restrictions 'for balance of payments purposes'.[103]

Paragraphs 9 and 11 are the principal provisions to Article XVIII. Article XVIII:9 provides that for the purposes of economic development, a country could place restrictions on the quantity or values of goods permitted for imports as long as the restrictions did not exceed two conditions of necessity. A country could therefore not continue the restrictions if there was no further need to 'forestall the threat of, or stop, a decline in its monetary reserves'; or 'in the case of a country with inadequate monetary reserves, to achieve a reasonable rate of increase in its reserves.'[104]

Under Article XVIII:11, it is expected that a country which adopted restrictions would keep in view the need to restore the lost equilibrium in its balance of payments and also that the policies it adopted would effectively employ the productive resources in the country. There was however a *proviso* to Article XVIII:11. The proviso stated that a country adopting quantitative restriction measures would not be required to withdraw or modify restrictions on the ground that a change in its development policy would render unnecessary the restrictions which it had put in place pursuant to Article XVIII:9.

The development objective of these provisions was at the centre of the dispute, *India Quantitative Restrictions on Imports of Agricultural, Textile and Industrial Products*.[105] In that case, the US[106] complained that India's continued maintenance of import licensing procedures and practices in respect of the agricultural and industrial products it had earlier notified to the Balance of Payments Committee[107] was contrary to India's obligations under Article XVIII GATT. In its defence, India claimed that the quantitative restrictions in place were not only necessary but also that it could not be asked to withdraw or modify the restrictions based on a change in its development policy which would have rendered the restrictions unnecessary, in line with the *proviso* to Article XVIII:11.[108] India further argued that in any event, it was required to phase out the restrictions *after* there was no longer any balance of payments problem.

To enable it to properly identify India's external financial position and make an objective assessment of India's programme of economic development, the Panel sought the opinion of the IMF.[109] The IMF was of the opinion that India was not experiencing a serious decline in its monetary reserves; that there was no threat of such a decline; and that India's monetary reserves were not inadequate.[110] Therefore India could not claim that imposing quantitative restrictions was "necessary" in the sense of Article XVIII:9.

The Panel then turned to review similar complaints brought under Article XVIII under the old GATT 1947 when the provisions on balance of payments had first been included in the rules of the multilateral trading system.[111] The complaints were: Germany (*German Import Restrictions Decision*),[112] Spain (*Report on the 1973 Consultation with Spain*),[113] and Italy (*Report of the Committee on Balance-of-Payments Restrictions on Consultation under Article XII:4(B) with Italy*).[114] Contrary to the assertion of India in the instant case, the Panel found that in these old GATT cases, the practice had been that countries were expected 'to remove their quantitative restrictions *as their balance-of-payments positions improved*'.[115]

The Panel was not satisfied that India had established that its balance-of-payments situation met the requirements of either Article XVIII:9 or of the additional provisions of Article XVIII:11. It was of the view that the quantitative restrictions were no longer necessary within the meaning of Article XVIII:9.[116] The Panel therefore recommended that India should bring its policies in line with its obligations under the General Agreement.[117] However, it did make a concession noting India's stage of development. In its recommendations, the Panel referred to the provisions of Article 21.2 DSU which states that 'particular attention should be paid to matters affecting the interests of developing country Members with respect to measures which have been subject to dispute settlement'.[118] The Parties were therefore advised to agree on a reasonable period of time in order to allow India being a developing country, to implement a phasing out period of the restrictions.[119]

One of the arguments raised by India is that Article XVIII is principally a special and differential treatment provision specifically included in the GATT for the benefit of developing country members.[120] This argument was based on Article XVIII:4(a) which states that Article XVIII was applicable to a Member State 'the economy of which can only support low standards of living and is in the early stages of development'; a provision noted by the Panel.[121] However both the Panel and the complainant the US, adopted a textual approach in interpreting Article XVIII:B. It would have been preferable that rather than adopting a textual approach, the Panel ought to have given fuller consideration to India's argument on the development nature of the provision, noted above. This would have allowed for a more objective assessment of India's economic and financial status, the country's development stage, and the general living standards of the society.

India had indeed argued further that the removal of the restrictions would cause decreased use of industrial capacity and increased unemployment, and would be inconsistent with 'economic employment of productive resources'.[122] Unfortunately the Panel was of the view that import restrictions could not be regarded as domestic policy.[123] In its view, since the removal of the quantitative restrictions did not imply a change of India's domestic development policy which would have made it unnecessary for India to eliminate the restrictions, the restrictions were void for their inconsistency.[124]

This dispute also highlighted the limited capacity of developing countries to sufficiently represent their arguments in the complex arena of international trade. Considering the proviso to Article XVIII:11, the Panel had pointed out that India has not been precise in specifying what it considered to be its development policy in the terms of the proviso.[125] But this failure on the part of India to present its claims effectively (bearing in mind that as a developing country it may not have the facilities and intellectual strength to do this compared with the complainant) should not have cost a developing country the benefits it ought to gain from a special provision. Incidentally, a Trade Policy Review (TPR) of India carried out a year after the dispute in 1998, pointed out the significance of quantitative restrictions as part of India's trade policy reforms, and the country's commitments to the trade liberalisation process.[126] Specifically, in the report by the Government of India, these policies were undertaken because, 'with increased liberalisation and globalisation of trade, India's focus is on areas of her strength and advantage to meet global competition, as also areas having trade potential'.[127] It cannot be denied that efforts such as these are for the proper purpose of building a trading capacity, and are invaluable for a country seeking to become a stronger participant in the global trading environment.

C. GATT Part IV – Trade and Development

Some considering the influence of the GATT in its early days have observed that:

> [...] the GATT was not a trade policy forum and the majority of its members, coming from the North, were not receptive to the political demand that an organic link be forged between trade and development, and that international trade should become a strategic means to be used by the international community to promote development in developing countries.[128]

It is no surprise then to note that in those early days, the idea that there was a nexus between trade and development found better acceptance in the United Nations. At the first United Nations Conference on Trade and Development in 1964,[129] the common positions of developing countries 'were embodied under a comprehensive trade and development agenda'.[130] An organisation dedicated to pursuing developing country integration and participation in the global economy took its name from the conference hence the acronym UNCTAD.

The UNCTAD agenda aimed to promote the development-friendly integration of developing countries into the world economy. The purpose of its work was 'to help shape current policy debates and thinking on development, with a particular focus on ensuring that domestic policies and international action are mutually supportive in bringing about sustainable development.'[131]

In the same year, a Committee on Trade and Development (CTD) charged with addressing the issues and concerns of developing countries was created under the GATT. Subsequently GATT Members adopted three new articles: Articles XXXVI (*Principles and Objectives*); XXXVII (*Commitments*); and XXXVIII (*Joint Action*) which were incorporated under a new 'Part IV' in the GATT. The new articles were collectively entitled '*Trade and Development*'[132] and as the title suggests incorporated the themes of trade and development into the chapeau of the GATT. In the statement of the Principles and Objectives to Part IV of the GATT, the Contracting Parties recalled that the main objectives of the General Agreement included 'the raising of standards of living and the progressive development of the economies of all contracting parties'.[133] They agreed that there was need for 'positive efforts designed to ensure that less-developed contracting parties secure a share in the growth in international trade commensurate with the needs of their economic development.'[134]

Article XXXVIII targeted six areas where the international trade regime could further the benefits of developing country participation.[135] These include for the Contracting Parties to make efforts to:

a. Provide stable market access for primary products of interest to less developed countries.
b. Collaborate with UN, its agencies, and UNCTAD in matters of trade and development policy.
c. Collaborate in analysing development plans and polices of less developed countries to determine the market prospects of the products of their industries.
d. Continuously review the rate of growth in world trade for developing countries and make recommendations for improvements where necessary.
e. Seek methods for improving harmonisation and adjustment of national policies and regulations which would assist the expansion of trade for the purpose of economic development including establishing facilities for increased trade flow information and market research.
f. Establish institutional arrangements to give effect to the scope of Part IV GATT.

The new Part IV codified development concerns and encouraged developed countries to assist in the trade and development objectives. It brought the developed countries under an obligation to extend special treatment to developing countries without the developing countries themselves expected to make any reciprocal concessions whether in respect of trade tariffs or other trade measures.

Criticism against Part IV has deemed that its language was 'cast in hortatory, rather than contractual, terms and led to very little concrete action'.[136] This sweeping commentary though harsh is not entirely without merit. Disputes brought under these provisions have not seen strenuous application thereof. We will consider two of such disputes: *EEC-Refunds on Exports of Sugar (Brazil)*[137] and *EEC-Restrictions on Imports of Desert Apples*.[138]

In *EEC-Refunds on Exports of Sugar (Brazil)* the Government of Brazil brought a complaint against the European Communities[139] claiming that the EC had acted contrary to the provisions of the GATT. It asserted that the European Community system for granting refunds on its exports of sugar had resulted in the Community countries having more than an equitable share of world export trade in sugar. Brazil contended that this action was not in conformity with the guidelines for Joint Action stipulated in Article XXXVIII which where provided to further the principles and objectives of Article XXXVI.

In its finding the Panel agreed with Brazil's assertions. Its reasoning was based on the fact that the EC had been able to make increased exports of sugar in the particular years complained (1978–9) owing to its use of subsidies. This resulted in reduced share of exports for developing countries in the world sugar market. Within the period and in respect of the adverse effect on developing country share of the world sugar market, the Panel found that the 'EC had therefore not collaborated with other contracting parties to further the principles and objectives set forth in Article XXXVI, in conformity with the guidelines given in Article XXXVIII.'[140]However although the Panel made reference to the efforts and commitment of the European Communities to the said Articles, there was no injunction issued to the Community to withdraw the subsidies, put a stop to their continued application, or make any concession to rectify the impaired benefits to Brazil, having found them in breach.

A later dispute on imports of desert apples brought by Chile against the European Communities was yet again silent on conclusive application of Part IV GATT. In *EEC-Restrictions on Imports of Desert Apples*, Chile's claim was against EEC import licensing procedures for desert apples which required a maximum 142,000 tonnes only from Chile out of a total quota of 500,000 tonnes from southern hemisphere exports. Chile complained that the quota was contrary to Articles I, II, XI, XIII and Part IV of the GATT. In its defence, the EEC argued that the quota was necessary to redress the surplus stock of apples in the market.

The Panel noted that consultations pursuant to Part IV GATT between the EEC and Chile had not been in the interest of developing countries. It however declined to make a finding under Part IV because it was of the opinion that the inconsistency of the EEC's import restrictions on the apples had already been established under Part I–III; in particular, under Part II GATT and so a Part IV consideration was not necessary.[141] Incidentally, the aforementioned Part IV subsists under the WTO which testifies to its continued relevance in the trade rules.

D. The Enabling Clause

The concerted efforts by developing countries lobbying under the UNCTAD resulted in a scheme which would provide preferential treatment to the benefit of developing countries. This became known as the *Generalised System of Preferences (GSP)* scheme.[142] In 1971, a waiver of Article I of the General Agreement [143] implemented this scheme. Resolution 21(ii) taken at the UNCTAD Conference[144] sets out the objectives of the 'generalised, non-reciprocal, non-discriminatory system of preferences in favour of the developing countries' to be: to increase their export earnings; to promote their industrialisation; and to accelerate their rates of economic growth.[145]

Under the GSP scheme, developed countries[146] granted reduced or zero-tariff rates (over the Most Favoured Nation (MFN) Rule) to selected products originating in developing countries. LDCs received this preferential treatment for a wider coverage of products and with deeper tariff cuts. The special treatment under the GSP as adopted by the GATT became permanent policy and was referred to as the 'Enabling Clause' in a GATT Decision of 1979.[147] Titled, *Differential and More Favourable Treatment Reciprocity and Fuller Participation of Developing Countries*, the Decision accorded non-reciprocal favourable treatment to developing countries alone.

The application of the Enabling Clause is set out in its paragraph 2 as follows:

(a) Preferential tariff treatment accorded by developed contracting parties to products originating in developing countries in accordance with the Generalized System of Preferences,[148]

(b) Differential and more favourable treatment with respect to the provisions of the General Agreement concerning non-tariff measures governed by the provisions of instruments multilaterally negotiated under the auspices of the GATT,

(c) Regional or global arrangements entered into amongst less-developed contracting parties for the mutual reduction or elimination of tariffs and, in accordance with criteria or conditions which may be prescribed by the CONTRACTING PARTIES, for the mutual reduction or elimination of non-tariff measures, on products imported from one another, and

(d) Special treatment on the least developed among the developing countries in the context of any general or specific measures in favour of developing countries.[149]

These 'special treatment' provisions have been the subject of a number of disputes. In *EC-Tariff Preferences*,[150] India challenged the conditions under which the EC grants tariff preferential treatment to other developing countries under an EC preferential tariff scheme to which India belonged.[151] Under *Council Regulation EC NO 2501/2001*,[152] the EC had provided for five different tariff preferential arrangements including special incentive arrangements for countries with policies for the protection of labour rights and the environment; special arrangements for combating drug production and trafficking; and special arrangements for LDCs. India alleged that these preferences were inconsistent with the MFN rule under Article I GATT, and paragraphs 2(a), 3(a) and 3(c) of the Enabling Clause.

We have previously cited the provisions of paragraph 2 of the Enabling Clause. Paragraph 3 provides that any differential and more favourable treatment provided under the Clause:

(a) shall be designed to facilitate and promote the trade of developing countries and not to raise barriers to or create undue difficulties for the trade of any other contracting parties;

(b) shall not constitute an impediment to the reduction or elimination of tariffs and other restrictions to trade on a most-favoured-nation basis; and

(c) shall in the case of such treatment accorded by developed contracting parties to developing countries be designed and, if necessary, modified, to respond positively to the development, financial and trade needs of developing countries.

In the opinion of the Panel, preferential treatment ought not to discriminate between recipient developing countries. By denying an extension of the preferential treatment to India (India had not fulfilled the EC criteria in respect of policy implementation for the purpose of combating drug production and trafficking and in respect of protection of labour rights and the environment), the EC had acted inconsistently with paragraph 2(a) of the Enabling Clause which required that preferential treatment had to be made on a non-discriminatory basis.

The AB upheld the finding of the Panel on this last issue although it adopted a different rationale for finding that the EC action discriminated against India. In the view of the AB, the EC's preferential arrangements were not supported by the Enabling Clause because the paragraph 2(a) provision on non-discrimination is substantiated in paragraph 3(c). Therefore, a proper interpretation of both paragraphs according to the AB, demands that identical treatment ought to be given to *all* beneficiaries in so far as these beneficiaries have the same '"development, financial and trade needs" to which the system in question is intended to respond'.[153]

This *EC-Tariff Preferences* case presented an opportunity for the DSB to determine the development question as it relates to the application of the trade rules (in this instance the rules under the Enabling Clause) on special treatment for developing countries. Notably, the DSB did make an attempt at an equitable interpretation of the term 'developing countries' and how this group ought to be construed in the implementation of preferential schemes under the Enabling Clause.[154]

The AB avoided grouping together all developed states, on the one hand, and all developing states, on the other, having regarded that each of the latter states has its own individual concerns and interests, strengths and weaknesses.[155] The AB noted that the needs of developing countries 'are varied and not homogeneous'.[156] It pointed out that paragraph 3(c) indicates that 'a GSP scheme may be "non-discriminatory" even if "identical" tariff treatment is not accorded to "all" GSP beneficiaries'.[157] To this end, it posited that so long as the objective of the Enabling Clause was complied with, the term "developing countries" in paragraph 2(a) should not be read to mean "all" developing countries. Accordingly, paragraph 2(a) does not prohibit preference-granting countries from according different tariff preferences to different sub-categories of GSP beneficiaries in that case.

A crucial question for the AB however was whether the EC Regulation had complied with the objective of the Enabling Clause in paragraph 3(a). This provision of the Enabling Clause states that differential and more favourable treatment '[...] shall be designed to facilitate and promote the trade of developing countries and not to raise barriers to or create undue difficulties for the trade of any other contracting parties'. In the summation of the AB, 'this requirement applies, *a fortiori*, to any preferential treatment granted to one GSP beneficiary that is not granted to another'.[158] Thus the reference to 'any other contracting parties' in paragraph 2 (a) of the Enabling Clause, was to *all GSP beneficiaries* under that particular scheme.

However, the DSB has pointed out that a preferential scheme is not an exemption from the obligations not to discriminate against other WTO

Members. In *EC- Export Subsidies on Sugar*[159] the dispute centred on an EC regime for import of sugars at low prices and at low duty in line with an arrangement pursuant to Council Regulation (EC) No. 1260/2001[160] and other supplementary legislation. The complaint was brought by Australia, Brazil and Thailand. They contended variously, that the EC sugar regime granted less favourable treatment to the sugars from producers and exporters not covered by the EC Regulation. They argued that the EC granted subsidies in the form of export refunds to producers contingent upon their use of EC domestic sugars and ACP/India equivalents. These export refunds enabled the exports of these sugars and their sale at prices less than their cost of production in the world market. It was also alleged that EC exports of sugar had exceeded the specified quantity commitment levels provided in the Schedule of Concessions for sugar and agricultural products notified to the WTO for the marketing period 2001/2002–2004/2005.

The discriminatory nature of the grants of subsidies and refunds were in the argument of the Complainants, contrary to the provisions on national treatment with respect to internal taxation and regulation (Article III GATT); the prohibition of subsidies made contingent upon export performance or use of domestic over imported goods under the *Agreement on Subsides and Countervailing Measures – SCM Agreement* (Article 3); and the provisions on export subsidy commitments under the *Agreement on Agriculture* (Articles 9; 10). In addition, both Australia and Brazil alleged that the EC regime was contrary to the general provisions of Article XVI GATT on subsidies.

The beneficiaries of the EC regime included as in the first case above, those in the EC-ACP/India partnership. In its defence the EC claimed that the sugar regime had not in actual fact nullified the benefits accruing to the complainants in respect of their share of world trade in sugar. The Panel disagreed with this submission. In its view, the EC argument was not sufficient to rebut the *prima facie* evidence by the complainants that the preferential treatment under the sugar regime had suffered an 'adverse impact' on the complainant's export as shown by the amount of trade lost by the latter as a result of implementation of the Council Regulation.[161] The Panel found for the Complainants, stating that the EC sugar regime was contrary to the relevant provisions of the Agreement on Agriculture. It did not go on to consider the SCM Agreement, deeming it sufficient that the former provisions had been proved to be breached, an action which was criticised by the AB even as it upheld the findings of the Panel.[162]

With respect to the impact of preferential schemes therefore, two things are to be noted. First, a preferential arrangement for the benefit of developing countries as provided subject to the Enabling Clause cannot be inherently discriminatory. In keeping with the non-discriminatory provisions of the Clause, any preferential tariff treatment applied under such a scheme ought to be extended to all the beneficiaries who sharing the same development, financial and trade needs, are participants in the particular scheme. Second, although a preferential treatment scheme operates as a waiver of the MFN provisions in the GATT, a contracting party irrespective of the obligations it assumes to extend preferential treatment cannot act contrary to the general obligations under relevant WTO Agreements.

There is no doubt that preferential arrangements hold great promise for direct assistance to developing countries by their developed country counterparts although the arrangements are not without their critics.[163] It must also be pointed out that although the Enabling Clause enhances the development-friendly potential of trade rules and is a significant contribution to the moves towards encouraging developing country participation in trade, it still has its limitations. While preferential treatment may provide a ready market for beneficiaries' products, it will not necessarily grant its beneficiaries an added advantage over other WTO Members who cannot in any event be prohibited from trading in that same market, as the *EC-Sugars* case buttresses.

E. Special Assistance to LDCs

LDCs also benefit under arrangements made pursuant to the Enabling Clause. For instance the EC *Everything But Arms* (EBA) initiative is made for the benefit of LDCs alone. The initiative is pursuant to *EC Council Regulation No. 416/2001*.[164] The EBA provides duty and quota free access to all agricultural products from LDCs apart from bananas, rice and sugar.[165] Thus excepting arms and ammunition (the suggestion that the low industrialised and poverty ridden societies of most LDCs have the capacity for producing weapons that can compete in the international arms market is remarkable), all agricultural products including beef and other meats, fruits and vegetables, maize and cereals, starch oils, processed sugar products, pasta and alcoholic beverages are duty and quota free under the EBA.

On the face of it, the EBA is a step toward extending this promise of direct assistance to the poorest developing countries.[166] Yet we are of the opinion that there is room for more effective assistance towards the development needs of the beneficiaries under the scheme. Whereas the initiative places much emphasis on the need to ensure that rules of origin are applicable to any goods claimed to have originated in an LDC, that fraud is averted, and that regulatory safeguards are applied in implementing the initiative, there is no indication of the grant of technical assistance or capacity building schemes to enable the farmers in these regions enhance their productive base in those sectors wherein they are offered preferential treatment. Such technical assistance will go a long way beyond extending special treatment; towards a strengthening of the production and hence, the trading capacity of the scheme's beneficiaries.

The above argument notwithstanding, in the general context of development action with respect of legal provisions on development related issues, LDCs do receive significant attention. In the Preamble to the *Decision on Measures in Favour of Least Developed Countries*,[167] the Member States acknowledge the less developed status of the LDCs, requiring them only to 'undertake commitments and concessions to the extent consistent with their individual development, financial and trade needs, or their administrative and institutional capabilities'. The Decision states the commitment of the WTO: in the implementation of special provisions in favour of LDCs, through reviews;[168] the autonomous implementation of concessions under the MFN (Article 1 GATT) rules for non-discrimination on tariff and non-tariff measures on products of export interest to LDCs;[169] for special consideration to be given to export interests of LDCs in the application of import relief measure under Article XXXVII GATT 1947 (on Joint Action);[170] sympathetic consideration to be given to concerns raised by LDCs;[171] for the provision of technical assistance;[172] and to seek positive measures which facilitate trading opportunities for LDCs.[173] Also, developing countries can enter into preferential tariff treatment arrangements with LDCs under the *Preferential Tariff Treatment for Least Developed Countries*.[174]

Other WTO initiatives for LDCs include the Plan of Action formulated after the 1996 Singapore Conference, the 'Integrated Framework' (a joint technical assistance programme with the IMF, International Trade Centre, UNCTAD, UNDP, World Bank and the WTO), a decision on preferential tariff treatment,[175] the 2002 Work Programme including support for agencies working on the diversification of LDC economies and assistance to ensure a speedier membership negotiation for LDCs, subsidised office space at the WTO Headquarters in Geneva, and fee exemption for use of the Advisory Centre on WTO law (ACWL).[176]

F. Special and Differential Treatment (SDT) Provisions

There are about 145 SDT provisions spread across the WTO legal framework, 107 of which were adopted at the conclusion of the Uruguay Round. 22 of these provisions apply to LDCs only.[177] In summary, the SDT provisions can be found in the following Agreements and corresponding citation:

(a) *Agreement on Agriculture*: Preamble; Articles 4.0 and Schedules; 6.1 and Schedules; 6.2; 6.4; 8 and Schedules; 9.4; 12.2; 15.1; 15.2 and Schedules; 16; 20; Annex 2 para 3; Annex 2 para 4; Annex Section B; Notifications.

(b) *Agreement on Sanitary and Phytosanitary Restrictions*: Preamble; Articles 9; 10.1; 10.2; 10.3; 10.4; 14; Annex B.

(c) *Agreement on Textiles and Clothing*: Articles 1.2; 1.4; 2.18; 6.6(a); 6.6(b); 6.6 (c); Annex: para 3.

(d) *Agreement on Technical Barriers to Trade*: Preamble; Articles 2.12 and 5.9; 11.1; 11.2 and 11.5; 11.3 and 11.4; 11.6; 12.2; 12.3 and 12.7; 12.4; 12.5 and 12.6; 12.10.

(e) *Agreement on Trade-related Investment Measures (TRIMS)*: Preamble; Articles 4; 5.2; 5.3.

(f) *Agreement on Implementation of Article VI (Anti-Dumping)*: Article 15.

(g) *Agreement on Implementation of Article VII (Customs Valuation)*: Articles 20; 20.1; 20.2; 20.3; Annex III.2; Annex III.3 ; Annex III.4 ; Annex III.5.

(h) *Agreement on Preshipment Inspection (PSI)* Preamble; Article 3.3.

(i) *Agreement on Import Licensing*: Preamble; Articles 1.2; 2.2, footnote 5; 3.5(a)(iv); 3.5(j).

(j) *Agreement on Safeguards:* Articles 9.1, footnote 2; 9.2.

(k) *Agreement on Subsidies and Countervailing Measures (SCM)*: Articles 27; 27.2(a); 27.2(b) and 27.4; 27.3; 27.5 and 27.6; 27.7; 27.8; 27.9–10; 27.11; 27.13.

(l) *General Agreement on Trade in Services (GATS)*: Preamble; III:4; IV:1; IV:2; IV:3; V:3; XV:1; XIX:2; XXVI:2.

(m) *GATS Annex on Telecommunications*: Para 5(g); para 6(a); para 6(c).

(n) *Agreement on Trade-related Aspects of Intellectual Property Rights (TRIPS)*: Preamble; Articles 65.2 and 65.4; 66; 66.2; 67.

(o) *Trade Policy Review Mechanisms*: Section D.

(p) *Understanding on Rules and Procedures Governing the Settlement of Disputes (Dispute Settlement Understanding)*: Articles 3.12; 4.10; 8.10; 12.10; 12.11; 21.2; 21.7; 21.8; 24.1; 24.2; 27.2.

Particular consideration given to LDCs under the respective Agreements include: longer transitional periods where these are allowed, provision of technical assistance, and consideration for importers products in the allocation of non-automatic licences.[178]

The justification for the inclusion of SDT provisions in the legal framework of the WTO has been observed to be based on a three-fold premise:[179]

- that developing countries "are intrinsically disadvantaged in their participation in international trade and therefore, any multilateral agreement involving them and developed countries must take into account this intrinsic weakness in specifying their rights and responsibilities";
- that the trade policies that would maximise sustainable development in developing countries are different from those in developed economies and

hence that policy disciplines applying to the latter should not apply to the former; and

- that it is in the interest of developed countries to assist developing countries in their fuller integration and participation in the international trading system.

The SDT provisions are acknowledged as an integral part of the WTO agreements.[180] However, it is the language of the provisions which determines their overall effectiveness since 'an important criterion for the assessment of special treatment in the WTO agreements concerns their binding character'.[181] The WTO lists six substantive categories of SDTs to include:[182]

(i) Provisions aimed at increasing the trade opportunities of developing country Members.
(ii) Provisions under which WTO Members should safeguard the interests of developing country Members.
(iii) Flexibility of commitments, of actions, and use of policy instruments.
(iv) Transitional time periods.
(v) Technical assistance.
(vi) Provisions relating to least-developed country Members.[183]

The SDT provisions are either 'mandatory' or 'non-mandatory'. The distinctions between mandatory and non-mandatory provisions apply to categories (i), (ii), and (v) and certain provisions of category (vi). These distinctions however do not apply to provisions under categories (iii), (iv), and certain parts of category (vi) because the latter provisions specify levels of flexibility and transition time periods that developing countries may choose to exercise of their own volition.[184]

Mandatory SDT provisions are distinguished from non-mandatory provisions based on the use of the words 'shall', which indicates a mandatory provision and 'should' which indicates provisions that are non-mandatory.[185] This distinction is however not absolute. Although there is the exclusive right of Members 'to adopt authoritative interpretations of their rights or obligations under the WTO Agreement'[186] as may be expected, this right is subject to any subsequent interpretations arising under a dispute settlement opinion.

The WTO itself has mentioned that 'a mandatory provision might not necessarily be effective'.[187] There are two ways by which non-mandatory SDT provisions could be made mandatory or confirmed to be mandatory:[188]

(i) through *amendment* of the WTO agreement in question which would convert non-mandatory provisions into mandatory ones, replacing the term 'should' with 'shall' without changing the rest of the provisions. This could be undertaken pursuant to Article X of the WTO Agreement;[189]

(ii) through *authoritative interpretation* of the provisions of the WTO agreement in question.

An authoritative interpretation is undertaken pursuant to Article IX of the WTO Agreement which provides:

> The Ministerial Conference and the General Council shall have the exclusive authority to adopt interpretations of this Agreement and of the Multilateral Trade Agreements. In the case of an interpretation of a Multilateral Trade Agreement in Annex 1, they shall exercise their authority on the basis of a recommendation by the Council overseeing the functioning of that Agreement. The decision to adopt an interpretation shall be taken by a three-fourths majority of the Members. This paragraph shall not be used in a manner that would undermine the amendment provisions in Article X.[190]

The DSB has not always interpreted the terms 'should' and 'shall' strictly. In *Canada-Measures Affecting the Export of Civilian Aircraft*[191] the AB had to interpret the term "should" in a relevant provision of the DSU which stated that 'a Member *should* respond promptly and fully to any request by a panel for such information as the panel considers necessary and appropriate'.[192] The AB was of the opinion that although the word "should" is often used colloquially to imply an exhortation, or to state a preference, it is not always used in those ways. It can also be used 'to express a duty [or] obligation'.[193] In its view, the word 'should' in the context of Article 13.1 DSU is used 'in a normative, rather than a merely exhortative sense', thus implying a duty. Similarly in *EC-Measures Concerning Meat and Meat Products (Hormones)*[194] the word 'should' was interpreted as implying a *duty*.[195]

The *Doha Declaration* proposes that 'all special and differential treatment provisions be reviewed with a view to strengthening them and making them more precise, effective and operational'.[196] The review done under the CTD is incorporated in the text of a later SDT Implementation document.[197] However, we will highlight areas which demand further action and which in our view will go a long way towards enhancing the efficacy of SDT provisions in addressing development considerations under the respective WTO Agreements.

As they are presently, the SDT provisions lack sufficient expression of the duties and obligations on WTO Members. The result is that even though the WTO Agreements are legally binding, the SDT provisions are not written in the style of a contract of obligations between developed country Members and their less developed counterparts. It is considered that it would lend clarity to the SDT provisions if like the provisions of a legal contract or statute, they are 'written with such a degree of precision that a person of Machiavellian cleverness, reading it in bad faith, cannot misunderstand it'.[198]

Some examples could be pointed out. For instance, there is provision for 'a study of questions' with respect to the implementation of the *Customs Valuation Agreement.*[199] Annex III.5 of the Agreement provides:

> Certain developing countries may have problems in the implementation of Article 1 of the Agreement insofar as it relates to importations into their countries by sole agents, sole distributors and sole concessionaires. If such problems arise in practice in developing country Members applying the Agreement, a study of this question shall be made, at the request of such Members, with a view to finding appropriate solutions.

The use of the phrase 'a study of this question', underscores the lack of clarity as to the intent of the provision. The provision begins by recognising the problems which may be faced by developing countries in applying the provisions of the Agreement as relating to Article 1 thereof. Reading the said Article 1,[200] this recognition is in fact necessary because the subject matter covered by the Article requires the significant collection of data and statistical analysis which may be cumbersome for any country without the basic infrastructural facilities to collate and analyse commercial import data for these purposes.[201] Developing countries need to have these resources not only for 'their own trade policies and practices, but also with respect to the interaction of their trade regime with the external environment'.[202] Rather than merely directing for a 'study of the question' to be made, the provision ought to have set out how developing countries can address the implementation of Article 1 of the Agreement insofar as it relates to importations into their countries by sole agents, sole distributors and sole concessionaires' as provided in Article III:5 cited above.[203]

The use of ambiguous language in SDT provisions is another case in point. Article 12.10 of the DSU is a good point of reference. The Article provides that:

> In the context of consultations involving a measure taken by a developing country Member, the parties may agree to extend the periods established in paragraphs 7 and 8 of Article 4. If, after the relevant period has elapsed, the consulting parties cannot agree that the consultations have concluded, the Chairman of the DSB shall decide, after consultation with the parties, whether to extend the relevant period and, if so, for how long.

In addition, in examining a complaint against a developing country Member, the panel shall accord sufficient time for the developing country Member to prepare and present its argumentation. The provisions of paragraph 1 of Article 20 and paragraph 4 of Article 21 are not affected by any action pursuant to this paragraph.[204]

In *Pakistan-Patent Protection for Pharmaceutical and Agricultural Chemical Products*[205] a complaint was brought by the US against Pakistan regarding patent protection for pharmaceutical and agricultural chemical products under the *TRIPS Agreement*. The representative of the US said that on 30 April 1996, his country had requested Pakistan to hold consultations with regard to the failure of Pakistan either to provide patent protection for pharmaceutical and agricultural products or to comply with the obligations under Articles 70.8 and 70.9 of the *TRIPS Agreement*. In a preliminary meeting of the DSB,[206] Pakistan, expressed its discontent with the provisions of DSU Article 12.10. It raised a number of issues affecting developing country interests which issues were not clarified by the language of the provisions. The issues were:

- The meaning and significance of the consultations stage;
- Whether a Member could decide unilaterally that consultations had been concluded.[207]

Pakistan sought reliance on Article 3.7 of the DSU in the face of this lack of precision. The referred DSU Article stipulates that before bringing a case a Member shall exercise its judgement as to whether action under the DSU procedures would be fruitful bearing in mind that the aim of the dispute settlement mechanism was to secure a possible solution to a dispute. The Pakistan representative at the meeting expressed disappointment with the US because despite Pakistan's assurances that it was making concrete efforts to address the issues raised by the US in their consultations, the latter proceeded with a request for the establishment of a Panel to hear the dispute. Highlighting its request for further clarifications on Article 12.10 of the DSU and on that basis, it could not agree to the establishment of a Panel as requested by the US.[208]

The *SPS Agreement* and the SDT provisions under its Article 10, presents another example of the limitations in these special treatment provisions. SPS measures demand a high degree of technical competence and bureaucratic capacity to meet the provisions of both international and private standards for imported food products. It is observed that apart from providing for longer time frames to allow developing countries to comply with the provisions of the Agreement, 'where the appropriate level of sanitary or phytosanitary protection allows scope for the phased introduction of new sanitary or phytosanitary measures', and for Members to 'encourage and facilitate the active participation of developing country Members in the relevant international organizations', the said Article 10 is silent on practical assistance towards the implementation of the *SPS Agreement.*

In addition, the mode of classification of SDT provisions does not adequately address the need for clarity in the provisions. In the *Implementation of Special and Differential Treatment Provisions in WTO Agreements and Decisions: A Review of Mandatory Special and Differential Treatment Provisions,* the SDT provisions are classified according to the following criteria *vis a vis* provisions which:

- require Members to achieve a certain result (obligations of result) or
- require Members to engage in a certain conduct (obligations of conduct) and;
- whether provisions stipulate obligations of Members taken individually or;
- stipulate obligations of Members taken collectively[209]

The CTD summarises the provisions in an Annex attached to the document.[210]

Unhelpfully, the CTD explains that 'the distinction between *obligations of result* and *obligations of conduct* is not invariably clear-cut'.[211] It states that SDT provisions which contain obligations of result require Members to achieve a certain outcome while leaving them free to identify and choose appropriate means of achieving that result; while SDT provisions which lay down obligations of conduct do not require Members to achieve any particular result but instead require them to adopt a certain course of conduct.[212]

For instance, Article 10.6 of the *Agreement on Technical Barriers to Trade (TBT Agreement)* which is an *obligation of result* provisions states clearly that:

> The Secretariat **shall,** when it receives notifications in accordance with the provisions of this Agreement, **circulate copies** of notifications to all Members and interested international standardising and conformity assessment bodies, and **draw the attention** of developing country Members to any notifications relating to products of particular interests to them. (Bold for emphasis)

The provision is clear in advising WTO Members to safeguard the interests of developing country Members. It instructs the Secretariat to provide copies of notifications to all Members and to alert developing countries to notifications on products of particular interest to them.[213]

Obligations of conduct on the other hand are imprecise and lack the potential for concrete application. For instance we may provide a contrast to Article 10.6 of the TBT examined above with Article 12.8 of the same TBT Agreement.[214] The latter provision identifies the problems of developing countries in applying the Agreement including institutional and infrastructural problems. It states that:

> It is recognized that developing country Members may face special problems, including institutional and infrastructural problems, in the field of preparation and application of technical regulations, standards and conformity assessment procedures. It is further recognized that the special development and trade needs of developing country Members, as well as their stage of technological development, may hinder their ability to discharge fully their obligations under this Agreement. Members, therefore, **shall take this fact fully into account**. Accordingly, with a view to ensuring that developing country Members are able to comply with this Agreement, the Committee on Technical Barriers to Trade provided for in Article 13 (referred to in this Agreement as the "Committee") is enabled to grant, upon request, specified, time-limited exceptions in whole or in part from obligations under this Agreement. When considering such requests the Committee **shall take into account** the special problems, in the field of preparation and application of technical regulations, standards and conformity assessment procedures, and the special development and trade needs of the developing country Member, as well as its stage of technological development, which may hinder its ability to discharge fully its obligations under this Agreement. The Committee **shall, in particular, take into account** the special problems of the least-developed country Members. (Bold for emphasis)

The provision unfortunately does not state any limits for the 'time-limited exceptions' which may be granted by the Committee. Also, should the Committee find that time exception may be needed by a developing country, the provisions do not provide for peremptory powers to enable it to grant any such exceptions even after 'taking into account' all the relevant facts before it. Rather, what is provided is for an affected developing country to *make a request* for exceptions, a condition which runs contrary to the provision's recognition that "developing country Members may face special problems, including institutional and infrastructural problems, in the field of preparation and application of technical regulations, standards and conformity assessment procedures."

One considers that the SDT provisions will be beneficial not only to the developing countries but also the trading system in general if these provisions can go beyond their present exhortatory nature. The drafting technique employed in respect of SDT provisions while it may have served the political purpose of conceding to demands for special treatment provisions, merely satisfies a superficial recognition of the presence of developing country membership in the WTO. What the drafting technique has not achieved is clarity on the practical results expected in the implementation of these provisions, particularly in the relevant areas of technical assistance and capacity building objectives.

G. The Committee for Trade and Development (CTD)

The CTD is primarily concerned with the development objectives agreed by WTO Member countries. It is the forum for discussions on all cross-cutting matters of special interest to developing countries.[215] The Committee:

- co-ordinates technical assistance work on development and its relationship to development related activities in other multilateral agencies;
- sets out the legal classification for SDTs which are mandatory and the implications of making mandatory those which are currently non-binding in line with the directives of the Doha Development Agenda; examines ways to make SDTs more effective and identifies ways to incorporate SDTs into WTO rules;[216]
- holds sessions on the trade related measures that could improve the integration of small economies and reports its conclusions to the General Council;
- provides an Annual Report; and
- structures its yearly work in line with its Work Programme which include overseeing:
  - Notifications to the Enabling Clause;
  - Technical Co-operation and Training;
  - Declining terms of trade for primary commodities; and
  - Other work arising from the Doha Development Agenda.[217]

As a regular WTO body, the CTD is comprised of all WTO Members including developing countries. As such, it is not only a focal point for considering and coordinating assistance to be given to developing countries, it actually provides a ready fusion of developing country representatives brought together to discuss (albeit with other countries) the trade and development agenda of the WTO.

Presently, the lack of a strong political cohesion between developing countries weakens efforts aimed at addressing the imbalance within the WTO. A weak coalition will find it almost impossible to achieve major successes in a bargaining arrangement. It has been observed, that 'the most important benefit of joint bargaining is the pooling of bargaining resources to allow greater negotiating weight to the weak'.[218] If developing countries can utilise the opportunity of meeting regularly under the aegis of the CTD, it can be argued that a stronger coalition can be facilitated as they will have both the number (presuming all developing countries attend) and the objective (given the focus of the CTD) to discuss issues that pertain to their needs and concerns at the multilateral trade level.

This is not to suggest that the present scope of reference of the CTD is without any impact. The argument here is that the CTD has more direct relationship with developing country representatives when they attend the meetings of the Committee, in assessing the trade and development activities of the WTO. Thus, attendance at CTD meetings and participation in the technical assistance and training activities coordinated by the Committee can further assist developing countries to produce cogent proposals on their concerns at WTO negotiations. A WTO Economic Research paper suggests that

> The best way to ensure that the WTO contributes to development is to move beyond the principle of differentiation to the substance of individual provisions, including in areas where new negotiations are proposed. Increased emphasis in recent years upon the need to see trade policy as an integral element of a broader panorama of development policies, rather than as an externally-imposed "add-on", supports such an approach. The core challenge is to link negotiating positions on liberalization commitments, WTO rules, and special and differential treatment to a clear and cogently argued identification of development needs and priorities.[219]

The CTD can be a forum for developing countries to analyse and link their negotiation positions in order to present strong and coherent proposals on integral issues including the scope of WTO obligations on development, the need for improved flexibility in the WTO rules, the concerns with the overall effectiveness of SDT provisions, and the general notion of special treatment in future trade negotiations. However for the CTD to have this desired greater impact in the trade and development work of the WTO, it must be utilised effectively. Effective utilisation here requires that developing countries must attend and participate in the CTD activities.

H. Technical Assistance and Co-operation with other Agencies

Most of the practical work on development carried out at the WTO is geared towards building trade capacity in developing countries. To this end, the WTO undertakes several activities in conjunction with other agencies such as the

International Trade Centre (ITC), World Bank, and UNCTAD.[220] It also undertakes Trade Related Technical Assistance (TRTA) and training programmes. The WTO carries out this work in co-operation with other international agencies and partners including external consultants, researchers and university lecturers who deliver the work at national or regional levels. Two bodies have been established to coordinate efforts in this respect: the Institute for Training and Technical Cooperation (ITTC) which was established in response to the development challenges posed by the Doha Round, and the Technical Assistance Management Committee (TAMC). The TAMC represents all WTO Divisions. It serves as a mechanism for coordinating and monitoring all TRTA work provided by the Secretariat.

The objective of the ITTC in its TRTA activities for the benefit of beneficiary countries is to:

- enhance institutional and human capacity in the field of trade,
- address trade policy issues,
- integrate more fully into the multilateral trading system,
- exercise the rights of WTO membership, and
- fully participate in multilateral trade negotiations.

The TRTA work of the WTO is set out in a 'Technical Assistance and Training Work Plan' prepared every two years.[221] The financing of the TRTA is carried out under the Doha Development Agenda Global Trust Fund (DDAGTF) established in 2002. The Fund is supervised by the Committee on Budget Finance and Administration and the CTD.

I. The Aid for Trade Initiative

More recently, the *Aid for Trade* (AfT) and *Enhanced Integrated Framework* (Enhanced IF) initiatives have been adopted in conjunction with other international bodies, as programmes which by targeting the *supply side constraints* in developing economies, can assist less developed countries to improve their industrial capacity and increase their market access potentials. The Enhanced IF builds on the earlier Integrated Framework programme.[222] The original Integrated Framework was formed as a response to a proposal in the first WTO Conference of 1996. That proposal focused on the need for special assistance to LDCs in their integration into the global economy. The programme was named the *Integrated Framework for Trade-Related Technical Assistance to Least Developed Countries*; in short form, the IF. Six multilateral agencies were involved: the International Monetary Fund (IMF), the International Trade Centre (ITC), the United

Nations Committee on Trade and Development (UNCTAD), the United Nations Development Programme (UNDP), the World Bank, and the WTO.

In a review of the IF in 2000, it was recommended that institutional changes should be made in order to make the programme more beneficial to a greater number of LDCs. The recommendations were for the IF: to mainstream trade into LDCs' Poverty Reduction Strategy Papers (PRSP) or other national development plans and to assist in the co-ordinated delivery of trade related technical assistance. The funds for the programme were for two purposes:

a. financing Diagnostic Trade Integration Studies (DTISs) and strengthening in-country structures; and
b. financing capacity building projects in the LDCs as identified in the DTIS Action Matrices.[223]

The enhancement of the IF arose out of the joint decision by the Development Committee of the World Bank and the IMF to provide the programme with more additional resources and expand the objectives of the IF to include[224]:

a. Increased, additional, predictable financial resources to implement Action Matrices.
b. Strengthened in-country capacities to manage, implement and monitor the IF process.
c. Enhanced IF governance.

The aim of the enhanced IF is to address the slow progress of the original IF which suffered from implementation setbacks. The priority areas of the DTIS identified under the original programme were not being addressed in the national investments in the LDCs. The Enhanced IF has the following key features:

a. increased resources,
b. strengthened governance structure with a secretariat,
c. strengthened in-country structures,
d. improved link between donours and recipients,
e. multiyear programmes of technical assistance and capacity building, and
f. possibility of extended coverage to other low-income countries.[225]

The AfT initiative is the wider category for long term development programmes set up for the purpose of assisting developing countries (including LDCs) to address the problems of supply side constraints in the bid for greater market access in the international trade environment. The *Doha Work Programme* set out at the Hong Kong Ministerial Conference adopted the view that the Aid Initiatives should have the objective of assisting all developing countries 'to build the supply-side capacity and trade-related infrastructure that they need to assist them to implement and benefit from WTO Agreements and more broadly to expand their trade'.[226] The rationale for the Initiative is that it will assist 'developing countries to increase exports of goods and services, to integrate into the multilateral trading system, and to benefit from liberalized trade and increased market access'.[227]

The AfT initiative established a Task Force set up by the WTO DG in 2006 to ensure that the programme meets its purposes. These purposes include: to help facilitate, implement and adjust to trade reform and liberalisation; assist regional integration; assist smooth integration into the world trading system; and assist in the implementation of trade agreements.[228] The Task Force recommends that 'projects and programmes should be considered as Aid for Trade if these activities have been identified as trade-related development priorities in the recipient country's national development strategies'.[229]

Areas which the AfT Task Force have identified as priority areas include:[230]

a. Trade policy and regulations including training trade officials; support to governments to assist them in implementing trade agreements.
b. Trade development which includes investment promotion; analysis and institutional support for trade in services; improving public-private sector networking.
c. Trade related infrastructure which would include building physical structures like ports, transportation links such as roads.
d. Building productive capacity of a country to increase production of goods.
e. Trade related adjustment including supporting developing countries to put in place accompanying measures that assist them to benefit from liberalised trade.
f. Other trade related needs.

Different developing countries and development agencies including development banks and WTO Members have offered their respective opinion on the expectations of the AfT programme.[231] The underlying agreement in these views however is the reiteration of the WTO commitment that the AfT initiative is not an alternative to the development agenda of the WTO. The Hong Kong Declaration is emphatic that although the AfT can be a complement to the DDA it 'cannot be a substitute for the development benefits that will result from a successful conclusion to the DDA, particularly on market access'.[232]

The argument against development aid is increasingly strong in current times.[233] The adoption of the new initiative has raised interesting questions.

Carin Smaller[234] assessing the AfT asks several key questions: Is Aid for Trade a consolation price for a failed Doha Agenda?; Will Aid for Trade be used to pressure developing countries to open their markets more than they otherwise would?; What are other potential consequences of bringing Aid for Trade into the WTO?; Are donors serious about embracing the expanded Aid for Trade agenda?; Will there be enough money?; Is the WTO the best forum to operationalise Aid for Trade?

Our concern is with the extent of involvement of the world trading system in the hitherto operational areas of the world development agencies. Granted, the initiatives are tied to trade related activities but can the WTO carry out this additional responsibility effectively given its limited administrative manpower and its prior obligations to development particularly those it has formulated in the latest Doha 'Development' Round?

Constituting the Task Force of WTO Members' Representatives under the AfT will undoubtedly stretch both the administrative and infrastructural capacity of the Organisation especially in consideration of the vast range of TRTA activity already undertaken under the ITTC and the TAMC. Although as was noted earlier, the WTO insists that the AfT is not a replacement of the objectives under the Doha agenda, it is possible that the main focus of the DDA and the WTO's commitments to assisting the development progress of its less developed Membership may suffer some neglect. It would have been preferable for an entirely independent structure to be composed out of the multilateral agencies which founded the two initiatives to oversee the programmes.

Nevertheless, the various forms of assistance enumerated under both the Enhanced IF and the AfT are distinctly technical assistance and capacity building contributions and so these areas will benefit from the WTO experience in technical assistance and capacity building programmes for improving a country's trade potentials. Although the WTO provides under the *Hong Kong Declaration*[235] earlier mentioned that initiatives are not to replace the WTO development agenda, whether the WTO will come to regard them as *additions* to their Organisation's commitments under the DDA or as *fulfilments* of the Organisation's mandate remains to be seen. Also, it is not yet clear how conflicts if they arise between the AfT and the DDA objectives, will be addressed, and resolved.

It must also be borne in mind, that there are other problems associated with aid initiatives when considered from the perspective of recipient countries. In particular the economic conditions prevalent in the communities of recipient governments make it difficult for the latter to unilaterally deviate from the views or programmes of a donor country or agency. Also the obligatory and at times mandatory financial commitments in the provisos to the legal agreements between donors and recipients may hinder the progress of other sectors of development within the domestic environment of a recipient country.

Several questions therefore arise: Will there be deference to the domestic conditions of the recipient country or will the views of the Task Force prevail where there are conflicts between the two? What happens where a country fails to follow through on its obligations under the aid programme? By what means are the projects carried out under the initiatives to be appraised as furthering the development goals of the programme and assisting the developing country to enhance its market integration? Will there be need for judicial resolution of any disputes? Will such disputes, seeing as they arise between the WTO and its member States, be settled under the WTO dispute settlement, mechanisms or should a different body, for instance, the International Court of Justice (ICJ) consider the dispute?

Presumably, answers to these and other questions would come to light as the Aid Initiatives are gradually implemented. One advantage of the Initiatives however is that they place the WTO in a position to oversee the enforcement of trade-related development policies in line with WTO targets in the domestic environment. To be able to do so without comprising its independence and whilst pursuing its development concerns will be in our view, a test to the capacity of the Organisation to address its development obligations within its legal framework and to respond to its developing country members' needs, and at the same time, cooperate with other development agencies in addressing trade and development issues in the global economy.

Chapter Three

DEVELOPING COUNTRY INTEGRATION

3.1. Developing Countries and Barriers to Trade

Prior to the adoption of a rules-oriented system, there were barriers or trade restrictive measures which were identified under the GATT as 'obstacles to international flows' of goods and services.[1] Such barriers made it impossible for producers and exporters to make meaningful gains from their economic endeavours, and for consumers to have a reasonable choice of goods and services. Davey et al[2] analysed these obstacles on four levels. Generally, these were:

1. Governmental explicit obstacle to imported goods e.g. quantitative restrictions, subsidies, government procurement practices.
2. Governmental internal practice or regulations which have protective effects e.g. regulations requiring a higher standard of safety for imports, requirement that importers be licensed. The authors point out here that there is often a valid domestic governmental purpose such as consumer health or protection addressed by the regulation and that the problem is balancing the application of governmental measures for a legitimate purpose against the requirements of the international trading system to minimise obstacles to imports.
3. Problems which arise due to the importing structure of the importing country e.g. government 'industrial policy', the structure of industry.
4. Business practice (non-governmental) e.g. governmentally-induced practices such as directing a private firm to refuse to purchase foreign goods, restrictive business practices of private enterprises such as exclusive dealing arrangements, business practice and structure such as habits and preferences of businesses, cultural barriers including a dislike of certain brand names, or a willingness to pay a premium for certain quality or specialty goods. Here, Davey et al note that these preferences may require marketing expertise on the part of particular companies in order to allow them penetrate the market.

These barriers are related to both developing and developed country alike. Given the efforts of the multilateral trading system in eliminating these restrictions by the provision of a uniform set of rules for the trading environment, why is it still difficult for developing countries to integrate fully into the world trading system?

In his seminal work on the integration of developing countries at the GATT, Hudec was of the view that the main factor limiting further improvements in market access for developing countries 'is the relative lack of economic power of developing countries'.[3] He noted that this difficulty contributed to the unrewarding relationship between developing and developed countries:

> The history begins with a legal relationship based essentially on parity of obligation, with only limited, almost token exceptions. Over the years the relationship has gravitated, in seemingly inexorable fashion, towards the one-sided welfare relationship demanded by the developing countries. This relationship is one in which developing countries are excused from legal discipline while developed countries are asked to recognise a series of unilateral obligations, based in economic need, to promote the exports of developing countries.[4]

Hudec was emphatic that such a welfare relationship ultimately caused more harm than good for developing countries. In his view, a strict enforcement of a reciprocal MFN policy in international trade relations would be more advantageous to developing countries than the endless pursuits of concessions from trade rules and of preferential treatment arrangements.[5]

Debra Steger in her study of the world trading system also notes this unbalanced relationship under the GATT, and its effects:

> Under the GATT, the concept of special and differential treatment for developing countries became embedded in the trading system. Prior to the conclusion of the Uruguay Round, most developing countries did not bind their tariffs and had numerous legal avenues to avoid the application of GATT rules to their trading regimes. Thus many developing countries retained high tariffs and imposed quantitative restrictions on imports for many years. In pursuing the agenda of special and differential treatment, developing countries withdrew from the trading system and allowed the development of special trade regimes by the developed countries for agriculture and textiles that were adverse to the interests of the developing countries. As a result, the trading system that evolved under GATT was two-tiered and unbalanced.[6]

Michalopulous points out that the divide between developing and developed countries may have been widened even further by the establishment of the WTO:

> Integration into the world trading system depends on whether countries and their trading partners establish policies and institutions that are conducive to the mutually beneficial exchange of goods and services, based on specialisation and comparative advantage.
>
> The establishment of the WTO has resulted in further changes that have placed additional demands on developing countries in respect of effective participation. First, the WTO covers a variety of new areas – such as services, standards and IPRs – in which new rules governing the conduct of international trade have been agreed and whose implementation requires additional institutional capacity on the part of member governments. Second the WTO negotiations on the liberalisation of various sectors require continuous participation by the members. Third, the new WTO Dispute Settlement Mechanism (DSM) enables developing countries to address their grievances, but it also poses tremendous challenges because of their very limited institutional capacity to initiate actions against developed countries.[7]

There is the possibility of a 'cultural dimension' to the problem of developing country integration. As R. Samuelson notes:

> Much of Latin America, for e.g abandoned trade protectionism and favouritism for local companies. Between 1985 and 1996, average tariffs fell from 5% to 10%. The results have been modest. What explains the contrasts? Perhaps culture. The gospel of capitalism presumes that human nature is constant. Given the proper incentives – the ability to profit from hard work and risk taking – people will strive. Maybe not. In a recent book, *Culture Matters: How Values Shape Human Progress*, scholars from the US, Africa and Latin America argue that strong social and moral values predispose some peoples for and against economic growth. As a result of history, tradition and religion, some societies cannot easily adopt capitalist attitudes and institutions. Even when they try, they often fail because it is so unnatural. 'Competition is central to the success of an enterprise, the politician, the intellectual and the professional' writes Mariano Grondona, an Argentine political scientist and columnist. 'In resistant societies, competition is condemned as a form of aggression'. Daniel Etonga-Manguelle of Cameroun contends that Africa suffers from a reverence for its history. 'In traditional African society which exalts the glorious past of

ancestors through tales and fables, nothing is done to prepare for the future' he writes. Once stated, culture's impact seems obvious.[8]

Most of the developing country membership in the WTO is from the regions mentioned in the above quotation, Africa, Latin America and Asia. Cultural perspectives certainly affect a people's disposition to adopting new ideas. Analysing these perspectives will help in identifying internal challenges to developing country integration and may even proffer innovations to the multilateral system.[9] As Hudec noted, 'the domestic impediments to trade liberalisation have to be understood if they are to be overcome'.[10]

We would add that the challenges to developing country integration into the multilateral system include:

3.1.1. Inequalities in Trading Power

That countries are allowed to self-adopt a developing status at the WTO is a clear indication of the disproportionate trade capacities of WTO Members. The World Bank has drawn a comparison with this issue of inequalities in the global market and in the rules-based system of the WTO. It acknowledged that the WTO processes could be perceived as unfair 'because of the underlying power imbalance between strong commercial interests and the public interest, in both developed and developing countries'.[11] At present, although the developing countries are in the majority of WTO membership, they do not account for a concurrent or even a comparable status in statistical analysis of world merchandise trade.[12] The UNCTAD *Trade and Development Report for 2005*, recognises that 'despite the increasing importance of the fast growing developing countries for international commodity markets, developed countries, which still account for two thirds of global non-fuel commodity imports, will continue to play an important role'.[13]

The fact that trade amongst developing countries is on the increase does not alter this perception. The UNCTAD Report stresses that:

> While increased South-South trade is a fact, recent developments in the developing countries as a whole require a careful assessment of the statistical data. Indeed, such an assessment calls for a number of qualifications to the prima facie impression that trade among developing countries has grown massively over the past decade or so, and that exports of manufactures account for much of that rise.
>
> The growing role of developing countries in world trade flows appears to be the result, above all, of the above-average growth performance of a few Asian economies, and the associated shifts in the level and composition

of their external trade. A substantial part of the statistical increase in South-South trade in manufactures is due to double-counting associated with intraregional production-sharing in East Asia for products eventually destined for export to developed countries. It is also due to double-counting associated with the function of Hong Kong (China) and Singapore as transhipment ports or regional hub ports. The important role of triangular trade in the measured rise of South-South trade in manufactures implies that the bulk of such trade has not reduced the dependence of developing countries manufactured exports on aggregate demand in developed-country markets.[14]

Economic statistics may show an overall improvement in world trade. However on closer inspection, improvements in world trade do not necessarily imply an elimination of the inequalities in trading power. An earlier academic assessment noted that although the share of developing world trade increases, 'global trade flows are dominated by exchanges within and between the three major regions of the global economy (the so-called triode): Europe, North America and East Asia'.[15]

The situation still obtains to a significant extent. The WTO Report on *International Trade Statistics 2005* reports an increased world trade growth in exports by 9% in 2004, from 4% in 2002.[16] Of the ten leading exporting countries in world trade, only one developing country, China, (ranked third) makes the list.[17] Trade in manufactures, a significant indicator of a country's industrial advancement also rose by 10% in 2004. However, in spite of Asia's increased share of about 30%, North America and Europe the geographical regions of the world's most developed countries with their combined share, accounted for nearly two thirds of global trade in manufactures.[18]

The 2006 *WTO International Trade Statistics* report does not reflect much positive adjustment for developing country merchandise export trade. The further increase of 8% recorded for the year 2006 was as a result of a boost in European and US exports.[19] Although China's trade expanded by 22%, developing country trade was significantly below average with export growth in South and Central America, the Commonwealth of Independent States (CIS), Africa, and the Middle East, largely exceeded by imports into these regions.[20]

In its *2006 Annual Report*, the WTO was more optimistic of developing country trade citing the increased exports of countries such as Brazil, China, India, Malaysia, Mexico and Thailand. The Report states that 'Africa' had increased exports in excess of 25% in the 3 years preceding the report.[21] However the suggested increase does not alter the fact that overall developing country contribution to world trade remains significantly low. Indeed much of the contribution is from the natural minerals sector with increased trade and profit from the fuels and other mining products from these regions due to increases in the world market demand for fuels and minerals, as noted in the 2007 *WTO Annual Report.*[22]

It must be kept in mind that while the less advanced countries have had to scramble to eliminate protectionist barriers as a condition of their accession to the Organisation, the stronger members who have had a longer history of harmonised trade and whose industries operate at full capacity have not suffered a comparable loss in the global environment. The terms of trade have proved favourable to developed countries because the latter have been able to negotiate better terms for themselves. Stiglitz observes that:

> It was not just that the more advanced industrial countries declined to open up their markets to the goods of the developing countries – for instance, keeping their quotas on a multitude of goods from textiles to sugar – while insisting that those countries open up their markets to the goods of the wealthier countries; it was not just that the more advanced industrial countries continued to subsidise agriculture, making it difficult for the developing countries to compete, while insisting that the developing countries eliminate their subsidies on industrial goods.
>
> Looking at the 'terms of trade' – the prices which developed and less developed countries get for the products they produce – after the last trade agreement in 1995, the *net effect* was to lower the prices some of the poorest countries in the world received relative to what they paid for their imports. The result was that some of the poorest countries in the world were actually made worse off.[23]

Most developing countries who carried over their membership from the GATT were colonies, trading partners with, or aid beneficiaries of, the original Contracting Parties to the GATT. For many of these countries, accession to the WTO has been a matter of political expediency and there is truth in the suggestion that developing countries accepted the Uruguay (WTO) Round 'without a full comprehension of the profoundly transformative implication of this new trading system'.[24] It is not uncommon to find developing country discussants still unable to identify exactly what their countries stand to benefit by membership of the WTO.[25]

Indeed Michael Finger suggests that the question of comprehension may be extended to both the developed countries and to analysts. In his view, 'we still have a way to go before we come to that 'full comprehension' of what the WTO is into, and of how to deal with it'.[26]

With an expansion of the scope of the WTO negotiations after the Uruguay Round, the scope of the modern international trade regime has also been extended including the potential for expansion in sectors in which developing countries may have believed they had comparatively strong positions but where they still face challenges in competing in the global trade environment. The result is that some Agreements inevitably are more beneficial to some countries than to others. For example, trade in services is a stronghold of the developed highly industrialised countries of the world with the European Union and the United States in the forefront of this sector.[27] With an apparently higher capacity for labour mobility owing to available human capital in developing countries, it may be assumed that the GATS offers developing countries a significant opportunity to benefit from this sector. This is not the case however.

The US and the EC with their advanced services in transportation, travel, insurance, banking, computer, consultancy, and other professional services, are current leaders in these areas of global trade.[28] The reality is that 'the participation of developing countries is more as importers of services rather than exporters of services'.[29] Less advanced economies may not be in a position to provide a wealth of export in the skilled services sector of global trade given the comparatively low skilled labour force in these societies. Where skilled workers from these countries are prepared to offer their services in the industries and civil sectors of the developed countries, domestic regulations and policies laying down specific credentials from immigrant workers restrict the free movement and trade in services across these borders.

Yet it could be argued that the service sector of some developing countries is strong. An example is India's activities in the area of outsourcing and offshore business, and Information and Communications Technology (ICT).[30] It must be noted however that while India's service sector has grown, her industrial sector has declined with the shift in manpower and finances from heavy industry and agriculture to services. It has been argued that '[F]or a country with close to 30% illiterate population (an official, understated figure), the service sector, given its inherent entry barrier by virtue of its requirement of a basic minimum skill set, offers a much limited employment potential for a vast sector of the population'.[31] Clearly, possession of 'unskilled' labour is only as beneficial to developing country trade as the possession of 'raw' goods.

The chance to participate in trade negotiations has not eradicated the inequalities. According to the 2005 *World Bank Report*, international trade negotiations are complex and the less advanced countries have 'less voice' in these processes. The Report admits that 'global markets are far from equitable, and the rules governing their functioning have a disproportionately negative effect on developing countries'.[32] The Report highlighted the fact that the international laws regulating global markets are the products of complex negotiations. As such, 'although the formal regulations resulting from these negotiations may be seen as equitable, the processes and outcomes are perceived as unfair'.[33]

Moreover, without the threat of competitive goods and possible retaliation in the event of trade disputes, trade policies of poor countries have little impact on their rich counterparts. The latter with their political and economic strength can adopt more coordinated trade alliances in their proximate locations effectively restricting market access to less competitive goods. Todaro notes that:

> Third world domestic policies generally have little impact on the economies of rich nations. Moreover, governments of developed countries often join to promote shared interests through coordinated trade and other economic ventures. Though these governments may not intend for such activities to promote their own welfare at the expense of that of poor countries, this is often the result [...]
>
> Rich country governments can influence world economic affairs by their domestic and international policies. They can resist countervailing economic pressures from weaker nations and can act in **collusion** and often in conjunction with their powerful multinational corporations to manipulate the terms and conditions of international trade to their own national interests.[34]

3.1.2. Strength of Participation in WTO Activities

Here, two areas are of particular interest – the political representation at the Ministerial Conferences and the capacity for effective use of the rules-based system of settling disputes under the compulsory jurisdiction of the WTO Dispute Settlement Body (DSB). In the first instance, WTO Trade Ministers represent the interests of their country. It is expected that they will put forward issues which are pertinent to their local trading interests – issues that will affect their farmers, fishermen, contractors, manufacturers. The WTO Director General Pascal Lamy explained the role of the country representative trade negotiators to the effect that they work in an 'authorising environment', representing the views of their parliament or collective democratic legislative assembly; their constituents.[35]

While it is expected that trade negotiators must have reached an agreement in their home countries on the issues which they intend to raise at the Ministerial Conferences, this may not be the case with developing country negotiators.[36] Trade negotiators especially those from countries whose governments are still struggling for legitimacy whether by military force or autocracy will be preoccupied with serving the personal interests of their leading government figures. The necessary communication between business enterprises and the government, the research and economic analysis which should generate background issues for trade negotiations, and the trade negotiating skills necessary in the modern trading system, are specialties that have not been fully developed in the developing countries. In the absence of a 'bottoms up' approach in domestic trade negotiations, the interests and concerns of the private enterprises who actually engage in trade may not be represented at international negotiations.

Second, it is not enough to have access to justice, one must also have the capacity to utilise the access to justice. Poor countries do not have the requisite legal expertise to analyse the Agreements, engage in legal negotiations for settlement of disputes, and appear before the DSB when necessary. Although the creation of a dispute settlement system with compulsory jurisdiction ensures equity in treatment, 'one also needs an adequate level of legal capacity and expertise to realise the full promises of such a system'.[37]

The WTO documents run to thousands of pages as do the collection of dispute settlement reports. The background research of facts and circumstances required prior to instigating a complaint against another country demands skill and expertise in law and economics, knowledge of domestic policies, international diplomacy, and international trade matters. The poorer members of the WTO may not have the indigenous independent talent for these purposes. Although there exists a WTO Advisory Body[38] which is available to assist developing countries in the preparation of claims and representation at dispute hearings, there is no question that developing countries who, apart from LDCs, have to pay for the services of the Advisory Body, will benefit more readily from access to an internationally competitive pool of analysts, academics and legal scholars, especially if these were indigenous professionals.

The strength of participation in WTO activities determines the quality of participation. Perhaps it is because developing countries are conscious of their limited strengths that these countries largely focus their negotiations on protectionist proposals. One attractive means of improving this strength of participation is for a stronger cohesion amongst developing countries. This they can achieve by pooling together their available human resources to address their common trade concerns and to support each other in trade negotiations and dispute hearings.

3.1.3. The Comparative Advantage Theory and the Modern Global Market

The early economist John Stuart Mill was a strong supporter of international trade. In his often quoted view, the benefit of international trade was 'a more efficient employment of the productive forces of the world'.[39] For Mills and the other early proponents, the free trade ideology holds significant opportunities for improving a weak economy because it 'promotes a mutually profitable division of labour, greatly enhances the potential real national product for all nations, and makes possible higher standards of living all over the globe'.[40]

Two modern enthusiasts of free trade remark upon the ease with which one may overlook the importance of this international exchange. They state:

> What are the economic forces that lie behind international trade? Simply put, trade promotes specialization, and specialization increases productivity. Over the long run, increased trade and higher productivity raise living standards for all nations. Gradually countries have realised that opening up their economies to the global trading system is the most secure road to prosperity.[41]

If opening up economies is the most secure road to prosperity as noted above, it is beneficial to examine in some relevant detail the ideas of 'specialisation' and 'increased productivity' mentioned above. We do this by referring to the original thoughts on how countries can profit from trading amongst themselves, according to Adam Smith. His idea is presented in his analogy below:

> What is prudent in the conduct of every private family, can scarce be folly in that of a great kingdom. If a foreign country can supply us with a commodity cheaper than we ourselves can make it, better buy it of them with some part of the produce of our own industry, employed in a way in which we have some advantage. The general industry of the country…will not thereby be diminished…but only left to find out the way in which it can be employed with the greatest advantage. It is certainly not employed to the greatest advantage, when it is thus directed towards an objective which it can buy cheaper than it can make.[42]

In simple terms, Smith's view was that whereas one country may be able to produce more than one good to its benefit, where it will be cheaper to purchase one such good from another country than to produce the good itself, it is even more beneficial and indeed prudent for the first country to purchase cheaply.

By the nineteenth century, another economist David Ricardo, had expanded on Smith's view and proposed the principle of 'comparative advantage'. This principle holds that 'each country will benefit if it specialises in the production and export of those goods that it can produce at relatively low cost'.[43] The view was that 'each country will benefit if it imports those goods which it produces at relatively high cost'.[44] The WTO embraces the postulations of Ricardo citing it as 'the single most powerful insight into economics'.[45] It sets out a theoretical assumption for Ricardo's theory:

> Suppose country A is better than country B at making automobiles, and country B is better than country A at making bread. It is obvious

(the academics would say 'trivial') that both would benefit if A specialised in bread and they traded their products. That is a case of **absolute advantage**.

But what if a country is bad at making everything? Will trade drive all producers out of business? The answer, according to Ricardo, is no. The reason is the principle of **comparative advantage.**

It says, countries A and B still stand to benefit from trading with each other even if A is better than B at making everything. If A is much more superior at making automobiles and only slightly superior at making bread, then A should invest resources in what it does best – producing automobiles – and export the product to B. B should still invest in what it does best – making bread – and export that product to A, even if it is not as efficient as A. Both would still benefit from the trade. A country does not have to be best at anything to gain from trade. That is comparative advantage.

[…]It is often claimed, for example, that some countries have no comparative advantage in anything. That is virtually impossible.[46]

The WTO in the above reference ends by inviting one to 'think about it'. Given the modern complex multilateral trade environment, this explanation of the theory of comparative advantage is not a convincing argument on the question of successful integration of developing countries into the modern global market. Even less appealing is the subtle attempt to present open trade as a problem-free solution which every country ought to pursue with haste. Our contention with the application of the theory stems from the following seven observations:

First, the comparative advantage theory was proposed with the understanding that countries are the entities that determine the processes of trade in the international arena. But countries are not the real parties in trading activity particularly in the modern world. Indeed Trebilcock and Howse, see it as an 'unfortunate semantic legacy' of the comparative advantage theory, which continues to cite *countries* as the parties in international trade.[47] It is the parties which give rise to international trading transactions, those participants in economic endeavour: the trading enterprises, individuals, SMEs, corporations, and multinationals who are the real parties to trade. Therefore, in presenting countries as the parties to trade, this issue of comparative advantage is not without conundrum. Will a country's comparative advantage refer to the income earning potential for a scarce resource which is in high demand (such as oil or diamonds), or does it simply refer to any factor of production or any natural resource which a country has in greater supply than its counterparts (for instance, vast arable land, unskilled labour, primary goods)?

In the first situation, great demand for scarce resources may appear to grant a country a comparative advantage. So, mining the diamonds may yield huge returns to a country's GNP. But will it improve the lives of the majority? The answer is: not necessarily. This is because it may not employ the most number of people. If a foreign technologically-proficient corporation is contracted by the host government to mine a scarce resource like diamonds, as is the case in the mining regions of Central and South Africa, the labour force utilised will be negligible.

For instance, the Botswana experience is always referred to as an example of significant progress and development owed to the high income from diamond sales in the global market, which principally go to the mining companies.[48] Generally, Botswana's economic growth can be ascribed to mineral and beef exports, tourism, and donor aid.[49] However, diamonds are by far the most important source of income for Botswana since their initial discovery in 1967, a situation which should prove of no surprise given the high demand and high price of diamond.[50] In the country's last TPR, the WTO Secretariat notes that the sector employs only about 3.5% in formal employment. The TPR notes that 'shortage of labour is a major constraint on the development of manufacturing industry'.[51] The Botswana Government Report notes that 'however, Botswana's economic base remains narrow, with one third of GDP in 1996 and some 50% of government revenues in the same year stemming from the mineral sector'.[52]

The combined earnings of the three mining operations in the country, all incidentally operated by a single private company – the De Beers Group, account for 77% of total export earnings and about 45% of the GDP of Botswana.[53] The Botswana government (with 15% shareholding) shares joint ownership with two others in the De Beers group: Anglo-American (45%) and Central Holdings (representing the Oppenheimer family with 40%). Its global mining operations employ approximately 20,000 people in its operating sites in Botswana, Namibia, South Africa, Tanzania and Canada and around the world; about 7000 of those employees are in Botswana.[54]

However, this phenomenal success has not countered the observation of Botswana economists about the low employment rate in the diamond industry and the threat of competition from the trade activities of other neighbouring countries. A WTO case study notes that:

> Botswana's own domestic market has been under threat since South Africa emerged from the apartheid era and has gradually opened up its market to foreign competition. The first real test was when South Africa negotiated a free trade agreement with the EU; this agreement was a de facto free trade agreement with all the SACU member states. The second eye-opener was the challenge faced by the EU in the WTO on its discriminatory preferential market access (under the Lomé Agreement)

to a select number of African, Caribbean and Pacific (ACP) countries. This meant that preferences enjoyed by Botswana (mainly for its beef exports) were coming to an end.[55]

On the other hand, the idea that a country's comparative advantage could lie in the availability of raw materials for finished goods is at best patronising. Lacking sophisticated industrial expertise, raw materials are sold in their primary state by most developing countries who supply the industries of developed countries with these materials including minerals such as oil and diamonds. In the sophisticated modern global economy with ever-changing consumer preferences and rapid technological advancements in manufacturing, possession of raw materials alone puts any country at a distinct disadvantage. Again the case of Botswana provides insight. A leading Botswana economist based at the Botswana Institute for Development Policy Analysis (BIDPA) comments as follows:

> While the diamond sector is by far the leading sector of the Botswana economy in terms of its contribution to gross domestic product and foreign exchange earnings, its contribution to employment is extremely low (under 3.6%) due to the high capital intensity of diamond mining and the fact that most of the diamond is exported in rough form. As a result of the low contribution to employment and fear of losing the market for beef in the EU, the authorities have adopted an industrial strategy aimed at promoting non-diamond industries both for export and local consumption.[56]

There is no doubt that countries must have to offer improved goods and labour; improved in the sense that goods will need to be processed into a secondary state in order to compete in the global market. It is the same with labour and the trade in services which benefit the more sophisticated service providers in the international market.

That is not all. Even the possession of a particular factor of production in abundance does not necessarily guarantee that a country will make any gains by that fact alone. A vast land mass may be restricted by government land-ownership laws or may be owned by a small section of the rich in the country. A huge labour force if it is largely comprised of unskilled persons may limit the comparative advantage to be exploited from skilled labour-intensive operations. For example, the huge undeveloped land mass and young labour force of the entire African continent has not detracted from the superior position of the EU and the USA in what may be referred to as their 'artificial comparative advantage' in producing agricultural goods. Apart from the sophisticated and technologically advanced agricultural practices of these countries, the clever subsidisation programmes in these countries consistently thwart the 'natural' comparative advantage which the African continent ought to have in agricultural enterprise.

Needless to say, abundant resources still need to be effectively harnessed towards producing goods or services that can compete in the global market. Without well structured policies to achieve this, a country may be blessed with land, natural recourses, labour, capital, and may yet remain unable to make anything out of this abundance.

Second, considering that the theory originated more than two centuries ago, it does not factor in the political underpinnings of the modern trade regime. The politics of bargaining and the demand for reciprocity operative under the multilateral system is in contrast to the basic considerations of the theory which envisions a simple agreement between two countries on which country will produce what goods. Trade liberalisation demands cross-border market access and a non-discriminatory trade regime. Presenting countries as being in an independent position to determine what they should produce and to whom to sell according to the WTO's explanation may be misleading to those who do not read beyond the apparent meaning of the theory. This is because the WTO basic principles – the MFN and the NT, demand non-discriminatory treatment across the Organisation's membership which in turn discounts the possibility of countries deciding with whom to trade without resorting to the exemptions under the WTO Agreements.[57]

Third, a comparative advantage is not static given the constant changes in demand and supply trends of goods and services in the global market. Thus, it is probable that in the modern global market, a country's comparative advantage may arise *as a consequence* of a profitable exercise in international trade. That is to say, as a country's trade activity in the global market increases and its goods maintain a significant market share, then the country may proceed to increase its production capacity for that good. China is a good reference point. One of the strong developing countries in the global market, China has become a strong industrial competitor for industrial and technical goods. It could be said to have a comparative advantage over such merchandise than most of its counterparts; indeed it presents a competition for developed country technical and industrial manufacture. Yet this comparative advantage only arose as a *consequence* of China's long and continued manufacturing activity which yielded lower costs for production stabilising its trading activity in this area to its advantage.

The point here is that a comparative advantage does not automatically arise on its own; it may well be dependent on the sales performance of a good or a trading activity, in the global market. It could be argued that it is possible, should developing countries have the enabling environment for productive capacity and the socio-economic improvements in living standards, that they may indeed gain comparative advantage in certain areas which have hitherto been considered areas of developed country advantage. In the multilateral trading system especially, it may well be that 'it is the gains from trade that implies the pattern of trade, not the reverse.[58] A country may thus have a comparative advantage *after* a rewarding pattern of trade and not before embarking on a trading arrangement.

Fourth, from the WTO's explanation of the theory, there is a presumption that countries are always in an equal bargaining position. This equality however does not negate the fact that in reality, under the WTO, inequalities exist both in the capacity to supply goods or services to trade, and in the capacity to participate in the trading system. The distinction between developed, developing, and least developed countries is instructive.

Fifth, there is a moral presumption in the theory which alludes to the fact that the two countries can trust one another to abide strictly with the terms of their agreement. In our view this presumption though compelling falls short of reality. The theory as it is demands that in the agreement between countries A and B, country B will be satisfied with its profits from bread making. Thus even where it assesses that with further R&D activities and with financial investments into its automobile industry it may match or even exceed country A's capacity in automobile production, it will not do so. Neither would country A attempt bread making, content to leave this industry to country B. The fierce competition amongst producers in the modern global market does not sustain this interpretation of the theory and it is impractical to retain the suggestion that a country is satisfied at producing a particular product when it can explore ways to find alternative and cheaper means of producing what it is forced to buy.

Sixth, basic 'needs' and 'wants' are no more the sole economic determinants of trade arrangements. The analogy with 'bread making' and 'automobile manufacture' is in the light of modern technological advancements and consumer preferences, simplistic. Emerging issues in modern living ranging from a ferocious consumer appetite for new products and the latest technologies, to environmental considerations, and including the threats of armed conflicts and terrorism will determine trade preferences and trade partnerships. Trade negotiations are consequently heavily influenced by political alliances.[59]

Finally, is *specialisation* alone sufficient for economic development? The theory makes no mention of the impact of industrial promotion policies and practices which assist industrial growth. Lee notes that:

> specialisation alone did not bring about economic development, and virtually all developed countries today applied industrial promotion policies to establish some manufacturing basis with the extensive use of subsidies and trade protections.[60]

Rodrik drawing on a number of studies also notes that contrary to the conventional understanding, specialisation according to comparative advantage is not an essential ingredient for development. He states that:

> Whatever it is that serves as the driving force of economic development, it cannot be the forces of comparative advantage as conventionally understood. The trick seems to be to acquire mastery over a broader range of activities, instead of concentrating on what one does best.[61]

Therefore, it is not entirely correct to assume as the WTO suggests that it is 'virtually impossible' for a country not to have a comparative advantage in anything. Whereas it may be naïve to suggest that a country does not have an economic sector in which it has the *potential* to become superior and thereby gain comparative advantage, given the constraints of the modern application of the theory, it is highly probable that countries may not *develop* a comparative advantage in any particular good. Also, if it is agreed that the economies of less industrialised countries are poor, that these societies have poor social and institutional systems, lack technological knowledge, and have low skilled labour, it is not far fetched to assume therefore that these countries may not have had the adequate opportunity to invest and grow a local industry to an advantageous position.

3.1.4. The Restrictions of the 'Single Undertaking' Requirement

One of the remarkable accomplishments of the Uruguay Round of trade talks, wherein the WTO was established, was the provision of a basic agreement to which Members would state their intention to be bound by the agreements emanating from the WTO. Thus, 'the vast bulk of the world's trading nations, agreed on the vast bulk of rules governing world trade'.[62] Article II:2 of the *WTO Agreement* explains the nature of this single undertaking requirement stating that the *WTO Agreement* and the provision relating to the multilateral agreement under Annexes 1–3 are integral parts of the WTO Agreement and 'binding on all Members'. To this end, the WTO would provide 'the common institutional framework for the conduct of trade relations among its Members in matters related to the agreements and associated legal instruments included in the Annexes' of the WTO Agreement'.[63]

This binding nature of the obligations on Members in respect of the respective WTO Agreements means that upon accession, every Member country regardless of economic status, wholly adopts all the provisions under the agreements as a 'single undertaking'. The difficulties this uniform application of the complex trade rules present to developing countries is immediately apparent.

Granted, there are time exemptions within the provisions (such as those exemptions which allow countries some time frame within which to ensure that the WTO obligations are adopted within the national trade frame work). However, it is submitted that these exemptions are not sufficient to address the development obligations of the rules based system and to ensure the effective participation of the developing country members. Schott and Watal argue that this requirement demands ever greater commitment to trade policy reforms by developing countries.[64]

It is further argued that there is indeed a fundamental contradiction in the pursuit of the Organisation's objectives of making trade work for development by the adoption of a single undertaking requirement. If developing countries are adjudged to be deserving of special treatment by way of provisional exemptions then why is it necessary to make them subject to the single undertaking requirement? The WTO CTD does not proffer the possibility of altering the single undertaking requirement allowing developing countries to opt out of restrictive Agreements, not even under the Doha Development Round. It warns that 'some Members might argue that the text of each existing agreement reflects a negotiated balance of interests and that to renegotiate one provision would require renegotiation of the entire Agreement'.[65]

This point is not convincing. Granted, any attempt to alter even one particular provision may require an entire alteration of the relevant agreement. It could be argued however that the negotiation of trade matters and interests is specifically pertinent to the idea of a world trade organisation in the first instance. If as the WTO suggests in its handbook, *Understanding the WTO*,[66] 'the first step is to talk', and that 'essentially, the WTO is a place where member governments go to try and sort out the trade problems they face with each other', then a reappraisal of the single undertaking requirement cannot be resisted on the basis that to do so would mean a renegotiation of the entire Agreement. Being a *negotiating* forum, it should be in accordance with the nature and mandate of the WTO to allow for renegotiations of its Agreements when and where required.

Besides, under the *WTO Agreement*, Articles X:1–10 set out the modalities for the amendment of any provision of the multilateral agreements including the conditions for acceptance on any proposals for amendment. Having already provided for the procedure for effecting a renegotiated provision, it is not in the spirit of the commitment to working for closer integration of its developing country membership for the WTO to delay in responding to the needs and concerns of its majority membership for increased flexibility in the legal framework of the multilateral trade system.

There is no doubt that developing economies find that the single undertaking requirement does not allow them the necessary flexibility they might require in implementing their concessions to the WTO legal provisions. The WTO

Agreements taken as an entire obligation including those which adversely affect developing countries' integration into the world market, also restrict what impact the SDT provisions can make on development since these are only limited non-mandatory exceptions.[67] Agreed, when countries cannot rescind an international commitment, it is safe to presume that the international rules can therefore claim 'security and predictability'. Jackson thus presents a well reasoned argument for a rules-oriented system. He identifies that in respect of economic affairs which affect 'more citizens directly, a rules oriented system, although it may be arrived at 'tortuously' (international negotiations and bargaining being increasingly difficult), 'when established will enable business and other decentralised decision makers to rely upon the stability of governmental activity in relation to the rule'.[68]

Jackson's view emphasises the importance of a rules-oriented system in the multilateral trade regime. However, 'tightly binding, unforgiving rules can have negative effects in the uncertain environment of international trade'.[69] This is especially so when the vision for security and predictability implied in the rigid and uniform application of a single undertaking becomes an impediment to the pursuit and realisation of the very economic development objectives which the WTO ostensibly promotes.

It could also be argued that the single undertaking requirement serves the further purpose of providing a fair treatment across the WTO membership. The advantage of a rules-based system is after all, to provide a level playing ground for all the participants in the global market. However, just as it would amount to inequitable treatment to treat countries of the same economic standards unequally, it amounts to inequitable treatment to subject countries unequal in their social and economic status to the same expectations as their more advanced counterparts. Arguing for the imperative on the WTO to accommodate the different legal systems and levels of economic development together with increased flexibility in negotiations, VanGrasstek and Sauvé, caution that 'although consistency is among the desirable attributes to which the multilateral trading system should strive, it cannot do so at the expense of all other desiderata'.[70]

Even in the light of the acclaimed successes of the world trading order under the WTO, it cannot be denied that 'obligations that demand too much from the parties and lack the *ex post* flexibility to respond to unanticipated problems or new developments may lead to an unravelling of the treaty as parties withdraw their participation'.[71] This reasoning can be applied to the present deliberations. It is clear from the protracted Doha Round of talks and the failure of the developed and developing countries across the negotiating divide to reach any sound conclusions on the issues of agriculture and non-agricultural market access (NAMA), that the aforementioned lack of *ex post* flexibility in

WTO Agreements is a major threat to the continued legitimacy of the modern international trade regime. The absence of an opportunity to redress the imbalances of the Uruguay negotiations which introduced the single undertaking requirement as part of the WTO legal framework has eroded the past achievements of the Organisation. A rejection of the calls for reappraisal of the inflexible nature of burdensome provisions in the multilateral trade rules defeats the stated goal of the WTO rules which is 'to help producers of goods and services, exporters and importers conduct their business, while allowing governments to meet social and environmental objectives'.[72]

It would have been preferable if at the time of accession especially, developing countries had the option of negotiating to opt out of Agreements that may prove burdensome. At present, where as is the case most developing countries have already acceded to the WTO undertaking, what is needed is for a reopening of talks on those aspects of the WTO legal framework and the areas of development-related policy issues which are fundamental to the development objective both of the WTO as an Organisation and of developing countries themselves. It is not for the WTO to refuse the reopening of negotiations or for the more powerful countries to reject the same because it is not in their best economic interests to do so. If the Organisation is to live up to its role as a negotiating forum and if the attempt at closer integration for the developing country membership is to go beyond mere rhetoric, then the strict undertaking requirement must be reappraised to allow for a flexible approach and a pragmatic application of multilateral trade rules by developing countries.[73]

3.1.5. *Internal Constraints*

Internal constraints to trade arise in respect of limited human, institutional, and infrastructural capacity. The WTO recognises that without these factors 'countries will not be able to expand the quantity and quality of goods and services they can supply to world markets at competitive prices'.[74] It notes that:

- **human capacity** refers to the professionals that the governments rely on for advice on WTO matters: trade lawyers, economists, skilled negotiators. A country that lacks these professionals is clearly at a disadvantage when implementing existing trade agreements, when negotiating new ones, and when handling trade disputes.
- **institutional capacity** refers to the institutions businesses and governments rely upon for trade, such as customs, national standards authorities, and the delegation representing the country at the WTO. Trade ultimately suffers if these institutions are inadequate.

- **infrastructure** refers to the physical setup required for trade to happen: roads, ports, telecommunications. Again, countries lacking infrastructure will find it difficult to develop trade.[75]

In the first place, knowledge of the WTO, its rules and structure and how it operates is extremely important. Although it is preferable that the WTO engages in greater awareness campaigns at the grassroots level, the tasks of the Organisation and the limited administrative and financial capacity of the Secretariat may not make this possible. However, knowledge and awareness of the WTO and of its functions and activities in the development arena is of utmost importance in the domestic environment as this will facilitate an understanding of the obligations under the respective Agreements. This means that a domestic government must properly identify the domestic relationship with the world trading system. An analysis of a developing country response to the challenges of participating in the WTO may prove instructive.

In Nigeria for instance, a bias against the opening up of markets to foreign corporations is supported by the view that 'the WTO Agreement operates effectively to prise open markets for the benefits of trans-national corporations at the expense of national economies'.[76] There is much play on the fear that developing nations face 'further marginalisation occasioned by the globalisation phenomenon'.[77] This fear only serves to obfuscate the principal issues: how can the country make significant adjustment in order to eliminate her supply side constraints; how can Nigeria address her institutional and administrative restrictions for improved global trade participation?

It must be pointed out that the promotion of this fear that Nigeria and the developing world are being 'marginalised' has not been without criticism from within the country itself. Reacting to a debate in the Nigerian House of Representatives as to whether Nigeria should continue her WTO membership in 2002, a Nigerian economist pointed out that such a debate betrayed a limited understanding of the functions of the WTO regime. He was of the opinion that 'if most members, are of the view that the WTO is the cause of poor industrial performance in the country, then the real issue is not being addressed.'[78] In his view, Nigeria's retrogressive performance in the industrial sector was due to 'the accumulation of bad domestic policies which made the cost of doing business in the country perhaps the highest in the world thereby reducing the country's competitiveness in the world market'.[79]

Apart from the constraints occasioned by government responses such as the above, other constraints faced by developing countries include the lack of consultation between government agencies and bodies in charge of trade matters and stakeholders both prior to and after WTO negotiations.[80] Again the absence of stability in the leadership of relevant government ministries and in the general political scene where officials of relevant national bodies are constantly replaced and government policies change with the political leadership affect the adoption of indigenous trade and development polices and their implementation.

In this respect, one considers that a 'domestic-needs' approach to trade and development legislation is preferable to what may be referred to as an 'external-conformity' approach. Countries have to concentrate on adopting long-term effective domestic policies rather than concentrating their efforts on arguing against the potential impact of trade rules or on trying to adopt domestic legislation as a last response to external pressures. Furthermore, less reliance ought to be placed on 'negative legislation' such as import prohibition strategies and more efforts towards finding ingenious ways to utilise the provisions of WTO Agreements for the benefit of developing countries.[81]

On a more basic level, the creation of an enabling environment where goods and services for the global market are made available demands serious institutional and infrastructural restructuring efforts by a domestic government to eliminate those factors which hamper an efficient supply.[82] These factors include: the absence of efficient power supply, lack of pipe borne water, ailing telecommunications systems, the absence of research and development facilities, inefficient transport systems, complicated and time consuming bureaucratic processes, limited credit facilities for the private sector entrepreneur, and the lack of support for business innovation and entrepreneurship in the local environment.

3.1.6. New Trade Rules

The multilateral trade environment is not only complex but also evolutionary. Areas such as agriculture, textiles, services, intellectual property, investment, hitherto considered within the ambit of national policy making, have now been incorporated into the global trade mandate.[83] The WTO DG has observed that the WTO owes its increasing relevance and indeed the controversy it attracts to the expansion of subjects in the rules of the multilateral trading system 'from tariffs and services to intellectual property rights, technical barriers to trade, rules of origin and a vast array of subjects which in spite of their bureaucratic names, have a bearing on the everyday lives of millions of people'.[84]

Developing countries are particularly vulnerable in some of these new areas. For instance, communities which require urgent food assistance will expectedly be less critical of potential adverse effects from GM foods, an issue with which the EU is very concerned and which developing countries were they to have better research facilities may be concerned with themselves. Many developing countries are ill-equipped to conduct scientific experiments into these issues and find the potential for increased food production by adopting bio-technological innovations in agriculture appealing regardless of scientific doubts as to the long term effects of these innovations in both human and environmental factors.

To elaborate on the earlier considerations on the GATS, the potential for increased trade may not be of immediate benefit to developing countries whose human resource potential is largely for unskilled labour. Granted, the advent of new technologies in the field of communications have had significant potential for the developing country labour market with the off-shoring of services and with a reduced necessity for physical presence for jobs which can be conducted by electronic means.[85] This gain notwithstanding and despite the fact that developing economies have a greater percentage of young persons and so a significantly higher labour force potential for the future, the *GATS* is one Agreement the provisions of which as it stands, have limited benefits to the services industry of the developing world.

The WTO has set out the rules for the operation of the GATS based on four modes of services supply across the constituent Member States[86]: *cross-border supply* – services are supplied within the territory of another, for instance by delivery of financial advice by telecommunications or email; *consumption abroad* – a service is delivered outside the territory of the Member to a service consumer of the Member, for example when a client of an investment company travels to the country where that company is locates to receive services. The other two modes of supply are with respect to *commercial presence* – a service is delivered within a Member's territory through the commercial presence of the supplier such as a representative or a wholly owned subsidiary or branch and *presence of natural persons* – a service is delivered within a Member's territory for instance, by persons working for a securities company of another Member.

Given the smaller scale of operations of many services suppliers in developing countries and their currently limited global presence, the other three modes are currently beyond the capacity of the less sophisticated service sectors of developing countries; the first two in particular. It appears developing countries have a real strength of participation in trade in services primarily in respect of the fourth mode of supply which refers to the movement of natural persons. However, this potential is not of remarkable impact to the economic development of these countries because a numeric advantage does not necessarily equate to an increase in the share of the services market for these economies. The practical demands of this fourth mode of supply are considered below.

Negotiations under the GATS rules will have to consider more effective means to provide for the needs and interests of developing countries; more effective that is than the provisions under Mode 4. It is noted that there are provisions on considerations for domestic regulations under Article VI and for increasing participation of developing countries under Article IV of the GATS. So far in the course of the Doha negotiations, the Working Party on Domestic Regulations (WPDR) has been concerned with adapting the GATS provisions on domestic regulations to the need for countries to ensure their domestic policies on services fulfil the requirements of 'necessity' and 'proportionality' pursuant to Article VI:4. The WPDR recommended that Members are to do this while taking 'account of the special development, financial and trade needs of developing country Members, with a view to ensuring that such measures do not create unnecessary obstacles to exports from developing countries'. [87]

In determining 'necessity' and 'proportionality' of domestic regulations, it will be important to address some limitations of the Mode 4 supply. [88] These include the restrictions for migrant professionals who must satisfy the demand for internationally accredited qualifications both academic and technical in order to compete in the modern global market. Also, restrictive visa and work permit requirements in the immigration policies of host countries significantly limit labour mobility of developing countries. Added to all these, the costs of migration and resettlement are often too high for private persons to undertake and domestic governments in the recipient countries ought to help alleviate these costs by reducing the charges and fees under migration policies.

Another new area has been Intellectual Property (IP) Rights. Here, because most developing economies have not successfully incorporated a culture of IP protection, they fear that the multinational companies and advanced research expertise of developed countries will make it easy for richer economies to acquire and register IP rights. Cultural and health practices in the territories of developing countries over which the latter have not previously claimed ownership will be susceptible to foreign acquisition. [89]

Although they may have legislation governing IP, developing countries also have comparatively low records of R&D and a concomitant lack of awareness of the need for IP protection over indigenous processes. The wide scope of the TRIPS Agreement including protection for drugs, foods, and other expensive technologies covered under the TRIPS Agreement remain a source of concern for developing countries considering the high cost of obtaining protected technology. As would be expected, some developing countries have been involved in disputes on IP protection before the DSB. [90]

Significantly, the DDA has clarified certain issues on developing country concerns for IP protection including recognition that some Members may face difficulties in making effective use of compulsory licensing provisions under the TRIPS agreement. [91] Paragraph 5(a–d) of the Doha TRIPS Declaration lists flexibilities afforded to each Member in applying the TRIPS agreement including the grant of compulsory licenses, and the freedom to apply IP rights on the condition that the non-discrimination and MFN rules are not violated. [92]

The *Decision on Implementation of Paragraph 6 of the Doha Declaration on the TRIPS Agreement and Public Health* also allows exportation of pharmaceutical product manufactured under a compulsory licence, a waiver of TRIPS Article 31(f) previously restricting such products to the domestic market.[93]

It has been suggested that developing countries may find solutions to any constraints under TRIPS by revisiting their domestic IP laws.[94] Considering the earlier reference to Nigeria and the challenges under the WTO, a revisit of the IP laws of Nigeria will be of relevance at this point.

Nigeria's legal protection of Intellectual Property exists under the *Nigerian Copyright Act*,[95] with amendments in 1992[96] and 1999.[97] Other intellectual property provisions are found in the *Trade Marks Act*[98] and in the *Patents and Design Act*.[99]. The *Copyright Act 1999* with the inclusion of a new Section 4f, extends IP protection also to WTO Members as envisioned under the National Treatment provisions in Article I:3 of the TRIPS Agreement. The said Article 1:3 provides that:

> Members shall accord the treatment provided for in this Agreement to the nationals of other Members.[[100]] In respect of the relevant intellectual property right, the nationals of other Members shall be understood as those natural or legal persons that would meet the criteria for eligibility for protection provided for in the Paris Convention (1967), the Berne Convention (1971), the Rome Convention and the Treaty on Intellectual Property in Respect of Integrated Circuits, were all Members of the WTO members of those conventions.

Under the Copyright Act Nigeria 1999, S. 4 A (1) extends copyright protection in Nigeria to every work where at least one of the authors is a citizen or body corporate of a country which is a party to any international agreement to which Nigeria is a Party. Under S. 4 (A) (1)b, the protection is also extended to any work first published in any country which is also a party to any international agreement to which Nigeria is a party. By extension, Article 4 of the WTO TRIPS Agreement providing for the application of the MFN principle is also protected with this extension of the rights to works not of Nigerian origin.

The Nigerian laws appear to have included the aspect of protection of cultural rights which developing countries fear may be exploited, under S.29 A of the 1999 Copyright Laws. The section provides for criminal liability for the infringement of any 'expression of folklore'. However, there is no further indication of the scope this provision is to cover – whether it extends to music, film, dance, literature, although it could be argued and we would agree, that the term 'expression of folklore' covers the indicated areas where they originate in the domestic cultural environment.

However Nigerian laws on IP Rights do not provide for the IP protection of indigenous innovation in areas of health and medicine, foods and agricultural processes, or any other processes of R&D. This is unlike the provisions of TRIPS which extend protection to copyrights, patents, industrial design, computer and computer data, wine and spirits, and lay-out designs of integrated circuits, including the control of anti-competitive practices in contractual licences. For instance under S.4(b) of the *Nigerian Patent and Designs Act*[101] patents cannot be obtained for 'plant or animal varieties, or essentially biological processes for the production of plants or animals (other than microbiological processes and their products'. S.5 of the Act states also that '[P]rinciples and discoveries of a scientific nature are not inventions for the purposes of this Act'. These provisions are in contrast to Article 27.3(b) TRIPS which provides that '[M]embers shall provide for the protection of plant varieties either by patents or by an effective *sui generis* system or by any combination thereof'. In effect research and scientific discovery into plant varieties in Nigeria do not have first protection under Nigerian IP laws. This makes it possible for foreign research bodies that have the requisite advanced technologies and can undertake scientific experiments, to claim first protection over the plant variety.

The consequences of such a *lacuna* could be appreciated in the light of a political dispute between India and the United States, over a product long associated with India, basmati rice. India had challenged the US government grant of patent to a US company (RiceTec Inc.) which allowed the company to label its cross-breed product of basmati and American long grain rice 'basmati'; a name hitherto used to refer to a variety of the rice plant grown in India and Pakistan. After a period of claims and counter claims on whom owned the rights to use the title 'basmati', the US Patent Office eventually upheld India's assertions that the term 'basmati' rice has been in public domain as it has always been cultivated in India and could not then be the subject of IP protection as sought by Rice Tec Inc.[102]

The principal conflict between the Nigeria's IP laws and TRIPS lies in the fact that the latter expects MFN principles to be applied in Nigeria whereas the country has not implemented the extensive range of IP property the TRIPS Agreement covers. Although the National Office for Technology Acquisition and Promotion (NOTAP) oversees the registration and transfer of foreign technology in Nigeria, provisions with respect to how and why such technology is to be used and how such imports can assist local manufacture are not included in the domestic rules. Notably, the NOTAP is concerned with ensuring that foreign technology imported into the country is not overpriced or obsolete but not with *what* technology and *how* such technology can be utilised.[103]

Generally, developing countries have themselves presented some of their concerns with IP at WTO negotiations. In a submission for the Doha Round negotiations, some developing countries set out the pertinent issues concerning the TRIPS Agreement:

> [t]he TRIPS Agreement has strengthened the rights of private ownership without providing for equivalent protection for the intellectual property rights of communities...In this regard, we call on the developed countries to consider proposals for new disciplines on disclosure of the source and country of origin of biological resources and traditional knowledge, and to secure prior informed consent and equitable benefit sharing. [104]

In sum, the position with respect to the challenges posed by the widening scope of WTO concerns is as follows. If the WTO seeks to address development concerns in terms of redressing the imbalance in socio-economic conditions of the Member States, care must be taken to ensure that developing countries are not handicapped by the introduction of rules on complex issues including investment and competition policy for which the developing countries are not equipped to consider given the rudimentary stages of their business environment. Institutionalising development issues into the international trade environment will require continuous efforts at understanding the needs of developing countries and the means for attaining the much required socio-economic development.[105]

Thus, negotiations on any new proposals must be subject to the effective participation of developing countries. By this it is meant that these countries must know about the proposals and are given time to review them in their domestic environment. This will also enable the sections of the private sector which will be affected to have the time and make the necessary consultations in order that they may appreciate the details of the proposals. To do otherwise would mean that 'more critical tasks, such as formulating strong negotiating positions in the traditional areas of trade liberalisation, and other non-trade areas of domestic development policy' are ignored to the detriment of developing countries' socio-economic progress.[106]

3.2. Current Action: The Doha Development Agenda

The WTO is very much aware of these difficulties to developing country integration, so much so that in 2001 at the start of the ninth Round of Trade talks, it adopted a 'Development Agenda'. Previously, the predominant subjects of discourse at the Rounds have centred on tariffs.[107] The nine trade rounds and the areas of interest are set out in the following table:

Year	Place/Name	Subjects Covered	No. of Countries
1947–8	Geneva	Tariffs	23
1949	Annecy	Tariffs	13
1950–1	Torquay	Tariffs	38
1956	Geneva	Tariffs	26
1960–2	Dillon Round	Tariffs	26
1963–7	Kennedy Round	Tariffs; Anti-dumping Measures	62
1973–9	Tokyo Round	Tariffs; Non-tariff barriers (NTBs); 'Framework' agreements	102
1986–93	Uruguay Round	Tariffs; NTBs; Rules; Services; Intellectual Property; Dispute Settlement; Textiles; Agriculture Creation of WTO	123
2001–	Doha Round	Trade and Development (to have ended April 2006, still on as at Sep 2009)	152[108]

Although the Round has suffered setbacks in negotiations owing to disagreements across its membership on certain areas of negotiations[109] there is no doubt that under the Round the Organisation is keen to emphasise its commitment to development and to developing country integration into the world trading system.[110] But what does the WTO really mean when it states in the Doha Declaration in respect of developing countries that it seeks 'to place their needs and interests at the heart of the Work Programme adopted'[111] under the Doha Development Agenda (DDA)?

We are of the view that a development agenda in the context of the WTO is invaluable to the Organisation in order to advance the integration of the developing economies into the global trade environment. But the concept of 'development' has been a part of the trade agenda for a long time as we have seen in the previous chapter. A 'Doha Development Agenda' suggests that the WTO has identified new areas of development-related activity which had hitherto not been emphasised before the current round of talks. It is therefore imperative to examine the objectives of the Doha mandate in order to determine what the multilateral trade system seeks to achieve in its bid for closer integration of its developing country membership in the global market.

The scope of the DDA includes negotiations on: Implementation-Related Issues and Concerns; Agriculture; Services; Market Access for Non-agricultural products; Trade-Related Aspects of Intellectual Property Rights; Relationship between Trade and Investment; Interaction between Trade and Competition Policy; Transparency in Government Procurement; Trade Facilitation; WTO Rules; Dispute Settlement Understanding; Trade and Environment; Electronic Commerce; Small Economies; Trade Debt and Finance; Trade and Transfer of Technology; Technical Cooperation and Capacity Building; Least Developed Countries; and Special and Differential Treatment.[112]

The DDA also mentions sustainable development as one of the areas of concern under the Doha Round. Paragraph 6 of the Doha Declaration states that the WTO is 'convinced that the aims of upholding and safeguarding an open and non-discriminatory multilateral trading system, and acting for the protection of the environment and the promotion of sustainable development can and must be mutually supportive'. The UN offers a perspective of sustainable development as an inclusive aspect of the general notion of development. In its view, 'development is a multidimensional undertaking to achieve a higher quality of life for all people. Economic development, social development and environmental protection are interdependent and mutually reinforcing components of sustainable development'.[113]

The objectives and the four point plan which we refer to here as the impact areas of the WTO Development Agenda as stated under the Doha Declaration are set out in paragraph 2 of the Declaration. The section provides:

> International trade can play a major role in the promotion of economic development and the alleviation of poverty. We recognize the need for all our peoples to benefit from the increased opportunities and welfare gains that the multilateral trading system generates. The majority of WTO members are developing countries. We seek to place their needs and interests at the heart of the Work Programme adopted in this Declaration. Recalling the Preamble to the Marrakesh Agreement, we shall continue to make positive efforts designed to ensure that developing countries, and especially the least-developed among them, secure a share in the growth of world trade commensurate with the needs of their economic development. In this context, *enhanced market access, balanced rules,* and *well targeted, sustainably financed technical assistance* and *capacity-building programmes* have important roles to play.[114]

This statement admits the obligation of the WTO towards development where it asserts the role of international trade in the promotion of economic development and the alleviation of poverty. It also reiterates the obligation of the WTO towards its majority membership, that of recognising the need for the peoples in these countries to benefit from increased welfare gains, and the opportunities generated by the multilateral system. Furthermore, there is a confirmation of the path through which the WTO is to achieve the objectives of development – in line with the Preambles of the *WTO (Marrakesh) Agreement*, to make positive efforts to ensure that developing countries secure a share in the growth of world trade commensurate with the needs of their economic development.[115]

The striking feature of the Doha Declaration is the express identification of the target areas in this renewal of the development commitments of the Organisation. These areas are enhanced market access, balanced rules, technical assistance and capacity building. The central theme of the Doha mandate is 'for all (our) peoples to benefit from the increased opportunities and welfare gains that the multilateral trading system generates'.[116] One may surmise that for the practical implementation of the DDA and with a focus on fulfilling the letter and intent of the Doha Declaration, every WTO action whether in the trade negotiations at the quasi- legislative bodies such as the Ministerial Conferences or Committees or in the dispute settlement processes must have these four objectives in mind.

Each of these areas can yield a substantial volume of research on its own. However, given the context of this work, it is important to consider how these factors can contribute to the work of the WTO trade and development agenda.

3.2.1. *Enhanced Market Access*

Enhanced market access for developing countries is an important and pertinent requirement for increasing developing country participation in international trade, particularly for the LDCs. Three central issues which developing countries confront in this area will be examined: trade barriers and the various arguments incorporated as 'a development box', the alternatives offered by increased developing country trade (south-south trade) under more proximate trade arrangements such as Regional Trade Agreements (RTAs), and the restrictions on access for developing countries arising by way of non-tariff barriers.

A. Barriers to Trade and 'Development Box' Arguments

If reliance is to be placed on the various publications of international development indices and these include accession countries which battle with economic instability as a result of war or other natural disasters, then developing countries especially those in sub Saharan Africa have not made significant progress in respect of market access. Some suggestions could be made on why this is so.

In most of these countries, agriculture is the means of livelihood and the principal occupation of the greater majority of the labour force is in subsistence farming which employs low skilled labour. Those which can rely on fuel and mineral trade do so at some cost: the reliance on this industry is at the cost of a diversified industrial economy and reduced opportunities for employment for a vast majority of the labour force. Without well structured government subsidies and the absence of sophisticated equipment and other infrastructure for storage and transportation, agriculture cannot yield significant incomes for the farmers. In order to compensate for the additional costs they incur in the agricultural process, these farmers offer to sell their goods at comparatively exorbitant prices. Unfortunately, their goods more often than not cannot withstand the competition from the more affordable, and sophisticated imports.

In 2003, developing countries addressed these issues by proposals for amendments to the WTO *Agreement on Agriculture (AoA)*. The proposals were set out in a 'development box'.[117] In general, the proposals sought an extension to Article 6.2 of the *AoA*. The said Article 6 provides that developing countries 'shall be exempt from domestic support reduction commitments that would otherwise be applicable to such measures'. The *Development Box* proposals included: the option to entirely exempt basic foodstuff from tariff reduction commitments and the increase of the *de minimis* threshold for developing countries from 10% to 25%. It also proposed that aid for rural development, employment programmes, food security, poverty reduction, diversification including investment and input subsidies for producers with low income should become part of the Green Box of permitted subsidies.

These proposals were not incorporated as part of the negotiations of the Doha Development Round. Nevertheless, it is essential to keep in perspective an overview of the development box proposals on market access as was initiated by developing countries at the start of the Doha Round:

Development Box Proposals Initiated Under the Doha Round[118]

General

Exempt certain products from AoA commitments, using either a negative or positive list approach. Under the positive list approach, all products would be exempt except those listed by developing country members. This approach is used in negotiations on industrial tariffs and services. Countries volunteer to include only those products in the Agreement they feel ready for. Under the negative list approach, products would have to be nominated by developing country members to be exempt from AoA commitments (it is envisaged that these would be products important from a food security perspective). In other words, all products are included unless a country explicitly decides to exclude one or more.

Market Access

Tariff reductions should be linked to reductions in trade-distorting support to agriculture in developed countries.

Basic food security crops should be exempt from tariff reductions or other commitments.

There should be a right to renegotiate (upward) the low tariff bindings that apply to food security crops where those bindings are low.

Special safeguards providing automatic increases in tariffs, with a provision to impose quantitative restrictions under specified circumstances in the event of a rapid increase in imports or decline in prices, should be allowed.

Developing countries should be exempt from any obligation to provide any minimum market access.

Domestic Support

De minimis support ceilings for product-specific and non-product-specific support in developing countries should be doubled to 20 per cent of the value of output.

Domestic support exemptions should be expanded, for example, by allowing subsidised credit and other capacity building measures as exemptions when provided to low income or resource poor farmers.

Developing countries should be allowed to offset negative product-specific support (i.e. where farmers are taxed) against positive non-product-specific support (i.e. where farmers are supported).

Developing countries should be permitted to use measures to increase domestic production of staple crops for domestic consumption.

Export Measures

Flexibilities for developing countries to provide export subsidies in certain circumstances, including those that reduce the costs of marketing and those that reduce charges for export shipments, should be continued.

While not recommending the suggestions in the 'box', the Doha document on *Implementation-related Issues and Concerns* however urged Members to 'exercise restraint in challenging measures notified under the green box by developing countries to promote rural development and adequately address food security concerns'.[119]

The removal of trade distorting support was further considered at the Hong Kong Conference of 13–18 December 2005. The Conference in the various provisions of the Declaration thereafter attached great importance to the DDA by emphasising the development dimension relative to the negotiations on market access. With respect to market access, the Ministers had stated:

> We agree to ensure the parallel elimination of all forms of export subsidies and disciplines on all export measures with equivalent effect to be completed by the end of 2013. This will be achieved in a progressive and parallel manner, to be specified in the modalities, so that a substantial part is realised by the end of the first half of the implementation period.[120]

Also under the Doha negotiations, developing countries submitted proposals for Special Products and Special Safeguard Mechanism as reforms of the agricultural trading arrangements under the WTO. The proposals were accepted as part of the *July 2004 package* by a General Council decision to allow developing country Members to designate some products as 'Special Products' (SP), and the establishment of a 'Special Safeguard Mechanism' (SSM). The decision states that in granting these flexibilities, the needs of food security, livelihood security and rural development will form the basis of the flexible treatment approved.[121] In spite of this decision, negotiations on the modalities for the percentage of produce to be identified as special products as well as the application of safeguard mechanisms under the July 2004 package have been part of the deadlock in the Doha talks.[122]

While the expected date for the elimination of all forms of export subsidies is awaited, it has been argued that the above demands of developing countries for special and different treatment from other WTO Member states in the recent Round of Trade talks, implies a return to protectionist trade policies which the WTO was established to counter. Peter Sutherland argues that whereas the Doha Agenda was intended to be 'the Development Agenda', the 'special and differential treatment' provided to developing countries is arguably 'an anti-development agenda'.[123] Yet he insists that the flexibilities that have been agreed at the start of the Doha Round cannot be ignored and is critical of the unwillingness of the WTO negotiators to reach a consensus in the Doha talks. He states that:

> Now, it will be argued that while industrial countries stand to concede much on market access, the developing nations — and especially the big emerging markets — are giving too little. It is certainly the case that the flexibilities and exclusions from which they 'benefit' have a real impact on the potential for opening their markets. Yet it was the US and EU, in their

anxiety to launch and move the round forward, that willingly and knowingly agreed on these flexibilities.

[…] In any event, it is no use coming back at this stage and claiming that the flexibilities were not intended for use.[124]

Alan Matthews has asked whether developing countries would not be more successful in this bid for enhanced market access by 'tackling the root causes of inequities directly rather than seeking to avoid the adverse effects of these policies by reinforcing their own protectionist policies in return'.[125] His opinion is that developing countries can achieve enhanced market access 'through seeking more effective market access conditions and greater disciplines on developed countries' use of trade-distorting support'.[126]

It would appear that developing countries have taken these suggestions into consideration in the Doha negotiations. In an emphatic submission by Argentina, Brazil, India, Indonesia, Namibia, Pakistan, the Philippines, South Africa, and Venezuela to the CTD on 28 November 2005, entitled *Reclaiming Development in the WTO Doha Development Round*[127] the countries asserting that 'agriculture is the central issue' of the Doha Round stated inter alia that a development round requires the removal of trade distorting domestic support in the developed economies, such support being anti-development measures which frustrate developing countries market access and inhibit integration into the global market.

The above notwithstanding, another limitation to market access may be pointed out. With respect to LDCs for example, in spite of the preferential tariff arrangements (such as the earlier mentioned EU-EBA agreement on duty-free quota-free market access for LDCs), these economies are still constrained by the strict application of rules of origin under the PTAs. The rules of origin demand that all the processes of production resulting in a 'finished' good should be undertaken in the territory which is granted preferential treatment. LDCs are of the view that simpler and more transparent rules are required in order to benefit from these preferential arrangements including those agreed under Annex F of the Hong Kong Ministerial.[128] One cannot but agree that a simplified approach is preferable. Finished goods need not necessarily be undertaken in the particular Member State which is party to a PTA. Co-operation amongst LDCs and within the developing countries in general could be in form of bilateral assistance between countries in the production process and ought to be permitted.

Granted, the rules of origin seek to deter countries from passing off their goods as those originating in territories which belong to a PTA. However it would not be any less preferential to accept that the 'origin' of a good can be determined by the country which offers it for sale in the market. There need not be a rigorous examination of the locations wherein production was carried out in order to apply preferential treatment for that good so long as the LDC in question is cited as the place of manufacture and the returns of sale are made to the LDC itself. In addition, the determination of a question in this regard is better suited for the DSB to determine, than for a situation where at the outset, trade rules (of origin) limit the opportunities for co-operation in enhancing production capacity between countries.

In the domestic environment however, the main impediments to access for developing country goods (including but not limited to agricultural goods) are twofold: *one*, ineffective domestic polices adopted by developing countries themselves and, *two*, limited globally competitive goods. Developing country producers stymied by inefficient domestic policy regulation and faced with the consequences of a lack of innovation and technical expertise in enterprise, appear satisfied with merely criticising the external issues (such as developed country subsidies) which present challenges to their potential for global market integration. It is suggested that rather, there should be efforts at pressuring the domestic governments to consider more inventive ways to boost domestic industrial growth.

This is because there is no evidence to show that there will be any significant increase in market access for developing country goods merely by a reduction in developed country subsidies. Granted, there are certain measures which can be taken in the context of making the rules or regulations affecting market access more flexible and beneficial and these measures are better addressed in specific terms.[129] However and more importantly, enhanced market access will be attained by trade-facilitation targeted improvements in the general industrial policy of developing countries and not by repeated arguments on improving access for a single trade sector, notably agriculture. Efforts between governments and stakeholders to diversify developing countries' economies and strengthen their trading capacity will necessarily be of more benefit on the long run.

Rodrik observes that it is 'increasingly recognized that developing societies need to embed private initiative in a framework of public action that encourages restructuring, diversification, and technological dynamism beyond what market forces on their own would generate'.[130] He suggests further that:

> market forces and private entrepreneurship would be in the driving seat of this agenda, but governments would also perform a strategic and coordinating role in the productive sphere beyond simply ensuring property rights, contract enforcement, and macroeconomic stability.[131]

Beyond this internal reform strategy however, as developing countries make advances towards improving their trading capacity, it is hoped that they would improve their trading relationship within their regions and in alternative trading arrangements which in our view presents a more pragmatic basis for cross-country trade.

B. Increased South-South Trade (and Alternative Trading Arrangements)

The alternative benefits of more proximate trading arrangements for developing countries ought to be considered. It could be argued that regional and bilateral trade is a more viable option for allowing developing countries goods greater access across borders as a prelude to global market integration.

The option for RTAs is provided for under the rules of the WTO. Like the preferential agreements discussed earlier, RTAs depart from the principle of non-discrimination in WTO agreements. However WTO Member States are not precluded from forming or joining RTAs so long as they comply with the conditions below:[132]

- Para 4–10 Article XXIV GATT on the formation and operation of customs unions and free trade areas covering trade in goods;
- Article V GATS on conclusions of RTAs in the area of trade in services for developed and developing country Members; and
- The provisions of the Enabling Clause, where applicable.

Not everyone is in support of RTAs. It has been argued that the WTO must redress the balance eroded in the multilateral trading system by the adoption of RTAs. Bhagwati is of the view that the former system embodies the fundamental principle of non-discrimination among trading nations while the latter is 'inherently preferential and discriminatory'.[133] It has also been argued that some factors which contribute to the setting up of RTA may detract from the inclusive nature of the multilateral system. These factors include:

- That while the two trading systems may share the common goal of trade liberalisation, RTAs may in some respect require participating countries to harmonise certain aspects of their national laws in order to achieve the objectives of the agreement where necessary;[134]
- Some regional groupings may not have any remarkable influence on trade due to political reasons;[135] and
- The provisions of RTAs may be wider or may vary from WTO rules dealing with issues such as enforcement of labour standards, investments, social mobility, and competition rules.[136]

The WTO is not of the same view. In allowing RTAs, the Organisation acknowledges that this alternative to the multilateral system can assist the flow of trade and services in line with the Organisation's rules.[137] This support of the WTO for RTAs has also been explained in positive terms by Michalopoulos who suggests that developing countries stand to benefit from RTAs (principally those between developed and developing countries) due to factors 'chiefly related to the dynamic effects accruing to developing countries from technology transfers through increased imports and investment as well as smaller trade diversion costs'.[138]

It could be added that RTAs operating in a closer area of proximity can have more direct positive effect with respect to the mission of global trade to achieve the raising of living standards and alleviation of poverty. In reaching for a more feasible alternative to the complex rules of the modern trading system, RTAs may be seen as '"laboratories" for the exploration of ways countries can manage their common problems while respecting their differences'.[139] It will necessarily be easier to apply rules negotiated in smaller groups and covering issues which are more pertinent to the needs of the citizens in a reduced trading arena, a fact served by the principle of direct effect of provisions under the EU Treaty.[140]

In particular South-South trade provides an opportunity for these countries to advance their interests within the more limited environment of their regions. It encourages the growth of specialised industries; it is cognisant of, and sympathetic to, the development-oriented trade policies adopted in their respective legal systems. These countries can also assist each other, particularly the least developed among them, in the technological processes of production. Where the countries themselves can reach agreement on their levels of co-operation, these bilateral or regional trading arrangements will in turn strengthen the cooperation amongst developing countries at the WTO forum enabling them to present more specific proposals on the rules and practical measures inhibiting their market integration.

One cannot ignore the agitation against a renewal of bilateralism, the fear of which has again arisen following the impasse in the market access negotiations under the Doha Round. The following arguments in a British newspaper portray the opposing views in this respect.

Robert Wade of the London School of Economics, while commenting on the failure of market access negotiations, pointed out that developing countries faced serious dangers of de-industrialisation if they accepted the basic terms of NAMA proposals. He stated that these countries risk becoming more specialised than at present in the production of primary commodities and simple, labour intensive products, and even less diversified in the production of more complex rich country foods. In his view, the situation 'may suit the collective interest of developed countries quite well, but it would be a bad result for the world'.[141] A response by the EU Commission Trade Spokesman raised the issue that a failure in reaching conclusions on these negotiations would result in developed countries returning to bilateral agreements to the exclusion of developing countries. In his view, developing countries would then 'lose out' on the benefits of an international trading system.[142]

While caution may be exercised with regard to the potential immediate impact of bilateral agreements which do not favour developing countries, this EU response is not entirely accurate. Apart from the fact that developed countries can also utilise the trading arena under bilateral or regional agreements of South-South trade to their benefit if they work towards this aim, there is no basis for the assertion that developing countries will necessarily 'lose out' in the event that developed countries seek exclusive bilateral or indeed regional arrangements. The EU spokesman's counter-argument is misleading on the question of the impact of bilateral agreements on the Doha agenda as they pertain to enhanced market access. This is because trade being a reciprocal arrangement, developed countries' businesses also need developing country markets. Developed countries benefit from access to developing country markets whose consumers are heavily reliant on developed country products. They also benefit from access to raw materials in developing countries often obtained at significantly cheap rates. Developing countries also present business opportunities for developed country services and are often viable business environments for expanding multinational corporations. Developing countries furthermore present opportunities for established firms in developed countries to harness or purchase local materials used to develop new technologies and new products. The cheaper labour market and less-stringent legal environment of most developed countries is also beneficial to developed country businesses.

It ought to be considered that in the alternative to the argument by the EU spokesman immediately above, should developing countries enter into exclusive proximate arrangements for their benefits which arrangements such as the ASEAN have proved to be of increasing success, there is no doubt that developed countries themselves may also lose significant market access.

What ought to be kept in mind rather than raising fallible counter-arguments such as the above is this: the superior benefit of the multilateral system is that the system focuses on the need to provide a regulated international trading environment which considers that cohesion amongst countries on the long run serves the interest of a greater number of peoples. Proximate trade agreements are therefore beneficial to the extent that they lead to a closer integration of the market area, and for the emerging economies of developing countries, these agreements may actually facilitate their global market integration process as highlighted earlier. The only question is whether developing countries themselves are willing to commit to such arrangements and how effectively they would utilise them.

C. Non-Tariff Barriers

It is not only subsidies and tariffs that constitute barriers to market access for developing countries. There are also Non-Tariff Barriers (NTBs) across the WTO Agreements so called because rather than the application of duties and charges these involve the application of domestic regulations and standards to imports. NTBs could arise by way of grant of subsidies to domestic goods, requirements in manufacturing or production processes of goods including SPS measures, or application of dumping duties or countervailing measures. Indeed most of the disputes brought under the WTO are with respect to NTBs.[143]

As may be expected, developing countries have concerns with NTBs in the domestic regulations of other WTO Member states which restrict market access to their products. The recent high profile dispute, *EC-Measures Affecting the Approval and Marketing of Bio-Tech Product* provides an example.[144] The dispute arose in respect of the EU moratorium imposed since October 1998 which restricted the importation into the EU of a number of bio-tech food products. Argentina had joined in the dispute, brought by the US and Canada.[145] A number of issues were raised by the Complainants, mainly under the SPS Agreement. They include *inter alia* that:

- The alleged moratorium violated the SPS rules against undue delay in approval procedures (Art 8; Annex C);
- The moratorium was not notified as an SPS measure (Art. 7);
- The EC did not publish risk assessments on the likelihood of harm from biotech products (Art.5.1);
- The moratorium was maintained without 'sufficient scientific evidence' (Art.2.2); and
- The EC had acted discriminately between domestic and imported products in 'comparable situations' because it regulated biotech products (e.g genetically modified seeds) more strictly that biotech processing agents (e.g enzymes used in food manufacturing) Art 5.5[146]

Argentina joined in the complaint as it is the largest developing country grower of GM crops followed by Brazil, China, Paraguay, India and South Africa.[147]

The Panel found that the EU had acted inconsistently with Annex C 1(a) and Article 8 of the SPS Agreement because there were 'undue delays' in the completion of the approval procedures for 24 out of the 27 imports restricted. The EU had also acted inconsistently with Articles 5.1; 2.2 of the SPS Agreement because the measures applied to restrict the imports were not 'based on' risk assessments and were 'maintained without sufficient scientific evidence'.[148]

This case presents interesting challenges to developing country market access. US contention that biotech products will address hunger in developing countries will understandably instigate a clamour for biotech products without any scientific assessment of risk whatsoever in these countries as indeed it has. Hungry people have little interest in waiting for scientific confirmation of the suitability of foods. Should developing countries restrict any such foods by adopting domestic SPS measures, they would require an 'assessment of risk and determination of the appropriate level of sanitary or phytosanitary protection' as set out under Art.5. Unless the national government already has agencies charged with this objective, it will not be an easy task for most developing countries. Neither will it be any easier to adopt control and approval procedures for such foods without 'undue delay' given the comparable bureaucratic inefficiency of poorer countries.

At dispute level, the challenges are not any less. Discharging the burden of proof also requires that relevant scientific opinion must be adduced either to contend against the measure or to support it. Thus, initially the complaining party has to establish an inconsistency with the SPS Agreement.[149] Then, when a *prima facie* case has been made, the burden moves to the defending party who must then counter the claim of inconsistency.[150] In either case, the burden is not easily discharged, a difficulty not only particular to developing countries.[151] The challenges under the SPS Agreement are considered in greater detail in the Appendix.

At present, in addressing the issue of NTBs and their influence on market access, the WTO and developing country governments should be concerned with how developing country exports can avoid the application of NTBs. Certain questions therefore arise: What factors inhibit developing countries from enhancing their production processes to suit international standards? Do developing countries require improvements in manufacturing processes for instance in the need for more sophisticated machinery and equipment? What training and skills support is required by individuals and others engaged in production processes? How can the indigenous processes be improved to conform to international standards?

A response to these questions should start from the premise that it is necessary to find ways of increasing the potential and capacity of developing countries to produce goods which will not be denied market access on the basis that these goods do not meet the domestic regulations of other States.

The importance of technical assistance in this area cannot be over-emphasised. But it could be argued that trade rules on technical assistance exist as guidelines on Members' obligations and cannot be expected to adequately address these issues. This is not the case. As earlier mentioned under the considerations of the Af T initiatives, the multilateral trade mechanism of the WTO effectively addresses the objective of economic development in its legal framework when it offers practical guidelines on how development can be achieved *through trade*. Dual action is important: practical normative provisions on technical assistance, and action by developing countries in negotiating for technical assistance both at the WTO and with individual trading partners.

Certainly, the objective of market access for developing countries is achievable under the WTO, post Doha. Technical assistance on ways to boost trading capacity and also, for internal industrial policy reform by developing countries is important. A stronger cohesion by developing countries towards facilitating effective regional trade agreements in line with the WTO provisions will also be of benefit. Added to this, stronger South-South integration in a more unified market area will help harmonise trade and development policies in line with international agreements including those of the WTO. The proximity of markets will also reduce protectionist trends and possibly increase production and trade across countries. The EU and the large American market have made successes on these platforms.

3.2.2. Balanced Rules

Here, two questions could be considered. In the first instance, are there still any benefits to developing countries under a rules-based system? Also, do the trade rules reflect the concerns of developing countries?

The first question does not present great difficulty. The security and predictability offered by the application of the multilateral trade rules is one of the strongest advantages of the rules-based trade system. So also is the opportunity for any disputes to be settled by a compulsory settlement mechanism. The MFN and NT rules in the multilateral system ensures that developing countries inclusive, all Member States of the WTO can be certain that their goods and services offered in the global market will not be subject to discriminatory treatment. Besides, although WTO Agreements are highly technical and the decisions of the DSB more often than not even more cumbersome to peruse, the rules-based system of the WTO as a consensual arrangement is laudably still 'Member driven'.[152]

The second question however addresses the relevant and current issue of how trade rules can facilitate development. The suspension of the Doha Round of talks in July 2006 by the Director General Pascal Lamy following the failure of trade negotiators to reach agreements on market access, tariff cuts, and on non-agricultural market access,[153] reflects the difficulties in achieving the requisite balance between the proposals of developing countries on the one hand and developed countries on the other. Be that as it may, the rules-based system itself needs some readjustment to certain provisions in order for a more balanced system.[154] Lee (2006) proposes that changes must be made in the wide range of rules governing specific areas of trade that have significant effects on development.[155] These changes will affect the Schedule of Concessions, subsidies, AD measures, safeguards, TRIMS, TRIPS and trade in services.[156] He also proposes an *Agreement for Development Facilitation (ADF)* which will incorporate special treatment and technical assistance provisions, though in a more binding form.[157] In addition, he sees the need for a more permanent body – a *Council* for Trade and Development which can address the complex and continuous nature of trade and development issues in an adequate organisational structure.[158]

In addition to Lee's support for the infant industry argument as a necessity for developing country economic development, further proposals could be made for a balance in the rules under the modern trading system.

A. The Case for New (and Vulnerable) Industry Protection

Hoekman *et al* have proposed that 'there is certainly a need to "get the rules right" from a development perspective which will require the re-opening of certain existing agreements'.[159] Balanced trade rules are integral to improving developing country trade particularly those developing countries that are dependent on a single sector with a limited employment of labour), those who either do not have a strong industrial base, or who do not benefit from significant levels of private entrepreneurship. Reference to a single sector with a limited employment of the available labour here is particularly concerned with countries which are dependent on sectors such as mining which sector is largely controlled by the activities of foreign multinationals or private groups and therefore do not employ a great percentage of labour. Previously, allusion to this area has been made in the earlier considerations of the impact of the diamond industry in Botswana.

Industrialisation is a significant boost to a country's trade capacity and is invaluable for expanding the goods and services which developing countries can offer making it possible for them to compete effectively in the modern trading arena. A counter argument may be made that some countries have not owed their economic progress to the production of manufactured goods. That may well be true. Countries such as New Zealand relying as it does on primary exports of meat, dairy, fruit and vegetables, fish, forestry products, or Australia with its highly rewarding services sector and mining activities, seem to succeed without dependency on manufacturing processes. However, the present reference to 'industrialisation' is not limited to the manufacture of goods alone. 'Industry' also refers to any branch of economic or commercial activity. Thus for the present purposes, industrialisation refers to a country developing industries on a wide scale whether for the production of goods or for the provisions of services; or any of those processes whereby a country builds its trading capacity.

The point is this: such countries have been able to consolidate on the gains of their long trading activities by embarking on macroeconomic and other structural and infrastructural reforms and beneficial trading arrangements in the region.[160] More importantly, these successes have arisen mainly because of reform policies undertaken in the domestic environment by the State.

It is the view that developing countries stand to benefit from State assistance in this area of infant industry growth, contrary to the objectives of the current trade rules which discount the need for State intervention. By contrast, a study of the early trading system reveals that the infant industry argument was used as justification for the protection of the infant manufacturing industries of Germany and the US in the nineteenth century. This argument was posited as early as 1791 by Alexander Hamilton, subsequently in 1841 by Frederick List and, by John Stuart Mills in 1848.[161] The argument justifies the use of trade restrictions on imports in order to allow the local industries develop to appreciable standards where they could withstand competition from imported goods.

Some economic thought is of the view that infant industry protection is not fundamental to the question of increasing developing country potential in the multilateral trading system. Trebilcock and Howse consider that the argument rests on the proposition that an advanced mature economy cannot be predominantly dependent upon agriculture or natural resources but rather on manufacturing.[162] They point out that certain countries have sustained high standards of living without substantial manufacturing sectors e.g New Zealand through agriculture as we noted above, and Middle Eastern oil-producing states through natural resources.[163] Other economics scholars have noted that protection of an infant industry does not necessarily determine the sustenance of that industry.[164]

However, these contrary arguments do not invalidate the present position. It must be said that the argument here is not for a return to protectionism. Rather, it echoes the basic idea in the infant industry argument: the idea of allowing weaker economies some measure of flexibility in adopting strategic policies and practices that will create new, diverse, and viable industries that can compete in the global economy. An analysis of modern developed economies points out that countries diversify over most of their development path.[165] It is only when they have reached an appreciable level of economic adjustment that their production patterns start to become more concentrated.[166]

One striking feature of countries in the process of economic development is that the number of export products offered in the international markets actually increase.[167] Furthermore, countries which have increased their export portfolios have owed their successes to the activities of a broad range of industries and not by sectoral concentration.[168] Rodrik also notes that the lack of innovation in developing countries export restricts economic growth.[169] In his view, 'it is innovation that enables restructuring and economic growth'.[170]

Innovation' requires an outlet – a well regulated industry in order to encourage further R&D and to maintain the viability of the new industry as it faces competition. Moreover, it is not only the domestic environment that benefits from the emergence of new innovations and industries, increasing global demand reflects an ever increasing diversity in consumer needs across a whole variety of goods. Enabling the creation and short term protection of 'new' industries in developing countries will also respond to these needs.

What is more, encouraging diversification in industrial activity by creating new, and protecting vulnerable industries can significantly offer fuller employment for a greater number of persons in the society. Developing countries need this diversification not only to increase the number of goods they offer in the international market but also to enable participation of the private sector both as entrepreneurs and as employees in competitive industrial and business activity. For international trade to bring about the gains promised by the rules-based system, the engagement of most of the labour force either as employers or employees of labour is fundamental to the issue of wealth creation and distribution in the society.

As Winters (2002) notes, whereas poverty is not a direct result of international trade, it however 'reflects low earning power, few assets, poor access to communal resources, poor health and education, powerlessness and vulnerability.'[171] Private entrepreneurship and employment in new areas of trading opportunities will to a considerable extent stimulate government activity in the provisions of adequate social infrastructure given the increase in national income and the increased participation of a stronger private sector. As a result, the crucial path to raised living standards, full employment, increased opportunities, etc, becomes a reasonable expectation.

B. Re-adjusting the Rules

Van den Bossche suggests that 'by means of a customs duty or an import restriction, national producers can be afforded temporary protection, allowing them breathing space to become strong enough to compete with well-established producers.'[172] A balance in the trade rules can only be based on provisions which meet the needs of both developed and developing countries. The provisions of

GATT Article XVIII on governmental assistance to economic development and the assistance which subsidies can provide to developing country industries are relevant to the achievement of this balance.[173]

GATT Article XVIII:7 provides that a developing country may enter into negotiations with other parties to modify or withdraw a concession in the Agreement where it 'considers it desirable, in order to promote the establishment of a particular industry with a view to raising the general standard of living of its people'. There is clearly an identifiable linkage in this provision between the need to establish a viable trading industry, and the opportunity to improve living standards for the benefit of the individuals in a society. The supplementary provisions to Article XVIII:7[174] extend the application of this provision to the establishment of a new branch of production in an existing industry and to the substantial transformation of an existing industry; to the substantial expansion of an existing industry *supplying a relatively small proportion of the domestic demand*. The provision also applies in the event of the reconstruction of an industry destroyed or substantially damaged *as a result of hostilities or natural disasters*.

The above italicised words reflect the spirit in which this GATT provision was drafted. Bearing in mind that the idea for the GATT took root in the aftermath of the Second World War and in the wake of the Great Depression of the period which resulted in severe unemployment and a marked reduction in industrial production, the provisions were to the benefit of those countries that needed to build or restructure their industrial capacity. Many developing countries in the WTO have undergone or still undergo the difficulties provided for in this GATT provision. They have small industries often operating as sole trading concerns which really supply only a small proportion of domestic demand. Their global influence has been marginal and unsurprisingly, the CTD noted at the beginning of the Doha Round that the establishment of industries has not been the basis of any claims pursuant to Article XVIII:7 before the DSB.[175]

An impediment to the application of Article XVIII may be the 'compensatory adjustment' requirement pursuant to Article XVIII:7(b). This rule is an encumbrance on poor countries. The effect of the said Article XVIII:7(b) is that a developing country has to agree on a 'trade-off' with another WTO Member before it can embark on implementing a relevant industrial policy. One may assess a scenario in this respect in the following hypothetical example:

> *Developing Country X wishes to establish a computer hardware factory manufacturing key boards using a recently discovered local durable synthetic material. It notifies Country Y from which it imports computer keyboards, and also the WTO Members (CONTRACTING PARTIES) that it will progressively restrict imports of computer keyboards over a period. Country Y, makes no objection but asks for monetary compensation for Country X's withdrawal from its WTO obligation not to restrict*

imports of other country products. Country X declines. It bases its objection on the fact that it cannot afford to make the payment given the costs of embarking on its industrial policy. It also states that its establishment of a computer keyboard factory is a development-based programme and therefore WTO-compliant under Article XVIII:7. Country Z informs Country X that it will immediately restrict Country X's palm oil exports. The palm oil industry is Country X's main income earner and employs the greatest number of its labour force. Country Z is its major trading partner.

The circumstantial issues behind Country X's action in the adoption of a domestic policy to grow an industry in the computer hardware sector should not be ignored. A Panel cannot make 'an objective assessment' of the instant facts as required under Article 11 DSU, without relying on the circumstantial issues behind Country X's action. Consideration ought to be given to Country X's special circumstances and the socio-economic objectives of its action including provision of jobs for the local labour force and diversification of its industrial activity. More so, the potential benefits to the multilateral trading system in the form of enhanced market access for non-agricultural goods from a developing economy, market integration for Country X, and increased competition in the global market for computer keyboard manufactures, are important.[176]

In addition, infant industries will also benefit from the grant of subsidies by their governments. Some exemptions beneficial to developing countries had been included under the *SCM Agreement* as non-actionable subsidies. These included: assistance for research activities conducted by firms, higher education or research establishments, assistance to disadvantaged regions within the territory of a member, for the purposes of regional development, and assistance to promote adaptation of existing facilities (existing for at least two years) to new environmental requirements imposed by law which proved burdensome to firms.[177]

With the lapse of these provisions on non-actionable subsidies pursuant to Article 31 of the SCM Agreement,[178] we are of the view that this issue ought to be revisited. Policies and measures adopted by developing countries which have the purpose of achieving development goals, including R&D funding, ought to be treated as non-actionable subsidies. Indeed this has been proposed under the *Doha Ministerial Decision on Implementation-Related Issues and Concerns.*[179] The Decision takes note of the proposal:

to treat measures implemented by developing countries with a view to achieving legitimate development goals, such as regional growth, technology research and development funding, production diversification and development and implementation of environmentally sound methods of production as non-actionable subsidies, [...] During the course of the negotiations, Members are urged to exercise due restraint with respect to challenging such measures.[180]

There is no escape from the fact that for developing countries, 'further development depends on diversifying into higher value-added activities in which they are not presently efficient'.[181] In this regard, the suggestion of the Zedillo Report which called for 'legitimating limited, time bound protection of certain industries by countries in the early stages of industrialisation'[182] is still pertinent.

Lee's proposals for the introduction of the concept of 'sliding scale' (differentiated treatment in accordance with development stages measured by GNI) in respect of tariffs, and subsidies under the WTO are of interest.[183] The former is to allow developing countries to impose additional tariffs over their maximum 'bound' commitments for the purposes of infant industry promotion. The latter seeks the authorisation of otherwise actionable subsidies to developing countries. Still of interest and significant here, are his views that trade rules on antidumping and countervailing duties greatly hinder developing country exports particularly those of new and emergent industries and should not be applied to exports of young industries.

3.2.3. Well-Targeted and Financially Sustainable Technical Assistance

The DDA notes the requisite technical assistance that the Organisation ought to provide for development purposes.[184] Technical assistance is required to enable all categories of developing countries including LDCs and economies in transition to adjust to WTO rules and disciplines, implement obligations, and enjoy the benefits of Membership. A number of WTO Agreements provide for technical assistance particularly the SPS Agreement, the TBT Agreement, the Customs Valuation Agreement, and the TRIPS Agreement.[185] Developed country members may provide technical assistance directly or under the technical cooperation programme of the WTO Secretariat.[186]

While the WTO has extensive activities related to TRTA as was mentioned in Chapter 1, effective participation by developing countries' at decision making and dispute settlement activities is extremely important. The modern multilateral trading system as it is, places demands on developing countries who lack the institutional capacity to implement their obligations under the wide variety of trade related activities covered by the WTO.[187] Apart from the problems of implementing the trade rules, there is also the basic problem of an insufficient engagement with the activities of the Organisation itself which may account for the wrong perception of the WTO as either a welfare organisation, or a rich countries' club.

To address this problem, well targeted technical assistance should apart from targeting the implementation of WTO Agreements, also consider those causes of poor developing country participation. Notably however, most of the considerations below will require the political will of individual governments particularly the developing country governments, and co-operative efforts among WTO Member States.

A. Capacity to Participate in WTO Negotiations

A WTO Member wishing to apply any measures in respect of matters covered by the Agreement ought to know exactly what is required to accomplish its objective. As has been observed, 'the ability to shape agreements depends on the capacity of countries to follow complex, wide ranging negotiations, an area in which some countries are distinctly more equal than others'.[188] Hence, technical assistance activities of the WTO are required to help those countries which lack this capacity to follow the trade negotiation processes at the Organisation. Increasingly and commendably however, developing countries are seizing the initiative to address the issues which limit their participation in WTO negotiations. An example is the recent communication by two developing countries to the Trade Negotiations Committee of the General Council identifying irregularities in the negotiation and decision making process of the organisation.[189]

The Communication *inter alia*, addressed the lack of sufficient capacity of developing Members to react to the large amount of documents emanating from Ministerial Conferences and meetings of the WTO in a limited time. It also raised the issue of procedural defects in meetings at the Conferences including the limited access which developing countries have to some negotiation groups, the lack of attention to proposals by developing countries, and the imposition of pre-determined texts. In its conclusions, the Communication expressed the view that 'the above-mentioned irregularities attempt against the full realization of the development dimension of the Doha Work Programme, an immensely relevant issue for developing countries which, as a matter of fact, make up the majority of members in this Organization'.[190]

While developing countries make up a majority of the WTO, the document referred to above suggests that reflections of their individual concerns and interests are still in the minority. There are a number of relevant factors here:

First, is the infrequent physical presence by representatives of developing country Members at the activities of the WTO. It is indisputable that politics and diplomacy demand the physical presence of participants – networking, exchange of ideas and informal talks are invaluable in enhancing relationships and understanding the workings of political groupings. Resource constraints are factors which will undermine the participation of developing countries here. Evidence of this limitation is found in the limited personnel and lack of office accommodation for a number of WTO Member States in Geneva. Real time presence of developing country representatives is a key requirement in the political background of the WTO and Member governments must place greater emphasis in this area, persuading and assisting developing countries to be more visible at the WTO.

Second, there are insufficient intellectual and research facilities in developing countries where preliminary study of the products of all WTO negotiations and other meetings (and not only those areas immediately relevant to them) can be analysed and disseminated. A significant problem of developing country Members is that they may not have adequate human manpower at their disposal for the purposes of analysing the voluminous pages of WTO rules and dispute settlement reports which in turn lead to an insufficient understanding of the rights and benefits set out in the Agreements themselves. An inevitable effect of this situation is that developing countries face further challenges in implementing the rules (and their rights) under the WTO Agreement and may occupy themselves with drafting ineffective proposals which would not be accepted at negotiations. This adverse effect was identified by the Chinese government in the timely establishment of the *Shanghai WTO Affairs Consultation Centre*,[191] prior to the Chinese accession to the WTO in 2001.[192] The WTO can encourage developing country governments to create such centres in their countries.

Third, the WTO needs to involve developing countries more fully in adopting projects for its technical assistance activities. In this respect, developing countries have to be clear what they expect from the WTO and the Organisation itself has to be clear on what it can offer. The form of technical assistance required by a country is dependent on the prevalent circumstances of the developing country. A country may need assistance in trade facilitation issues while another requires assistance with respect to determining the application of a particular WTO Agreement for a complaint before the DSB. Targeting a country's area of need is thus important for successful technical assistance projects.

Finally, it is also important to stress the need for available funds to meet clearly identified programmes. Rather than periodic contributions from developed countries, it would be preferable that at the start of each financial year, a budgeted sum is placed at the disposal of the WTO Secretariat responsible for technical assistance programmes.[193] Developing countries who can, should also be encouraged to make the least minimum contribution to this fund from their domestic budget. It should not be left to developed countries alone as this only accentuates the wrong idea of the WTO as a welfare Organisation.

B. Effective Use of the Dispute Settlement Process

The DSU has a number of provisions which take into cognisance the fact that developing countries require special provisions to substantiate their participation at the DSB.[194] However, a major obstacle to developing country participation is the lack of, or insufficient legal expertise and administrative infrastructure at the domestic level to help developing Member States in their recourse to the DSB.[195] Another limitation is that developing countries may not have successfully internalised the WTO rules in their domestic legislation and in their domestic trade disputes.[196]

The WTO Membership can engage in co-operative efforts to develop the legal expertise and skills of developing country representatives. Such assistance would contribute significantly to relieve some of the difficulties developing countries may have in aligning their domestic trade arrangements with the requirements of their multilateral agreements, and in utilising the dispute settlement process.[197] The WTO Secretariat is already charged with providing secretarial and technical support by assisting Panels in legal, historical and procedural aspects of the matters to be dealt with (Art 27.1); provision of a qualified legal expert from the WTO technical cooperation services on request by a developing country disputant (Art 27.2); and the conduct of special training courses on dispute settlement procedures and practices for interested Members (Art 27.3), all of which go a long way towards the provision of technical assistance.

Knowing when and how to use the dispute processes is also an area where the WTO can educate its less developed Membership. Well targeted technical assistance would also address an underlying imperative of the dispute settlement mechanism: that the dispute settlement mechanism should be used in good faith to resolve disputes and not to further contentions.[198]

3.2.4. Capacity Building Programmes

The DDA confirms that capacity building is a core element of the development dimension of the multilateral trading system.[199] The objective of the WTO in this aspect of the development initiative falls largely on providing:

a. particular assistance to LDCs to enable them participate effectively in the negotiations on market access for non-agricultural goods;[200]
b. support to developing countries in policy analysis and development objectives in respect of trade and investment;[201]
c. support in policy analysis and development objectives in respect of trade and competition policy;[202]

d. support in policy analysis and development objectives in respect of transparency in government procurement;[203]
e. support in trade facilitation involving expediting the movement, release and clearance of goods including goods in transit;[204]
f. encouraging Members to share expertise with others especially LDCs wishing to perform domestic environmental reviews;[205] and
g. general capacity building for the benefit of LDCs and for their accession and also call for an increase in contributions to the Integrated Framework for Trade-Related Technical Assistance to Least Developed Countries (IF) fund and the WTO extra-budgetary trust funds in favour of LDCs.[206]

These objectives dwell on certain aspects of multilateral trade which it is argued are not fundamental to the needs of developing countries at present: investment; competition; government procurement. This is not to say that developing countries should distance themselves from negotiations on these matters since they must be present if only to state their opposition. However, capacity building objectives such as these reflect the paramount interests of developed countries and focus on areas which are not material to the current development agenda. Capacity building objectives if they are to meet the purposes of the Doha Mandate must first support policy and development initiatives in areas where developing countries lack sufficient capacity to participate in the multilateral system.

Capacity building programmes should also be extended to the provision of public funding for researchers and scholars from developing countries. Training programmes ought not to be limited to government officials or to particular countries alone but should be made open and transparent, and should cover academic and research purposes. It is hoped that developing country representatives will realise the need to inquire into and participate in academic research funding, scholarships, and exchange programmes organised by the WTO Secretariat to meet the demand for local expertise in International Economic Law in their domestic environment.[207]

3.3. Administrative Responsibility of the WTO Secretariat

The WTO Secretariat has an implied mandate to ensure that its activities reflect favourably on the adopted objectives of the Organisation including in the efforts at developing country integration, and work on the four impact areas of the DDA. The Secretariat bears some responsibility in respect of those development programmes which it directly implements particularly with regard to technical assistance and capacity building.[208]

In the Doha Declaration, the Ministers 'instruct the Secretariat, in coordination with other relevant agencies, to support domestic efforts for mainstreaming trade into national plans for economic development and strategies for poverty reduction.'[209] It is not unreasonable to consider that if developing countries do not reflect improvements in the areas of technical assistance and capacity building, it may be an indication that the Organisation's administrators have not fully delivered on its responsibility pursuant to the Doha Declaration which identifies technical cooperation and capacity building as core elements of the development dimension of the multilateral trading system.

However it cannot be denied that the greater responsibility is on developing countries to take advantage of the opportunities for technical assistance and capacity building programmes organised by the WTO Secretariat. Technical assistance such as workshops for government officials, the use of the Advisory Law Centre, and other technical initiatives will only be of value if developing countries detail precisely what assistance they need particularly to address the challenges at grassroots level.

Finally, the 'terse mix of economics, business and law'[210] which constitutes the trade rules calls for greater action in information dissemination for the general public. The WTO efforts in this regard – online accessibility for information on the WTO and its activities, and by the annual public seminar sessions it holds at Geneva are commendable efforts in bringing the WTO closer to the grassroots. Again developing countries will do well to encourage its citizens to access this facility both for information and awareness purposes.

Chapter Four

JUDICIAL REVIEW OF THE DEVELOPMENT QUESTION

4.1. Addressing the Development Objective in Settling Trade Disputes

In the preceding chapters we have examined development in the context of the rules, the implementation, the challenges, and the initiatives adopted by the WTO. But the issue has not been left out of the dispute settlement process of the WTO. Particularly in the course of judicial review, the concept and how it is interpreted, indeed to what extent it is acknowledged, is fundamental to the perception of the WTO as an Organisation for development through trade.

Some developing country Member States have not been entirely satisfied that the dispute settlement process has furthered the development objective. They are not convinced that the DSB has always interpreted developing country domestic policies from a development perspective. They have expressed the view that 'the Panels and Appellate Body have displayed an excessively sanitised concern with legalisms, often to the detriment of the evolution of a development-friendly jurisprudence'.[1] To counter this perception, Qureshi first engaged in a careful study of several disputes which have centred on the development question. He subsequently opined that the development question 'needs to be factored in at the level of drafting WTO Agreements; institutionalised in the very process of interpreting WTO Agreements; engineered in actual interpretations of WTO Agreements; and facilitated through the introduction of development friendly material in the judicial process'.[2]

Some efforts have been undertaken at Secretarial level to facilitate developing country utilisation of the dispute settlement mechanism. The WTO Legal Affairs Division engages in training and technical assistance programmes designed to assist developing countries in their participation at WTO dispute settlement. Also, the ACWL established in July 2001 as an independent body created by an Agreement separate from the WTO Agreement provides assistance to developing countries in this area.[3] It provides free advice on WTO law and requests a nominal charge to represent developing countries at the DSB. In particular, LDCs are granted fee exemptions at the ACWL.

The ACWL provides free advice on WTO matters to its developing country members and to all LDCs who are members of the WTO or who are in the process of accession. For a small fee, it represents these countries in WTO dispute settlement proceedings. Its main activities pursuant to paragraph 2 of its establishing Agreement are:

- Legal advice on WTO law;
- Support to parties and third parities in WTO dispute settlement proceedings; and
- Training of government officials in WTO law through seminars, traineeships or other appropriate means.

In spite of these support, the lack of human and infrastructural capital at domestic level, to support a developing country's participation in the dispute settlement process is still a source of concern. As has been observed:

> The complainant's level of development speaks directly to its capacity for recognising, and aggressively pursuing, legal opportunities as a complainant. Having this capacity, a complainant is in a much better position to hit the right legal buttons in the request of consultations, to pressure the defendant on its weakest legal points during consultations, and to give the impression that the issue might well be pushed to a successful conclusion.[4]

At the multilateral level however, the concern is with the interpretation of development objectives in the course of judicial review at the DSB. For this reason it is important to assess the DSB activity in respect of the interpretation of the development question by considering three scenarios: (a) where development considerations form the basis of a complaint; (b) where development considerations do not form the basis of a complaint; and (c) whether development considerations can be the basis for a non-violation complaint.

4.1.1. Where Development Considerations Form the Basis of a Complaint

A dispute brought on the basis of developing country needs is *EC-Antidumping Duties on Imports of Cotton-Type Bed Linen from India*.[5] In this case, India claimed that the EC had pursuant to a Council Regulation,[6] imposed definitive duties against imports of certain types of bed linen from India. In its submissions, India stated that the EC had not taken into account the special situation of

India as a developing country as required under Article 15 of the Antidumping Agreement.[7]

India maintained that despite repeated and detailed arguments stressing the importance of the bed linen and textile industries to India's economy, the EC failed to acknowledge India's status as a developing country let alone consider possibilities of constructive remedies.[8] The disputed Article 15 provides:

> It is recognised that special regard must be given by developed country Members to the special situation of developing country Members when considering the application of anti-dumping measures under this Agreement. Possibilities of constructive remedies provided for by this Agreement shall be explored before applying anti-dumping duties where they would affect the essential interests of developing country Members.

India argued that the EC had not explored constructive remedies before imposing the anti-dumping duties as provided for in the second part of the article. The EC claimed that its practice when developing countries are involved in an antidumping investigation is to give special consideration to the possibility of accepting undertakings from their exporters. It however stated that the difficulty that frequently arises in relation to undertakings, that of effective supervision, also applied in the case of developing countries. The EC argued that the reason no undertaking was accepted was that none had been offered within the time limit set by the EC Regulation.[9]

The Panel stated that it did not consider the first sentence of the Article since the Parties were in agreement that that sentence imposed no legal obligation on developed country Members and there was no claim in that regard.[10] In the Panel's opinion, the issue was in relation to the 'possibilities of constructive remedies' being explored 'before applying anti-dumping duties' as the Article stated. It was the view of the Panel in its findings, that Article 15 imposed an obligation on the EC authorities to actively consider 'with an open mind' the possibilities of price undertakings (which the Panel held to constitute a constructive remedy[11]) with Indian exporters prior to the imposition of final anti-dumping duties in the bed linen investigation.

In the opinion of the Panel:

> [...]Article 15 imposes no obligation to actually provide or accept any constructive remedy that may be identified and/or offered. It does, however, impose an obligation to actively consider, with an open mind, the possibility of such a remedy prior to imposition of an anti-dumping measure that would affect the essential interests of a developing country.[12]

The Panel found that the EC rejection of an expression to offer undertakings communicated by the Indian authorities in the course of the dispute indicated an outright rejection. In their opinion, this failure of the EC 'to respond in some fashion other than bare rejection particularly once the desire to offer undertakings had been communicated to it, constituted a failure to explore possibilities of constructive remedies'.[13] It thus found that the EC had acted inconsistently with its obligations under Article 15 of the Anti-dumping Agreement. The Panel Report was adopted by the Appellate Body with modifications.[14]

In spite of the fact that the dispute raised the claim for special consideration to the development status of India, there was however no indication in the adopted parts of the Panel Report nor in the modifications in the Report of the Appellate Body that the rationale for this finding was based on the fact that the interests of a developing country had been prevalent in the considerations of the Panel, of the particular circumstance of the dispute.[15] In our view the DSB, and in particular the Panel with its principal role of making an examination of the facts in a dispute, ought to have reflected on the question of special consideration for India's development status. [16]

Indeed, it appears that such considerations have been limited in the context of WTO judicial review. In one of the early cases arising under the WTO, the dispute involved Indonesia and its issuance of a Presidential Decree in February 1996 for the purposes of a national car programme. The case was *Indonesia-Certain Measures Affecting the Automobile Industry*.[17] Under the Decree, only one company was designated a 'pioneer' company and only national cars manufactured by this company were made eligible for special tax breaks and customs duty benefits under specific local content requirements. The EC, Japan, and the United States, whose automobile manufacturing companies were adversely affected, raised a complaint at the DSB.

The Panel set up to settle the dispute found that the local content requirements linked to certain sales tax benefits and customs duty benefits violated the provisions of Article 2 of the TRIMS Agreement. The sales tax discrimination aspects of the Indonesian Decree were also found to violate Articles I and III:2 of GATT 1994. For these reasons the Panel found that there was serious prejudice to the interests of the European Communities contrary to the provisions of Article 5(c) of the SCM Agreement.

In the instant case, although there was sympathy to Indonesia's attempt to lift itself out of poverty and lessen its dependence on foreign automobile manufacture, its desire to grow its automobile industry ran counter to a literal interpretation of the letter of the WTO Agreement. In general, the twin guiding principles of the GATT, the MFN rule under Article I that countries do not discriminate against each other, and the NT requirement under Article

III demanding reciprocal treatment in the application of trading measures amongst countries, could not be departed from even for the purposes of economic advancement or development. Therefore, since the tax exemptions granted by Indonesia were not extended to non-indigenous manufacturers, it was considered that these had nullified or impaired the benefits accruing to the complainants.

The circumstances of this case are interesting. At the time the complaint was made to the DSB, Indonesia faced severe economic problems, a lack of employment opportunities, and financial crisis. In essence the DSB was faced with a dispute in which it could not avoid development considerations both of the country's status and of the rationale behind the adoption of the policies for the national car programme which was the subject of the dispute. The DSB ruling records its observation that Indonesia's action was for the purposes of development:

> [...]we would like to refer to some of the arguments put forth by Indonesia regarding the steps taken by Indonesia to diversify production and to deregulate international trade so that the country could continue in its commitment towards economic reform... Although we agree that these statistics have no direct bearing on the issues for consideration before the Panel, we would like to highlight the fact that developing countries often need to take steps to bolster their economy and to overcome problems of imbalances in regional development. *We would suggest that the multilateral trading system examines the initiatives taken by these countries in the overall pursuit of economic development in their context.*[18]

It is regrettable that the Panel, although it referred to the statistics on Indonesia's external debt situation, did not consider the significance of Indonesia's action to bolster its indigenous automobile industry production while reaching its conclusions. We cannot reconcile how the Panel could have 'agreed' that India's efforts at economic reform 'have no direct bearing on the issues for consideration before the Panel' and yet found the need to suggest 'that the multilateral trading system examines the initiatives taken by these countries in the overall pursuit of economic development in their context'?

In any event, these DSB suggestions for a holistic consideration of the developmental needs of developing countries in the context of multilateral trade did not deter the economic problems Indonesia would encounter. The country already suffering crisis in its economic and financial sectors slid further into a recession. An emergency recourse for financial assistance from the International Monetary Fund (IMF) in 2002 had to be made even though this loan appeal extended the already huge debt surplus of the country.[19]

What is apparent however is that where it is made a basis of the complaint, the DSB as in the *EC- Bed Linen case* will examine arguments for development considerations even if it does not undertake a detailed examination of these issues. But before such an examination can be made, a developing country must have to make a strong claim for development considerations in its arguments. In such circumstances, the DSB cannot avoid interpreting the development considerations arising within the relevant provisions of the Agreement which is the subject of the dispute. Some other disputes wherein the DSB has had to undertake this task of interpretation could also be considered.

The earlier mentioned dispute involving non-trade concerns affecting agriculture and the impact on developing countries can be considered here, in greater detail. This arose in the complaint by Argentina, a developing country with a growing potential in agricultural production of GMO foods in the *EC-Bio-Tech* case.[20] In this case, Argentina highlighted in particular, Article 12 of the TBT and Article 10 of the SPS Agreements which respectively provide for SDT provisions on behalf of developing countries.

The Panel did not find the special concessions for special treatment to developing country members in these provisions applicable to Argentina in the instant case. The reasons for this finding was that in the first instance, Argentina had not established that by applying a general moratorium for the period complained ie June 1999–August 2003, the EC had acted contrary to the provisions of Article 10.1 of the SPS Agreement.[21] The said Article provides that WTO Members ought to take account of the special needs of developing country members in the preparation and application of SPS measures. In the opinion of the Panel, by not establishing that the EC had acted inconsistently with Article III:4 (NT rule on internal distribution of imports excepting transport charges) in respect of any of the product specific measures complained of by Argentina, there was no need for the Panel to rule on Argentina's alternative claim under Article 12 of the *TBT Agreement*.[22]

It would have been preferable if the Panel had deliberated on the question raised by the aforementioned general provisions of Article 10.1 *SPS Agreement* and reached a finding even if it were an *obiter* pronouncement determining whether the impact of the EC moratorium had adversely affected Argentina with respect to its more vulnerable economy than was the case with the other complainants. Doing this may have demanded a *prima facie* examination of the applicability and effectiveness of the relevant SDT provisions raised and a helpful interpretation of the development objective in the provisions could then have been given.[23]

In another earlier case in which Argentina was also a party, the Panel had also found insufficient evidence for the developing country's claims which while they did not rest on SDT provisions, appealed for deference to the development needs of Argentina. The case is *Argentina-Measures Affecting the*

Export of Bovine Hides and the Import of Finished Leather.[24] Therein, the dispute centred *inter alia* on the application of GATT Articles X:3(a) which provides for the requirements of uniformity, impartiality, and reasonableness in the publication and administration of trade regulations by a WTO contracting party; and Article III:2 which prohibits tax discrimination of foreign products that are like, directly competitive or, substitutable with domestic products.

Also in dispute was the application of Article XX(d) of the GATT under which the Panel had to consider the overall justifiability of the imposition of further tax on operators of imported goods into Argentina. The exception under Article XX(d) under the GATT is applicable to laws:

> necessary to secure compliance with laws or regulations which are not inconsistent with the provisions of this Agreement, including those relating to customs enforcement, the enforcement of monopolies operated under paragraph 4 of Article II and Article XVII, the protection of patents, trade marks and copyrights, and the prevention of deceptive practices.[25]

Argentina for its part argued and it was noted by the Panel that, the 'overriding reason why the Argentine Republic established the withholding and collection regimes at the root of the dispute is, without any doubt, tax evasion'.[26] The Panel observed that this problem of tax evasion which was more acute in 'unstable economic situations' was 'much more pronounced in developing countries'.[27] It noted that 'indeed, these latter countries often lack a reasonable degree of political and economic stability and are likely to display many of the features that lend themselves to tax evasion.'[28]

Having noted the circumstances in this area of developing country financial needs, in its interpretation of the reasoning behind the adoption of the measures by Argentina, the Panel could therefore not agree with the EC allegation that Argentina's regimes of tax and the timing of the tax payments (at customs) were intended to alter the competitive conditions for goods imported into Argentina. The Panel was of the opinion that the measures were indeed to address the problem of tax evasion which was of greater incidence in developing countries.

This opinion notwithstanding, it however found that the tax regulations applied under the measures to counter the incidence of tax evasion in Argentina were not applied consistently with the stated GATT provisions. Argentina had most importantly not been able to prove sufficiently that the tax measures were justified as exceptions to the MFN rule. Although they fell under Article XX(d) itself, the measures and the tax regulations applied did not satisfy the *chapeau* of Article XX requiring that 'such measures are not applied in a manner which would constitute a means of arbitrary or unjustifiable discrimination between countries where the same conditions prevail, or a disguised restriction on international trade'. Thus placing less weight on the development status and the challenges of Argentina in the circumstances, the Panel held that the tax regulations themselves were not justifiable under the aforementioned provisions of the GATT.[29]

In *Brazil-Export Financing Programmes for Aircraft*[30] the complainant Canada, challenged the export subsidies granted under the Brazilian *Programa de Financiamento às Exportações* (PROEX) to foreign purchasers of Brazil's *Embraer* aircraft. Canada alleged that the subsidies were contingent upon export performance, contrary to the general letter of Articles 3, 27.4, and 27.5 of the *SCM Agreement*. Brazil did not dispute the complainant's allegations. However in its defence it claimed that the payments were permitted under the Illustrative List of Export Subsidies pursuant to Article 3 and Annex 1 of the *SCM Agreement*. Canada was insistent that Article 27.4 and 27.5 which provided for the circumstances under which a developing country could apply and maintain export subsidies had in fact not been complied with by Brazil. The relevant sections of Article 27 are as follows:

> Any developing country Member referred to in paragraph 2(b) shall phase out its export subsidies within the eight-year period, preferably in a progressive manner. However, a developing country Member shall not increase the level of its export subsidies, and shall eliminate them within a period shorter than that provided for in this paragraph when the use of such export subsidies is inconsistent with its development needs. If a developing country Member deems it necessary to apply such subsidies beyond the 8-year period, it shall not later than one year before the expiry of this period enter into consultation with the Committee, which will determine whether an extension of this period is justified, after examining all the relevant economic, financial and development needs of the developing country Member in question…

Article 27.5 provides that:

> A developing country Member which has reached export competitiveness in any given product shall phase out its export subsidies for such product(s) over a period of two years. However, for a developing country Member which is referred to in Annex VII and which has reached export competitiveness in one or more products, export subsidies on such products shall be gradually phased out over a period of eight years.

Although the Panel noted that Article 27.4 provides that 'panels should give substantial deference to the views of the developing country Member in question',[31] it found that Brazil had not acted within the limits set out by the special provisions. This was because as the facts of the dispute revealed Brazil had not only increased the level of export subsidies it granted under the programme but also by failing to phase out the subsidies after the date on which they should have been terminated, it had not complied with the phase out period set out under the provisions.[32]

Revisiting the interpretation difficulties observed by the Panel in its earlier finding on facts, the AB[33] while it did point out that 'to take no account of inflation in assessing the level of export subsidies granted by a developing country Member would render the special and differential treatment provisions of Article 27 meaningless', confirmed the Panel's earlier conclusion relating to the Brazilian adjustment for inflation of its export subsidies.[34]

This interpretation of technicalities (with respect to time limits and periods) in the provisions of the SCM Agreement above is unduly strict.[35] A more flexible interpretation would have considered the circumstances which informed Brazil's actions although given the lack of flexibility in the rules on subsidies themselves, the DSB would have to be 'inventive' or 'activist' in order to allow 'substantial deference' to the views of Brazil as counselled by Article 27.4.

Two other possible means of assisting the DSB in its role of interpreting the development needs of a disputing party could be suggested. One, is the importance of referring to the relevant Committee set up pursuant to an Agreement and in particular in respect of assessing developing country needs – the need for greater action by the CTD. Another, is the necessity of referring to the factual findings of a country's development, financial and economic circumstances under the Trade Policy Review Mechanism (TPRM).

Under the Doha Work Programme, Article 12 directs the CTD to assess the cross-cutting issues bordering on special treatment for developing countries. The Panel in the *Brazil-Aircraft case* had referred to the SCM Committee as being in a better position to determine the relevance of subsidies and export performance on a developing country's needs.[36] In similar fashion, the CTD set up with the mandate to oversee the incorporation of special and differential treatment into the architecture of the WTO rules, also has a part to play in the determination of the impact of subsidies and export performance on developing country needs. Whereas other Committees can assess the impact of the respective provisions which they oversee, it is only logical that the CTD should be able to provide advice to the DSB on questions of the development situation of a party to a dispute and the impact of trade provisions on the country's development initiatives. The political nature of the body notwithstanding, the CTD's mandate to oversee cross-cutting issues under the current Doha work programme will not take it beyond its brief.

In addition or in the alternative as the case may be, advice on the impact of trade measures to developing countries can be obtained from the TPRs of countries involved in the dispute. Although they are fundamentally legal bodies as the Panel noted in the latter case, a Panel cannot without factual and well researched evaluation of the domestic political and economic environment in a Member State, come to an effective interpretation of the development needs of a particular developing country. This is because the duty of the Panel as the first reference in a judicial dispute settlement review, is 'to examine, in the light of the relevant provisions, the matter referred to the DSB and to make such findings as will assist the DSB in making the recommendations or in giving the rulings provided for in that/ those agreement(s)'.[37]

To this end, for the examinations of questions on developing country circumstances for which any disputed domestic policies or measures have been adopted, more reliance ought to be placed on the trade policy reviews of these countries. The TPRM conducts 'surveillance of national trade policies'[38] and its purpose as agreed under the Uruguay Round of Trade talks is to contribute to a smoother functioning of the Multilateral trading system 'by achieving greater transparency in, and understanding of, the trade policies and practices of Members'.[39]

Annex 3 of the WTO Agreement which states that the TPRM *inter alia* 'is not, however for dispute settlement procedures [...]'[40] constrains the potential for more efficient fact finding and assessment of developing country needs at the DSB. Reference to trade policy reviews will be of great benefit even to the dispute settlement system because it will afford the Panel access to reliable information which may be relevant to the claims or defences of a developing country involved in a dispute. Even further, the DSB should be able to place more reliance on such development-related reviews under the TPRM than on information provided by bodies such as the IMF or World Bank who are primarily concerned with general welfare statistical data and not as is pertinent in the WTO context, the impact of trade policies on the domestic trade and development paradigm *per se*.

The function of the review mechanism is 'to examine the impact of a Member's trade policies and practices on the multilateral trading system'.[41] The TPRM document further establishes that this examination 'takes place, to the extent relevant, against the background of the wider economic and developmental needs, policies and objectives of the Member concerned, as well as of its external environment'.[42] The observation of the Panel in its interpretation of Article 27.4 of the SCM Agreement in the *Brazil Aircraft case* above where it cited the inadequacy of a Panel as a legal body, to review inquiries of a peculiarly political and economic nature is illuminating. The Panel stated:

> We note that this element of Article 27.4 is troubling from the perspective of a panel. Article 27.4 provides in relevant part that a developing country Member 'shall eliminate [its export subsidies] within a period shorter than that provided for in this paragraph when the use of such export subsidies is inconsistent with its development needs'. We recognize that as written this clause is mandatory, and a conclusion that this clause was not susceptible of application by a panel would be inconsistent with the principle of effective treaty interpretation. On the other hand, an examination as to whether export subsidies are inconsistent with a developing country Member's development needs is an inquiry of a peculiarly economic and political nature, and notably ill-suited to review by a panel whose function is fundamentally legal. Further, the SCM Agreement provides panels with no guidance with respect to the criteria to be applied in performing this examination.[13]

It is therefore more appropriate that the practical development concerns of countries appraised which necessarily include economic and political considerations and which is adequately reviewed under the TPRM mechanism should be relied upon by the DSB in the course of judicial review. Incorporating the advice of the CTD and the TPRM particularly at the factual evaluation stage of the Panel proceedings will aid in more rounded judicial review of the development, financial, and economic needs of WTO Members States.

In both cases it is noted that there may be impediments. In the first place, there is no provision in the DSU for the DSB to request a TPR of a party to a dispute. Second, TPRs are not annual events and the frequency of review is a function of a member's share in world trade.[44] The four major trading nations – the EU, the US, Japan and Canada are subject to review every two years; the next sixteen largest traders every four years; and the other countries, every six years.[45] A longer period may be established for LDCs.[46] Thus available reports may not reflect the prevalent circumstances which gave rise to a dispute complaint. Also, meetings of the CTD are neither convened concurrently with DSB sittings nor is there again a provision in the DSB directing the CTD to convene a meeting for the purposes of appraising the impact of a trade measure on a developing country.

However, a provisional inclusion to this effect in the DSU and in the WTO Agreement can be undertaken similar to Article 13 of the DSU (and Appendix 4 DSU which sets out the rules and procedures relating to the formation of expert review groups) to address the situation. Particularly with respect to TPRs, the DSU rules which provide that the Panels have a right to 'seek information from any relevant source and may consult experts to obtain their opinion on certain aspects of the matter',[47] can be expanded to include available reports of the TPRM (in the absence of express rejection by the parties) as relevant advice to the Panels where questions on developing country circumstances and needs arise.

4.1.2. Where Development Considerations are not the Basis of a Complaint

Where development considerations do not form the basis of a complaint that is, where a request is not made for the Panel or AB to consider the development needs of a disputing party, and where there is neither an appeal for special treatment nor for considerations of SDT provisions in the course of a dispute, it is understandable that the DSB need not undertake to examine such matters.

Such a situation arose in *United States-Subsidies on Upland Cotton*.[48] In that case, Brazil contended that US grants of prohibited and actionable subsidies to US producers, users and exporters of upland cotton, as well as all the legal instruments providing such subsidies and grants were contrary to US obligations under the WTO agreements.[49] The Panel addressed its considerations to the obligations of the Respondent under the relevant covered Agreements. It found that the US domestic support programmes were not protected by the Peace Clause[50] and that some of these programmes resulted in serious prejudice to Brazil's interests in the form of price suppression in the world market. In its view, by applying the said export subsidies, the US had acted inconsistently with its obligations under the WTO, a charge which the Respondent had not rebutted.[51] To that extent, the US had 'nullified or impaired benefits accruing to Brazil under these agreements'.[52]

Although the parties in the *US-Upland Cotton* case included developing countries and the subject matter was one of significant interest to developing countries, there was no reference to the fact that the subsidies harmed the development of Brazil's cotton industry and thus adversely affected the country's development progress. In all probability, this was because hindrance to the development progress of Brazil was not made a claim in the complaint.[53] That the DSB therefore did not make any pronouncement on the issue could be explained as an operation of the principle of judicial economy. As the Appellate Body noted in another case, panels 'need only address those claims which must be addressed in order to resolve the matter in issue in the dispute.' [54]

This calls for careful action by developing countries at dispute settlement proceedings. Even if they join as third parties, developing countries must take up the opportunities offered in the relevant special provisions of WTO

Agreements. They would have to present their arguments making a detailed representation for a consideration of their economic and development needs at the DSB. Without presenting development considerations in their arguments before the Panel, there is little scope for the Panel or the AB to examine any needs or concerns they may have in respect of dispute complaint against them or, one brought by them.

4.1.3. Development Considerations as the Basis for a Non-Violation Complaint?

There has been no clear definition of what constitutes a non-violation complaint by the DSB.[55] The complaints which have addressed the non-violation provisions since the formation of the WTO in 1995, have been in the course of disputes between developed countries,[56] in particular, disputes between the US and the EC.[57]

Larouer is of the view that even with the inclusion of non-violation complaints under Article 26 DSU, the disparity between developing and developed country recourse to this provision 'proves that non-violation complaints constitute an unaffordable luxury for the immense majority of WTO Members, which neither participated in the design of this remedy nor tries to use it'.[58] This can be taken to imply in a sense, that because developing countries have less developed legal infrastructure and expertise, they may not have the resources to perform the background research and present detailed justification on which to base a non-violation complaint as required by Articles 26.1(a); 26.2(a) of the DSU.

The WTO itself has questioned the relevance of non-violation complaints.[59] The Legal Affairs Division of the Organisation wonders on the continued retention of the non-violation complaint given that the WTO Agreement contains all the rights and obligations which Members agreed in this negotiation. It asks: 'Why shall there be a remedy against actions that are not inconsistent with the rights and obligations, in other words, means that the WTO Agreement does not preclude?'[60]

Be that as it may, criticism against the continued operation of this category of complaints rather emphasises the importance of the provision particularly in the possibilities of utilising it as a means of enforcing the WTO development objectives. In respect of Article XXIII:1(b) GATT (the non-violation complaints provision) which was subsequently included under the DSU,[61] the following criticism was made:

> Of all the vague and woolly punitive provisions that one could make, this seems to me to hold the prize place. It appears to me that what it says is this: In this wide world of sin there are certain sins which we have not yet discovered and which after long examination we cannot define; but there

being such sins, we will provide some sort of punishment for them if we find out what they are and if we find out anybody committing them.[62]

The response to the opinion above is that the current imperative for the rules-based system of the WTO towards furthering an effective development through trade objective establishes the probability that some 'sin' has been discovered: the sin of neglecting development needs of developing countries. Consider the novelty of the WTO development agenda and the christened 'Development Round' of the Doha negotiations. The focus on development concerns as a WTO objective in the new millennium and as the goal of the latest round of trade talks was certainly 'not yet discovered' under the GATT 1947 when the provisions of Article XXIII were set out. The wordings of Article XXIII can thus be seen as an attempt by multilateral negotiators under GATT 1947 to give room for considerations on future matters which give effect to the overall objectives of the multilateral trade regime.

The trade negotiators under the old GATT recognised that the *General Agreement* may not support a particular complaint by a Member where the circumstances of the complaint were not covered by the provisions of the General Agreement. The non-violation complaint would however allow the complainant to seek redress from the general Membership (and subsequently under the WTO, from the DSB, pursuant to Articles 26:1(a–d); 2) in order to determine whether the complaint actually inhibited the complaining Member from attaining the benefits of multilateral trade.[63]

This view subsists under the WTO. Article 26(1) DSU incorporates the non-violation provisions of Article XXIII:1(b) in respect of complaints not within the scope of any covered Agreement.[64] Also, the WTO apart from a moratorium agreed in certain covered Agreements,[65] maintains the provisions of the non-violation complaint in other covered Agreements.[66] It states that:

> In general, disputes in the WTO involve allegations that a country has violated an agreement or broken a commitment. But in some situations a government can go to the Dispute Settlement Body even when an agreement has not been violated. This is called a non-violation complaint. It is allowed if one government can show that it has been deprived of an expected benefit because of another government's action, or because of any other situation that exists.
>
> The aim is to help preserve the balance of benefits struck during multilateral negotiations. For example, a country may have agreed to reduce its tariff on a product as part of a market access deal, but later subsidized domestic production so that the effect on the conditions of

competition are the same as the original tariff. A non-violation case against this country would be allowed to restore the conditions of competition implied in the original deal.[67]

Therefore, a non-violation complaint can address development considerations in WTO jurisprudence. A complaint that another Member State's activities consists of 'impediments to attainment of the development objective' could be brought under the non-violation provisions of Article XXIII:1(B) GATT 1994 and Article 26 DSU of the WTO.[68] Failure to provide technical assistance and adequate capacity building programmes by both developed country Members under relevant SDT provisions, and by the Organisation itself in its development assistance projects, could form the grounds of non-violation complaints. The remedy offered under Article 26 DSU which enshrines the non-violation complaint into the WTO dispute settlement *acquis* is a 'mutually satisfactory adjustment' of the measures complained against, and only in exceptional cases, an offer of compensation.

To retain the spirit of a mutually satisfactory adjustment of the circumstances complained against, compensation here need not be financial. It would suffice for the DSB to make a recommendation for a defaulting country to render technical assistance or engage in co-operative action in a relevant sector in the complainant country.

4.2. Improving WTO Development Jurisprudence

The recourse to the dispute settlement process is one of the greatest benefits of the multilateral trading system. Indeed in its Article 3, the DSU provides that the dispute settlement system *is a central element in providing security and predictability to the multilateral trading system*. To this end, the Understanding reiterates that 'recommendations and rulings of the DSB cannot add to or diminish the rights and obligations provided in the covered agreements'.[69]

In a Report by a Consultative Board to a former WTO DG, the Consultative Board highlighted some areas which needed greater consideration particularly in the realm of WTO 'post-judgement' jurisprudence.[70] The importance of preserving the rights and obligations under the WTO Agreements is also pertinent to a preservation of the *intent* of the *WTO Agreements* with respect to the need to consider the areas of concern to developing countries in WTO dispute settlement. The following are three such areas of concern:

1. An objective assessment of development considerations in judicial review.
2. Enforcement: compensation and retaliation.
3. Detailed opinions and development-oriented recommendations.

4.2.1. Objective Assessment of Development Considerations

In making an objective assessment of the facts of any case before it, the DSB often deliberates on what is referred to in WTO jurisprudence, as the standard of review. The 'standard of review' in WTO jurisprudence refers to the extent of consideration given to the national policies and domestic conditions which give rise to a WTO dispute by a WTO dispute settlement Panel or Appellate Body. Determining the standard of review involves defining to what extent reference is made to national or regional authorities in WTO adjudication.[71] For example, can a WTO Member justify legislation banning certain imports into the country? Will reasons of danger to public health or cultural sensitivities suffice to counter allegations that a ban on another country's goods is not protectionist and contrary to WTO obligations?[72]

In its finding in the *Hormones case*,[73] the AB relied on the provisions of Article 11 DSU as a basis for defining a specific standard of review. The dispute arose on an appeal from an earlier Panel decision in the case. In its arguments on appeal, the EC had submitted that the two panels established in the instant case and which panels had found a violation of the SPS Agreement by the EC, 'erred in law by not according deference to […] aspects of the EC measures'.[74] In particular, in the opinion of the EC, the Panels had not deferred to the EC reasoning behind its application of a higher level of sanitary protection and, its basis for invoking the precautionary principle.[75]

The EU argued that in highly complex factual situations (e.g. relating to a risk for human health) panels need to defer to relevant member state authorities and not to make *de novo* review.[76] The AB rejected this argument stating that the proper standard of review was for an 'objective assessment' of the matter to be made in line with Article 11, DSU. The said Article provides that a 'panel should make an objective assessment of the matter before it, including an objective assessment of the facts of the case and the applicability of and conformity with the relevant covered agreements'.

The AB followed the earlier *Underwear* panel report[77] which in applying an objective assessment test pronounced that its review should neither completely substitute national determinations nor totally defer to member states' findings.[78] The objective assessment according to the panel, ought to be based on whether national authorities: (1) had examined all relevant facts before it; (2) had given adequate explanation of how the facts supported the determinations; and (3) whether the determination made was consistent with the international obligations of the member state.[79] The AB thus suggested that a standard of review must represent the balance set out in an Agreement between the WTO, and the Member country. In its view, 'to adopt a standard of review not clearly rooted in the text of the Agreement itself, may well amount to changing that finely drawn balance; and neither a panel nor the Appellate Body is authorised to do that'.[80]

It has been suggested that the DSB could adopt the treatment of standard of review in US jurisprudence which allows for deference to national agency authorities under the US-Chevron doctrine.[81] Critics of this suggestion note however that there must be a balance between the authorities' interest in protecting their sovereignty, on one side, and broader interest in realising the gains of international coordination, on the other'.[82]

In disputes involving developing countries, in order to make an 'objective assessment' of disputes wherein developing country policies and programmes for economic development are challenged, the 'standard of review' adopted by the WTO DSB will have to consider the basis of these countries' national policies, and their domestic trade regulations. As long as they cannot be said to be arbitrarily protectionist, developing country trade policies which are geared towards improving domestic production of a good or for restructuring local industries in order to enhance their competitive capacity in the global market, merit extensive consideration.

To this end, the instructions of Article 11 DSU provide further room for the evaluation of developing country needs. What the provision demands is 'an objective assessment of the facts of the case and the applicability of and conformity with the relevant covered agreements'.[83] The principle which ought to guide WTO judicial review in this instance is not whether the measures taken are *prima facie* contrary to the provisions of a relevant WTO Agreement. Rather, in making an objective assessment of the facts of the matter, the DSB must pay attention to the facts of the case; to the development objective pursued; and then consider whether these factors are in line with the overall theme of recognition for developing country needs stated in the Preamble to the WTO Agreement and in the particular Agreement at the centre of the dispute. Only then can it be said that the appropriate level of deference has been given to the national policy or measure complained against.

4.2.2. Enforcement: Retaliation and Compensation

Article 21(5) DSU provides that parties can, in the event of a disagreement with the implementation of recommendations or rulings of a settlement 'wherever possible resort to the original panel'. Articles 21(2); (7); (8) provide that attention should be paid to the implementation of a dispute settlement where a developing country Member is a party to the dispute. In particular, sub paragraph 8 provides that in considering the appropriate action to be taken, the DSB shall take into account 'not only the trade coverage of measure complained of, but also their impact on the economy of developing country Members concerned'.

Article 22 DSU makes further provision for the measures a winning party may take where the other party does not comply with the recommendations of the dispute settlement finding. Article 22 (1) provides for voluntary compensation to be agreed between the disputants pursuant to negotiations. Compensation refers to a temporary measure (not necessarily a monetary payment[84]) available to a winning party for failure by the defaulting party to implement recommendations or rulings under the settlement. Where no satisfactory compensation is agreed within 20 days after the expiration of a reasonable period of time afforded to the losing party to bring itself into compliance, the winning party may request authorisation from the DSB to suspend concessions applicable to the defaulting Member.[85]

To counter the possibility of retaliatory measures, some countries may agree on prior arrangements or measures to take in the event of non-compliance by a defaulting party pursuant to Article 22 DSU. Such an arrangement is referred to as a 'sequencing arrangement'. Sequencing arrangements are becoming a practice of dispute settlement cases even if they have not received provisional legitimacy in the WTO legal framework and there is no restriction against developing countries in seeking to reach an agreement on a sequencing arrangement if it has the legal expertise and diplomatic relationship with the other party in the dispute to do so.[86] A developing country may be able to reach an agreement on a sequencing arrangement if it has the legal expertise and diplomatic relationship with the other party in the dispute to do so.[87]

However there is a potential risk to developing countries in the 'trade-retaliation' provisions in Article 22 DSU. Article 22(2) provides for this principle of retaliation where no satisfactory compensation has been agreed within twenty days after the expiry of a reasonable period of time agreed for the expected compliance with the DSB recommendations. It states that any party having invoked the dispute settlement procedures 'may request authorisation from the DSB to suspend the application to the Member concerned of concessions or other obligations under the covered agreements'.[88] The suspension of concessions is a temporary measure lasting until the measure found to be inconsistent with a covered agreement is removed or another mutually satisfactory agreement is reached.[89] The level of suspension of concessions or other obligations authorised shall also be equivalent to the level of nullification or impairment.[90]

Depending on the circumstances, it is expected that the complaining party should first seek to suspend concessions with respect to the same sector in the covered agreement as that wherein a violation was found.[91] Where this is not 'practicable or effective', suspension can be carried out in other sectors under the same violated agreement[92] or, in other covered agreements where the circumstances not only make it impracticable or ineffective but also are serious enough to warrant suspension of concessions or other obligations under another covered agreement distinct from that under which the violation occurred.[93]

Article 22(3) (d) in sub paragraphs (i) and (ii) exhort[94] disputing parties to take into account:

(i) The trade in the sector or under the agreement under which the panel or Appellate Body has found a violation or other nullification or impairment, and the importance of such trade to that party;

(ii) The broader economic elements related to the nullification or impairment and the broader economic consequences of the suspension of concession or other obligations.

As developing country participation in multilateral trade increases, the possibility for retaliatory measures also increases. This potential risk of retaliatory measures adopted in a dispute involving a developing country is important bearing in mind the impact on the economic progress of the developing country.[95] Where it is the winning party, a developing country may find itself at a disadvantage in negotiating adequate compensatory measures under Article 22. Where it is the losing party, the resultant measures taken to counter its non-compliance under the relevant afore-mentioned provisions of the DSU may debilitate its economy.

Apart from the fact that a WTO Member cannot treat its obligation to comply with a settlement finding as non-mandatory, with their vulnerable position in international trade, developing countries cannot adopt a *laissez-faire* approach to their obligations to comply with a DSB ruling or recommendation especially if the other party is economically at an advantage. Thus while a developed country may not suffer comparable hardship in implementing compensatory measures or withstanding retaliation given its stronger position in the global market, a developing country is at potential risk in similar circumstances.

This is not to suggest that developed countries do not suffer any losses on the application of retaliatory measures. The appeal by the EC against the Panel's decision in *United States/Canada-Continued Suspension of Obligations in the EC-Hormones Dispute*[96] is a case in point. The Panel had considered the continued suspension of concessions and the application of retaliatory measures by the US and Canada in spite of a new Directive (2003/74/EC) adopted by the EU to redress the inconsistencies of the previous Directive (which was held 'unjustified' in the absence of sufficient scientific evidence to support the restrictions on meat imports treated with hormones from the US and Canada in *EC-Hormones*.[97]

First, the Panel noted that with respect to the claims of the European Communities concerning the violation of Article 23.2(a) read together with Articles 21.5 and 23.1 of the DSU, the United States had acted inconsistently:

1. by seeking, through the measure at issue — that is the suspension of concessions or other obligations subsequent to the notification of the EC implementing measure (Directive 2003/74/EC) — the redress of a violation of obligations under a covered agreement without having recourse to, and abiding by, the rules and procedures of the DSU, the United States has breached Article 23.1 of the DSU;
2. by making a determination within the meaning of Article 23.2(a) of the DSU to the effect that a violation had occurred without having recourse to dispute settlement in accordance with rules and procedures of the DSU, the United States has breached Article 23.2(a) of the DSU.[98]

It however concluded having addressed the claims raised by the European Communities concerning Article 23.1 read together with Articles 22.8 and 3.7 of the DSU, that:

1. to the extent that the measure found to be inconsistent with the SPS Agreement in the *EC - Hormones* dispute (WT/DS26) has not been removed by the European Communities, the United States has not breached Article 22.8 of the DSU;
2. to the extent that Article 22.8 has not been breached, the European Communities has not established a violation of Articles 23.1 and 3.7 of the DSU as a result of a breach of Article 22.8.[99]

Whereas developed countries may be able to handle the impact of retaliatory measures, however given the current imbalance between trading nations, it is probable that rather than seeking retaliation, developing countries may yield to the attraction of 'buy out' solutions which may not be favourable to them in the long run. As the Report of the Consultative Board (2004) noted:

> To allow governments to 'buy out' of their obligations by providing 'compensation' or enduring 'suspension of obligation' also creates major asymmetries of treatment in the system. It favours the rich and powerful countries which can afford such 'buy outs' while retaining measures that harm and distort trade in a manner inconsistent with the rules of the system.
>
> For poorer WTO Members, especially the least-developed countries with their narrow participation in world trade, the 'buy out' attitude can nullify

the value of their pursuing dispute settlement cases. These countries normally cannot effectively use the weapon of retaliation without imposing damage on themselves and on the goals of trade liberalization.[100]

Where they request for it, it is understandable that most developing countries would be keen to pursue monetary compensation, seeing this as an avenue to boost their domestic finances. Monetary compensation in the absence of infrastructural and institutional ability to apply the monetary gains from a WTO dispute settlement victory will not sustain the goal of developing country integration in the world market. Neither will it make valuable contribution to domestic socio-economic development in the poorer countries of the world.

Proposals offered as a solution by the Report include the substitution of compensatory market measures from the winning party with monetary compensation from the party required to comply with the dispute settlement report as a temporary approach pending full compliance. The other solution is for losing parties to reimburse successful complainants for legal costs incurred. In both cases, the Report spots potential draw backs. It notes that the monetary compensation option may still yield to 'buy out' problems. The burden of legal costs may in respect of the second alternative, inhibit poorer countries access to the DSB.[101]

An alternative proposal by Yemkong, is for a Pre-authorised Contingent Financial Commitment (PCFC) by WTO Members. By this, Members commit themselves to a specific amount of money to be paid to the WTO annually. If a Member is found to have breached obligations pursuant to a DSB finding and failed to comply, instead of authorising retaliation, the winning Member/s would be authorised to withdraw an amount equivalent to the level of nullification and impairment from the non-complying Member's PCFC every year till compliance is achieved; the larger the economy and the frequency of violation, the higher the amount to be requested by the WTO Members in negotiations.[102]

This proposal is yet to be tested. If the Members can overcome reservations on the practicability of this method which we envision as an impediment to its success, poorer economies stand a better chance at effecting the DSB decisions in their favour. The DSB will also find that its rulings will attract better compliance by defaulting Member States. But whether the poorer Member States of the WTO can make this contribution and indeed whether it is practicable to expect them to do so given their economic condition is questionable. Considering that some developing countries hardly ever use the dispute settlement process, it is also doubtful whether this proposal would appeal to these countries.

A. The Option of Cross-Retaliation

It must be mentioned that the potential efficacy of cross-retaliation provisions under Article 22.3(c) of the DSU is often overlooked. The provision states that in respect of a party seeking authorisation for retaliation:

> If that party considers that it is not practicable or effective to suspend concessions or other obligations with respect to other sectors under the same agreement, and that the circumstances are serious enough, it may seek to suspend concessions or other obligations under another covered agreement.

Incidentally, the argument against the efficacy of this provision remains the same as that which contends that the general trade retaliation provisions are not very useful to developing countries.[103] Yet these provisions were relied upon successfully by Ecuador in *EC-Bananas III* before the Arbitration Panel set up to consider the level of suspension of concessions after the original Panel had found the EC to be in breach of its GATT/GATS obligations. It was the first attempt at retaliation by a developing country and the first time approval for cross-retaliation had been sought.[104] After the US sought authorisation for retaliatory measures against the EC, Ecuador followed suit. It argued that its merchandise imports from the EU were too small to allow full retaliation against imports of EU goods.

The Arbitrators noted that Ecuador should first seek to suspend concessions or other obligations with respect to the same sectors as those in which the original panel had found violations. They however found that Ecuador may request authorisation from the DSB (which was subsequently given) to suspend concessions under other agreements. These included[105]: under GATT 1994 (not including investment goods or primary goods used as inputs in manufacturing and processing industries); under GATS with respect to 'wholesale trade services' in the principal distribution services; and to the extent that suspension requested under GATT 1994 and GATS was insufficient to reach the level of nullification and impairment determined by the arbitrators; under TRIPS in the following sectors of that Agreement: Section 1 (copyright and related rights), Article 14 on protection of performers, producers of phonograms and broadcasting organisations), Section 3 (geographical indications), and Section 4 (industrial designs).

Ecuador successfully argued that retaliation against EC exports of goods or services was not 'practicable or effective'. The Arbitration Panel interpreted the term 'practicable' to include considerations as to whether retaliation would harm the developing country. It concluded that retaliation which increased the cost of industrial inputs would not be 'practicable'. In its interpretation of the term 'effective', it considered whether retaliation would have a meaningful political impact on the defendant country.[106]

In his assessment, Hudec noted that the answers by the Panel on these questions were 'rather superficial and inconsistent'.[107] In his view, the Panel did not develop a full analysis of the developing country claims against the adequacy of trade retaliation. He however observed that the Panel's response to Ecuador's claims showed an inclination to support the claim of inadequacy of trade retaliation particularly against industrial products.[108] Moreover, developing country officials could now consider the possibility of cross retaliation in dispute settlement cases.[109]

All things considered, the fact is that the key to enforcement of dispute findings rests more on the strength of political persuasion on the country in violation to redress the harm its domestic measures have occasioned.

Certain limitations to cross-retaliation for developing country purposes mean that this option can only be exercised with utmost care. It is no surprise that it has never been put in practice despite the authorisations obtained at the DSB.[110] Poor countries dependent on the richer countries for aid and other assistance are wise to be hesitant in seeking cross-retaliation. Not only can this be injurious in the political realm, it also invites the possibility of withdrawal of unilateral trade preferences such as GSP arrangements by developed countries against which cross-retaliation is applied.

Furthermore, procedures for cross-retaliation also require significant amendment of domestic rules in order to apply them. For instance, domestic regulation on IPRs would need modification to include provisions on the practice and procedures for the withdrawal of IP protection which withdrawal must be equivalent to the level of impairment caused by the violation. Extensive legal and economic analysis would be required in the domestic environment as the Panel in the Ecuador Arbitration noted.[111]

Also, an Agreement such as the GATS presents further challenges. The Agreement (GATS) remains subject to negotiations and there is such a substantial difference between the commitments made by each Member State that executing cross-retaliation under the Agreement, always bearing in mind that 'the level of the suspension of concessions or other obligations authorized by the DSB shall be equivalent to the level of the nullification or impairment',[112] may prove to be more burdensome than profitable.

Therefore the importance of mutually acceptable solutions as a preferable option to the complexities identified in effecting compliance with a WTO dispute decision cannot be over-emphasised in the area of WTO development jurisprudence. Even the Sutherland Report earlier mentioned is clear on the fact that regulation of multilateral trade in this aspect of compliance with WTO settlement findings may not find its practicability in the DSU provisions. In its considered view, the Consultative Board noted that effective compliance will not really depend so much on specific remedies including retaliation or compensation contained in the DSU, but more on the general attitude of WTO Members particularly the very large and powerful ones.[113]

Further assistance may also be found in the form which DSB recommendations are made. A Panel or Appellate Body may direct disputants (where a developing country is involved) on those aspects of the rulings which can and ought to be mutually agreeable thereby lessening the dependence on the goodwill of richer countries which may not necessarily be forthcoming. Such a direction will of course require that parties will have to have stated in their claims, the form of compensation they would wish to have in the event that the dispute is in their favour. This would mean that they present their claims and 'prayers' just as the litigants in a civil claim at a domestic court. With this in mind, the DSB can assess the viability of implementing the demands and can set out what can and cannot be implemented given their findings in the dispute.

4.2.3. Detailed Opinions and Development-Oriented Recommendations

In the domestic environment, the success of a rules-based system of governmental administration rests largely on the capacity of a State's enforcement machinery: the police or military, the physical prisons which restrict movement and also act as further deterrent, and the government machinery which assists in the recovery of fines or other imposed financial penalties such as seizure of property or freezing of assets. Domestic courts have the added aid of institutional means of enforcing its decisions, and the poorer individuals of society are confident that the courts' orders in their favour will be enforced.

Proponents of a 'direct effect' for WTO DSB rulings in national courts, (if there are any, given that the WTO Agreement itself does not make any allusions to this idea, save for the TRIPS Agreement wherein the private Intellectual Property Rights of nationals are to be granted the same protection across WTO Member States), may argue that there would be more effective enforcement of WTO Agreements using domestic institutions to ensure compliance with settlement findings. It is however considered that the question of 'direct effect' of the WTO agreements is not principal in considering how developing countries can gain from the dispute settlement process.

For the principle of direct effect to have application, the notion implies that all the Member States of the WTO are willing and able to apply the provisions of WTO rules homogenously and will employ their institutional machinery to protect the implementation of WTO rules in the national polity as demanded by the individual citizens and businesses who will have direct recourse to the rules. Such a level of acceptance has not been reached within the domestic setting of WTO Members, certainly not amongst the developing countries. For the latter also, the capacity to undertake such a responsibility is extremely questionable.

At present, the DSB currently has no means of enforcing the outcome of a dispute settlement process. At the end of a dispute settlement, the losing party is expected to make the required adjustments to a domestic policy which has nullified or impaired the benefits accruing to the successful party. There is however no institutional machinery to force the losing party to comply with the DSB ruling or recommendation. There are also no sanctions imposed on a Member State who defaults in implementing the DSB rulings. The complaining party is left with an appeal to the compensation or trade-retaliation provisions of the DSU discussed above.

While the DSB may not be equipped with the enforcement machinery of its domestic counterparts, the DSB could further enhance WTO jurisprudence by providing more detailed advisory opinions on the WTO development objective and the development needs of developing countries in its dispute findings. The WTO dispute settlement mechanism can include such advisory opinion as is undertaken by the International Court of Justice, in the event of a necessity to ascertain the weight to be given to development considerations in the circumstances of a developing country policy or action in the event of a dispute.[114] Such detailed reasoning is especially relevant where a complaining Member State alleges that another State's trade policies or practices while not an outright violation of a WTO covered Agreement, is deemed to be of potential harm to the development interests of the complainant. A detailed advisory opinion would also appraise the areas where the WTO Agreements need a development-friendly interpretation.

Adopting a more extensive explanation of SDTs and a deeper consideration of the circumstances of developing countries involved in disputes (more extensive than at present), it would be beneficial if the DSB provides detailed reasons why these considerations ought or ought not to be bear on the dispute at hand. Further still, DSB opinions on matters involving development considerations ought to show an appraisal of the socio-economic circumstances prevalent in a country and the domestic trade policies provided to tackle these. They ought not to rely solely on textual interpretation of applicable WTO provisions. When this happens as it often does, it presents an unflattering critique of the Panels and Appellate Body; that they cannot adequately evaluate complaints and arguments on development-related questions, which questions, affect the majority of the Organisation's membership.

With respect to development-oriented recommendations, rather than directing a party to bring its policies in line with its WTO obligations in the generic format of DSB recommendations, the DSB can direct the parties on practical measures to undertake which would facilitate the development needs of a developing country disputant. In earlier analysis of the SDT provisions it was noted that certain provisions including those setting out technical assistance and capacity building support for developing countries are not binding and so do not command a legal obligation. While it is hoped that this category of SDT provisions are made more precise and more normative, it is important to reiterate the earlier suggestion that the DSB can make recommendation to the effect that a country should deliver technical assistance or capacity building as part of the compensatory measures pursuant to a dispute. This may be more beneficial to a developing country (if mutually acceptable agreements can be reached) rather than the latter pursuing retaliatory measures or monetary compensation.

Furthermore, the DSB can recommend that a party where it is in a position to do so (and irrespective of the fact that it may be the winning party to the dispute) may undertake to provide assistance to a country in breach, as a means of averting further dispute complaints. Again, this moral obligation will depend on mutually satisfactory negotiations and willingness of countries to extend a hand of 'fellowship' in the profit-oriented sphere of global commerce.

Chapter Five

THE WAY FORWARD: MULTILATERAL CO-OPERATION AND INTERNAL REFORM

5.1. The Merits of International Trade

Considering all the difficulties faced by developing countries in adapting to the rules-based system, why do they still remain in the WTO? Since the WTO has been careful to maintain a distance from those who wish to categorise it as a development organisation, why do the Member States still drive negotiations on a development platform especially under the Doha Round? One may ask whether indeed there is a correlation between the creation of trade rules and the attainment of increased opportunities, full employment, welfare gains, poverty alleviation, and higher standards of living. Since these issues are essentially those which are relevant in the domestic social and economic arena, how does multilateral co-operation assist the attainment of such objectives? Do trade rules not in fact undermine the ability of an internal government to decide on a trade and development regulatory structure which will respond to the particular needs and concerns of its internal environment?

This final chapter points to the incontrovertible response to all these questions: that indeed trade does offer an opportunity for development *but* it is an opportunity which can only be obtained by collective responsibility both at the multilateral, and at the domestic level. The arguments go back and forth on the merits of international trade rules. On the one hand, international regulation for the buying and selling of goods and services under the open trade conditions of the WTO system may adversely affect the national industries without domestic governments adopting restrictive measures to safeguard its domestic trade environment. Thus from one perspective, it could be considered that 'under certain conditions, open trade in goods leads to factor price equalisation with reduced returns to factors that are relatively abundant in other nations'.[1] An example would be for instance, that should low-skilled labour be relatively abundant outside the United States, open trade in products intensively utilising such labour will lead to lower income for low-skilled American workers.[2] In recent times, there may be more to this argument considering the resurgence of queries on the benefits of free trade and international rules to America which became a key issue in the 2008 American presidential race.[3]

However, not many accept the view that international trade hinders domestic regulation. These include Cass R.A & Haring, who considered the arguments immediately above[4] and argue however that trade encourages competition and efficiency and trade rules promote rather than distort efforts at economic growth.[5] Likewise, the WTO advances multilateral trade co-operation and presents multilateral trade as an attractive means of addressing economic growth. The Preamble to the *WTO Agreement* states the intents of the Parties as follows:

> *Recognizing* that their relations in the field of trade and economic endeavour should be conducted with a view to raising standards of living, ensuring full employment and a large and steadily growing volume of real income and effective demand, and expanding the production of and trade in goods and services, while allowing for the optimal use of the world's resources in accordance with the objective of sustainable development, seeking both to protect and preserve the environment and to enhance the means for doing so in a manner consistent with their respective needs and concerns at different levels of economic development,
>
> *Recognizing* further that there is need for positive efforts designed to ensure that developing countries, and especially the least developed among them, secure a share in the growth in international trade commensurate with the needs of their economic development,
>
> *Being desirous* of contributing to these objectives by entering into reciprocal and mutually advantageous arrangements directed to the substantial reduction of tariffs and other barriers to trade and to the elimination of discriminatory treatment in international trade relations[6]

The elimination of discriminatory treatment is easily understood as a necessity to efficient cross-border trade. But what is the relevance of rules which go beyond eliminating barriers to trade and dwell on specific issues including food safety, animal health, agriculture, intellectual property and such like? In spite of the Seattle and Cancun protests and the deadlock of the Doha Round, the Organisation continues to exist and to carry out the implementation of its Agreements. The reason may not be far-fetched. As Ortino points out, the WTO, 'is no longer limited to the reduction at the border- of trade barriers and the elimination-within the border-of discriminatory treatment, but deals increasingly with national regulation that is "unnecessarily" or "unreasonably" trade restrictive'.[7]

The point is that there are in fact merits to the regulation of international trade and these merits are found in multilateral co-operative efforts at limiting those unnecessary and unreasonable barriers to cross-border trade. Added to this, internal reforms by domestic governments who accede to the WTO also create an enabling environment for trade, thereby boosting wealth creation and redistribution in the domestic environment. We will consider these twin elements: multilateral co-operation, and internal reform.

PART I: MULTILATERAL CO-OPERATION

5.2. Open Trade

In assuming multilateral trade to be a proper vehicle for development, there are three basic factors which are considered relevant. *First*, the antecedents to the emergence of a world trading system clearly define the overarching need for rules on cross border trade which were to alleviate the poverty and weakened domestic industrial capacities of the allied nations in the late 1930's. Trade was seen as a means to this end: that with a larger market environment and greater uniformity in trade practices participating countries had the greatest potential to achieve greater employment, increase industrialisation, and bring about improvements in the social and economic life of citizens.

The *second* factor is evident in the overall statements on the objectives of the *WTO Agreement* itself and in the various Agreements providing for the rules on multilateral trade. The preambles to these Agreements exhibit the same acknowledgement of the multilateral trading system as a catalyst for economic growth of citizens and Member States alike. The legal framework of the WTO supports the notion that the multilateral trading system is concerned with the life and economic well being of individual citizens as well as the economic advancement of the Member State. Friedl Weiss in an article *WTO Dispute Settlement and the Economic Order of WTO Member States* commenting generally states that, 'the central function of the WTO is to safeguard the interests of citizens of small countries, developed and developing'.[8]

These observations are true. Nowhere in the vast documents included in the dispute settlement reports of the WTO has it been indicated that the goal of the Organisation is anything less than economic development across its Membership. The key to this unique characteristic of the WTO is that it is in a position to effect development by assisting developing country governments to build their trading capacity, a task which the WTO is making efforts through its TRTA programmes to address.

The *third* factor hinges on the fact that at present, the Organisation has over a hundred and fifty members. Of this number, over a hundred are developing countries. With a significant two thirds majority at the WTO, it becomes extremely important that the needs and concerns of the majority membership must be a priority for the Organisation.

These factors notwithstanding, the promotion of the 'free trade' theory as the solution to developing country problems of integration and the attainment of welfare gains is rather over stated. Apart from the fact that an examination of the economic history of the modern world's developed nations reveals that this has not been the case, there is a subtle almost deliberate disregard for the differences in theory and practice when the free trade principle is defended. While 'the defence of the free trade principle is an integral part of economic theory', there is a marked contrast between the international trade theories (and the emphasis on comparative advantage and specialisation) and the reality of practice.[9] It is also important to point out that the potential of open trade as the route to development is more limited than it appears given the WTO's case for open trade. It has been noted previously that the WTO is keen to emphasise that it is not a panacea for development. This defence of the nature of the Organisation is actually more suited to a proper characterisation for open trade: that is, *that open trade is not a panacea for development.*

Rodrik (2002) has noted that the limits of open trade 'is a lesson of particular importance to countries such as those in Africa that are in the early stages of reform'.[10] He points out that:

> [...] the benefits of trade openness should not be oversold. When other worthwhile policy objectives are competing for scarce administrative resources and political capital, deep trade liberalisation often does not deserve the high priority it typically receives in development strategies.[11]

The promotion of free trade and the urge to liberalise markets puts undue pressure on these countries to free up their market restrictions. In the attempt to liberalise their fragile markets, developing countries encounter shocks to their domestic environment: the diversion of local demand for foreign goods, the potential loss of jobs to foreign professionals particularly in the services sector, the limitations of employment opportunities for the local labour force and most importantly, a potential decline in indigenous efforts at production. The needs and concerns of developing countries at present rest on the urgent demand for a strong economic base; strong enough to withstand any shocks to the domestic environment; strong enough to compete in a global open market economy. Without a strong economic base, 'poor countries may find it particularly hard to buffer these shocks and to bear the costs they incur, and they typically have weak safety nets, or none at all to protect the poor.'[12]

Deborah Cass is of the opinion that 'free trade is not an objective of the [WTO] system'.[13] She insists that 'the overriding *telos* of the WTO is economic development through non-discriminatory trade'.[14] She finds that this view is 'the only possible reconciliation' of the contradictions which arise when one confronts the contrasts between 'the principles of non-discrimination, multilateralism, liberalisation, and transparency in trade, and the numerous departures from, and indeed contradictions with them both within the terms of the agreement and its contextual interpretative background.'[15]

Therefore the task before the WTO, if it is to fulfil this *development obligation*, is for the Organisation to reorient its activities. Greater action towards encouraging its developing country members towards a 'production and employment-oriented approach to poverty reduction' is one such means.[16] This paradigm is one which will not only assist international development objectives but will also guarantee that poverty alleviation, increase in opportunities, and better socio-economic living conditions will be available for a greater majority of persons. As the UNCTAD LDC 2006 Report noted, this would entail 'a development-driven approach to trade rather than a trade driven approach to development'.[17]

At the multilateral level, there are five ways in which the WTO can facilitate this development approach:

1. Mainstreaming development into current WTO action.
2. Closer co-operation between developing countries
3. Policy space in the implementation of trade rules.
4. Special Treatment and Committee Action
5. Keeping the WTO Development Agenda in focus.

5.2.1. Mainstreaming Development into Current WTO Action

Mainstreaming development into current WTO action demands that certain factors must be borne in mind.[18] *First,* is for a clear and appropriate definition of what the WTO ought to have as its goal in pursuing development. Development is not purely an indication of national economic strength; rather it is a measure of the individual's ability to avail one's self of the opportunities for personal development and financial security, and the access to the basic social amenities which can sustain modern standards of living. Incorporating development into the agenda of the WTO requires a proper identification of what constitutes development and of the human element intrinsic to the realisation of this concept.

In doing this, trade negotiators and those who carry out the WTO mandate under the Organisation's development agenda ought also to bear in mind that a well-focused development programme will have a long term effect not only for the present developing countries. Mainstreaming development into WTO action ensures that any future declines in the economies of any WTO Member States affecting the socio-economic standards therein, will receive appropriate development action. In such circumstances, facilitating that society's development through international trade would be practicable because the foundations and modalities for development action have already been entrenched within the framework of the WTO.

Second, the wholesale presentation of trade liberalisation as *sine qua non* to a country's economic development and poverty elimination strategy without more is flawed and should be resisted. This is because this view is posited without due consideration of the limitations in the pure economic theories of specialisation and comparative advantage, which bear on the potential of developing country capacity to trade.

Third, the single undertaking requirement which demands a uniform approach to the obligations of membership at the WTO is another constraint to the flexibility required by developing countries in the adoption of policies suited to their level of development. A review of this requirement is neglected at the expense of finding solutions to the restrictions placed by WTO Agreements in their implementation by these countries. WTO negotiations including those strongly contested debates on the integration of developing countries into the global trading system will merit from a consideration of developing country proposals for some flexibility in their WTO commitment under the Agreements. While this consideration may appear as a restriction on the application of a uniform rules-based system, it is essentially a demand for a more equitable system that acknowledges the needs and concerns of the majority of its Members.

Fourth, the dispute settlement system of the WTO in particular judicial review at both the Panel and the Appellate Body has to be imbued with development-based jurisprudence. It is not only a balance in the negotiations that must be achieved; there also ought to be equity in the interpretation of WTO Agreements where developing countries are concerned. As has been argued, the duty before the DSB is for the Body when presented with any relevant dispute, to properly assess the circumstances of the complaint and make an objective assessment of the facts while keeping the development objective both of the country and of the Organisation, in focus. This will require that recommendations in dispute decisions do not ignore the individual needs of a developing country and do not compromise the Member State's efforts towards market integration by restricting the potential for new, infant or vulnerable industry growth.

Fifth, the WTO oversees the implementation of its objectives through the activities of the WTO Secretariat, in co-operation with other international bodies, and under its TRTA programmes. Equipping the Organisation with financial and technical assistance in order for the development mandate to be achieved is one of the principal obligations of the richer WTO Member States. The AfT Initiative has already attracted some financial assistance from some donor countries. More so, the technical assistance programmes and the capacity building projects organised by the Secretariat pursuant to the DDA, require the close attention of all WTO Member States to ensure that these programmes and projects are targeted to the areas of need in recipient countries.

5.2.2. Closer Co-operation Between Developing Countries

One may question whether developing countries will benefit more from the multilateral system if they pursue their interests at the WTO on an individual basis. It is not suggested that developing countries should neglect to advocate their development concerns in WTO negotiations, or that they should not bring disputes against the actions of another developing country if they find that their interests have been nullified or impaired. However, in the general context of addressing development objectives within the WTO, it is argued that a consensus approach is more beneficial. If developing countries yield to pressure domestic or international, to engage only in negotiations which affect them individually, or to engage only in policy debates which serve their immediate needs, this would prove detrimental to the collective bid for global market integration for developing countries.

In effect, the developing countries' greater majority in the WTO rule making bodies must be appropriately and effectively utilised. This may require less emphasis on the political perspectives of special treatment *per se* and more reliance on reviews of particular WTO Agreements' provisions which inhibit market access, create an imbalance in the rules, or relate to improving the efficacy of technical assistance and capacity building programmes. The earlier mentioned suggestion that the 'best way to ensure that the WTO contributes to development is to move beyond the principle of differentiation to the substance of individual provisions, including in areas where new negotiations are proposed'[19] is of relevance here.

Strength in a negotiation forum is undoubtedly fundamental to a favourable conclusion for a trade negotiator. In the international trade environment, it is invaluable that trade proposals are backed not only by persuasive representatives but also by sound arguments backed with empirical data. The 'South-South appeal'[20] at trade negotiations will rest on well researched and carefully argued proposals which identify the issues which within the WTO legal framework are reflective of the development goals both of the developing countries themselves and of the Organisation.

Strong coalitions will also encourage more intensive participation by developing countries in the Organisation's working bodies. Appointments to

WTO bodies are based on criteria which developing countries may not be able to satisfy individually.[21] These criteria include that Members in financial arrears for over a year may not chair WTO bodies. Another criterion requires that a person considered for appointment to a WTO body must have the capacity to undertake the special responsibility demanded of that particular position.[22] Developing countries can strengthen their participation and hence their influence in negotiating Agreements when they join resources to facilitate their collective strength at international trade negotiations and at dispute settlement processes.

Furthermore, inter-developing country trade on a bilateral or regional level will boost local production of commonly consumed products including foods, and encourage trade facilitation by addressing supply side constraints. These include improving inefficient transportation networks thereby reducing transportation costs which greatly influence the final price of goods and increasing R&D activities. A stronger South-South integration and a more proximate market area will help harmonise trade and development policies in line with international agreements including those of the WTO. The proximity of markets will also reduce protectionist trends.

On the long run, closer trade relations with other developing countries will adequately prepare developing countries particularly LDCs to ease into a larger trading environment. Closer co-operation will also facilitate information exchange flows between countries and where possible, enhance technical assistance at the bilateral and regional level.

5.2.3. Policy Space

While the WTO may make rules which affect the domestic legal framework, national trade and commercial laws still have to reflect the socio-economic needs of the society. Developing country studies in relevant research have always stressed that policy support ought to be given to those areas of national development programmes that can advance industrial growth and domestic production.[23] As Stiglitz argued, it is not equitable to compel developing countries under the aegis of the free trade theory to comply with rules based on those practiced in developed countries and which have been secured by the latter's advantages in production technology and infrastructural capacity.[24]

It must be borne in mind that national rules have to consider primarily, the areas for improvement in a community and the areas where investment in commercial activities will boost employment and create the necessary conditions for raising the standards of living in the community. Thus the policy space required by developing countries in the WTO points to the need for flexibility in the trade rules. This flexibility will allow developing countries to adopt reforms and policies in their trade and economic development regime which address their deficiencies in expanding their base of tradable goods.

Countries can take advantage of this policy space to adopt trade rules which can facilitate their peculiar needs. As Eeckhout noted:

> In principle, the WTO Agreement could have specified what effect its provisions are to have in the domestic legal order of WTO Members. However, it did not do so. Therefore, although each Member must execute fully the commitments which it has undertaken, it is free to determine the legal means appropriate for attaining that end in its domestic system.[25]

In any event, any complaint arising from such domestic action can be brought before the DSB. For their part, developing countries have a duty to study carefully, the legal provisions of the WTO Agreements in order to implement policies and regulations which are appropriate to their needs and yet not contrary to their WTO obligations.

5.2.4. Effective Special Treatment

The inclusion of SDT provisions in the WTO Agreements has been a significant success in the struggle by developing countries to have their concerns acknowledged within the trade rules. However since these provisions are not legally binding obligations, they are severely limited. For these provisions to have any real meaning and impact, the special provisions particularly those on technical assistance and capacity building must move beyond exhortations to normative provisions.

Action at Committee level across the several Committees set up under the rules will also be advantageous in implementing the special treatment provisions. The work of the SPS Committee shows a clear commitment to address development concerns even if the commitment is not matched by specific successes. More particular, the work of the CTD which directly oversees the special treatment provisions across the WTO Agreements needs more bite to it. The CTD is in the best position in relation to developing countries at the WTO, to direct multilateral action towards greater integration, beyond the special treatment provisions of trade Agreements.[26] Besides reviewing SDT provisions, CTD should be seen as the nerve centre for collating developing country concerns with the trading system. Meeting and participating at the Committee meetings, identifying issues of common interest, and co-operating in the preparation and presentation of proposals on such issues will undoubtedly influence the preparation of cogent and specific proposals on the cross-cutting areas of trade and development under the trade Agreements.

5.2.5. Keeping the Development Agenda in Focus post-Doha

The WTO insists that the multilateral cooperation under the AfT Initiatives cannot replace the commitments under the DDA and should not be seen as a fulfilment of the WTO development goals. It may well be that while the DDA remains as negotiable instruments of the WTO commitments under the Doha Round, the AfT Initiative will at least find the WTO undertaking practical action towards implementing its commitments to developing countries. In any event, in the wider context of a sustained multilateral system of international trade, the afore stated focus areas of the DDA remain critical to the goal of closer market integration for developing countries beyond the Doha Round.

PART II: INTERNAL REFORM

5.3. Developing Country Responsibility

While multilateral cooperation is incidental to developing country integration in general, it would be misleading to disregard the importance of internal reform in developing countries.[27] Trade, and development regulations, which do not factor in the needs of the producers in society while they may satisfy the demands of the WTO rules, cannot assist the trading capacity of developing country members. In seeking compliance with the demands of the free trade theory, countries will necessarily have to make adjustments to their national economic programmes. Such programmes may include but are not limited to: the privatisation of previously State owned enterprises, the public sale of government interests in national companies, elimination of restrictive barriers on imports, and macroeconomic reforms including unilateral trade liberalisation policies.[28] These attempts at economic restructuring will often call for radical changes and will be blamed for any ensuing destabilisation of the economy.

However, most of the problems of wealth distribution and the absence of good living standards are not primarily caused by multilateral trade participation contrary to widespread belief in developing countries. Inefficient policies and poor governance structures are mainly to blame particularly where trade policies are not fragmented along provisions which guarantee the efficient redistribution of national wealth to the citizens. The question that ought to be raised by developing country governments is not just how to enhance their participation at the WTO, but, what is the primary and urgent need of their society? What should take precedence in domestic strategies: membership of the WTO and participation in open trade or institutional reforms? Rodrik (2002) makes the often overlooked observation that 'a high-quality institutional environment has greater economic payoffs than a liberal trade regime or adherence to WTO rules'.[29]

There are five factors which we consider to be of paramount importance to developing country internal reform measures:

1. Understanding the WTO structure and functions.
2. Effective governance.
3. Engagement with stakeholders.
4. Improved WTO-information flow.
5. Creation of an enabling environment for trade.

5.3.1. Understanding the WTO Structure and Functions

A main cause for disenchantment with the WTO is the lack of proper understanding of what this Organisation is and what it does. Despite the shared obligations under the WTO Agreements, both developed and developing countries still ascribe some welfare-system function to the WTO. Developing countries continually demand exceptions while developed countries reluctantly agree by accepting the inclusion of vague 'special' provisions. The greater damage is done to developing countries who rest on the false promise that the WTO can improve domestic economic conditions and yet do not appreciate the demands such improvement will make on their domestic systems. This point can be elaborated on again using the case of Nigeria.

In Nigeria, the country's accession was not communicated to the public and there were no public debates or publications which outlined the obligations arising from the country's WTO Membership. Perhaps it was this last consideration that prompted the Nigerian government in 2004 almost ten years after accession to the new WTO, to set up a Committee presumably to review the WTO Agreements and the impact on the country's industrial activity. Explaining the rationale behind this objective, the government at the time suggested that the proposed Committee would analyse the WTO Agreement, with a view to "'reviewing and ensuring that Nigerian industries are protected" and that the national economy is "encouraged to grow and expand and that everything will be done within the approved regulations to ensure that the dumping of goods into the Nigerian economy is prohibited"'.[30]

This view offers an insight into the general, albeit naïve perceptions of the WTO. Three provisions of the WTO Agreement effectively dissuade on the above suggestions: *First*, under Article XII of the WTO Agreement, there is presumed to be a capacity to enter into the WTO Agreement, by Nigeria. The provision refers to 'any State or separate customs territory possessing full autonomy in the conduct of its external commercial relations and of the other matters provided for in this Agreement and the Multilateral Trade Agreements'. Such entities have the requisite capacity to accede to the WTO

Agreement, on terms agreed between that entity and the WTO. Nigeria may rebut this presumption of capacity to accede in the view that the country's accession to the WTO was as we earlier stated, a politically motivated act by the unpopular military government at the time. This however does not remove from the fact that Nigeria had the necessary capacity to enter into the multilateral agreement with other countries which she did, as a developing country member.

Second, the suggestion that the WTO Agreement may be 'reviewed' is not an entirely accurate interpretation of the provisions which enshrine a Member State's commitments under the rules-based system of the WTO. Article II:2 of the WTO Agreement provides that 'the agreements and associated legal instruments included in Annexes 1, 2 and 3 (hereinafter referred to as "Multilateral Trade Agreements") are integral parts of this Agreement, binding on all Members'. The practicalities of the 'single undertaking' requirement have already been considered. Therefore, regardless of earlier considerations on its effect on developing country progress and the need to review this requirement in pursuit of the WTO Development Agenda, it must be pointed out that as it stands, not only has Nigeria entered into an agreement to be a Member of the WTO, the country has undertaken the binding nature of obligations arising under the various multilateral Agreements.

Third, the WTO Agreement expects a practical implementation of the Agreements in the legal realm of Member States. Accordingly it provides that 'each Member shall ensure the conformity of its laws, regulations and administrative procedures with its obligations as provided in the annexed Agreements'.[31] Furthermore, Article XIV:2 provides that a Member which accepts the WTO Agreement after its entry into force shall 'implement those concessions and obligations in the Multilateral Trade Agreements [...]starting with the entry into force of this Agreement as if it had accepted this Agreement on the date of its entry into force'.

Given the government remarks criticised above, it is questionable whether trade liberalisation as a necessary instrument of socio-economic advancement is a theory that is understood, nay accepted in the country. The popular view is that the WTO is one of the many international organisations which exists to determine domestic policies without due regard to the interests and concerns of the country itself. In other words, there is suspicion as to the exact role of the Organisation in influencing domestic trade activity.

It is important that the full extent of the radical global initiative of market access and open trade as envisioned by the WTO is understood by developing countries, in the present instance, by Nigeria. This is necessary in order that there is a sound identification of the nature and scope of Nigeria's obligations under the Organisation and the benefits the country and her citizens ought to expect from participation in the trade liberalisation process. The same may be said of other developing countries.

5.3.2. Effective Governance

There is also a responsibility on the part of developing countries to review their development initiatives and the implementation of development programmes and projects in the domestic legal framework. Accusing the WTO of robbing developing country rights to development is no answer to administrative incompetence, financial mismanagement, and poor social infrastructure. Neither does it resolve the issue of badly conceived domestic development programmes and the inappropriate implementation of trade policies.

The 1933 inaugural speech of US President F. D. Roosevelt which was made at the time of the economic recession brought on by the Great Depression offers an insight into the thinking and spirit behind effective domestic trade and economic policy making for the purpose of socio-economic development in such challenging circumstances. President Roosevelt addressing the reality of developmental needs of the US for the period bearing in mind the importance of maintaining international trading relations said:

> we face our common difficulties [...] the means of exchange are frozen in the currents of trade; the withered leaves of industrial enterprise lie on every side; farmers find no markets for their produce...a host of unemployed citizens face the grim problem of existence, and an equally great number toil with little return
>
> Our greatest primary task is to put people to work...the task can be helped by definite efforts to raise the value of agricultural products...it can be helped by national planning for and supervision of all forms of transportation and of communications and other utilities that have a definitely public character
>
> Our international trade relations, though vastly important, are in point of time, and necessity, secondary to the establishment of a sound national economy [...] I shall spare no effort to restore world trade by international economic readjustment; but the emergency at home cannot wait on that accomplishment.[32]

The above thoughts are not offered as a call for protectionist policies for developing countries today. Rather as some observers have emphasised:

> The important thing for governments – rather than privileging trade as a magic wand or dismissing its relevance – is firstly to assess whether and how

trade can support a wider strategy of balanced economic development, and secondly what kind of trade policies are needed specifically for poverty reduction.[33]

The trade sectors of national governments together with other government institutions are best placed to address issues of poverty, unemployment, and social insecurities. Yet, other WTO Member governments should also weigh the domestic needs of their counterpart Members in demanding compensatory adjustments for new trade polices or in negotiating concessions in international trade.

While TRTA programmes including the AfT Initiatives will continue to be significant to developing countries, these countries must adopt effective governance systems to address their needs at domestic level. Governments have to identify new trading opportunities in response to the changing demands of the global market. Relying on agriculture as the most viable enterprise and therefore the only sector which should be protected from the strict international trade regime is not without its risks to developing countries. The world market for agricultural products is not as vibrant as it used to be. There is a growing market for services, cheaper manufactures, and new varieties of foods including GMO foods amongst others. This means that reliance on a single sector is detrimental rather than beneficial. Identifying new trading opportunities will also free up the resources for reinvestments towards a diversified economy.

At grassroots level, the gains from trade will be measured by a government's efforts at wealth creation and wealth redistribution in the domestic environment. Thus, institutional reforms in the banking and financial sectors, well administered taxation policies, and efficient regulatory institutions, are fundamental to the government's control of, and success in, the domestic trade and development agenda. In sum, effective governance will entail identifying new trade opportunities, building domestic trade capacity, and reinvesting the gains from trade into the social setting by establishing efficient infrastructure – schools, health facilities, welfare systems, etc, to meet the socio-economic needs of the society.

5.3.3. Engagement with Stakeholders

In the realm of domestic policy making also, the suggestions of local traders, entrepreneurs, research officers, academics, economists, legal professionals, and others whose activities centre on trade relations including the government trade officials, are necessary for effective policy making. It is within a network of these persons and groups of persons that governments can set out policies and regulations that will keep the overall development progress of the country in focus.

In Nigeria's case for instance, without this grass-roots partnership, it is inevitable that representations on Nigeria's WTO membership and her trade potentials in the global market are 'government-led' responses to the trade negotiating proposals at the Organisation. As earlier noted, such responses retain the bias against the opening up of markets to foreign corporations with recurring themes such as that 'the WTO Agreement operates effectively to prise open markets for the benefits of trans-national corporations at the expense of national economies'.[34] Inevitably, strong policies which can redress the imbalance in favour of domestic businesses are not pursued. Rather there is much play on the fear that developing nations face 'further marginalisation occasioned by the globalisation phenomenon'.[35]

Stakeholders can ferment a better understanding of the obligations under the WTO and can provide answers to the problems faced by a country in its trade sector. For governments therefore, consultations with the grassroots is fundamental both for receiving feedbacks on the impacts of implementation of the trade rules in the trade environment and as a source for collating those concrete proposals to be presented at WTO negotiations. This is so because the outcome of such consultations will undoubtedly reflect the needs and concerns of the society.

5.3.4. *Improved WTO-Information Flow*

Information flow here refers to a number of issues. One is the need for greater participation at the WTO meetings, seminars, TRTA programmes. Another is for government-stakeholder information flow as discussed immediately above.

While the WTO operates at the inter-national level, it can reach the grassroots even better than national governments can; a capacity well utilised by the Organisation's website accessibility and by its public seminar programmes. Such information flow can be replicated by governments. National governments may find it beneficial to request copies of free publications of the WTO for their government offices, for public and research libraries and for general public use. They may also organise public seminars relating to the country's multilateral trade activities in order to create and sustain awareness of the trade rules and of the working of the WTO.

5.3.5 *Creating an Enabling Environment*

Finally, apart from engaging with the TRTA programme at the WTO, internal reform programmes for the purposes of building trade capacity must also factor in the need to create an enabling environment for producers of goods and services. In the internal environment as well, domestic rules must have the necessary flexibility to allow more people get involved in entrepreneurship. This will demand less stringent procedures for business creation, clearly delineated roles for respective government agencies to avoid duplication of functions, and a review of commercial regulations to reduce proliferation and unnecessary bureaucracy.

Furthermore, financial assistance for local enterprises where this is needed is important as are R&D activities in local production and manufacture. Governments also need to actively encourage the growth of new businesses. Institutional and infrastructural restructuring is also required. Limiting the *supply side constraints* in the local environment – inefficient power supply, poor transport and communication networks etc, will be invaluable for efficient and sustained production ventures whether they are in respect of goods or, of services.

CONCLUSION

The importance of trade to countries is two-fold: one, it provides a country with income; and two, it directly provides a country's citizens with income as well. In a sense, facilitating access to markets is the best form of direct investment a country can undertake towards its socio-economic development.

Throughout this work, we have emphasised that trade is instrumental to a people's socio-economic development. We started first with a review of trade and development at the WTO. The emphasis was on understanding the exact nature of the Organisation in order to provide a preliminary foundation for future consideration of what the WTO can and cannot do for its developing country Members. When we examined the classifications by international organisations on development status, it was clear that the international community through these various organisations understands that the principal element of 'developing country' status is the level of poverty and the limited capacity for individual growth and opportunity. These are elements which motivated the world trading system even from the time of the GATT, to lay out provisions in the international trade rules to address the challenges of developing country participation in organised global trade.

Developing country integration however has faced and still continues to face teething problems. Apart from the general barriers experienced across the global market which a uniform rules-based system was expected to resolve, developing countries' circumstances have not been improved in the face of challenges like the inequalities in trading power, internal constraints, an ever-expanding body of rules, and the single undertaking requirement which demands commitment to every single WTO rule irrespective of the capacity to execute the obligations therein. In addition, we also argued that the application of the comparative advantage theory to the modern market is more of a constraint than a true reading of the political economy of the times. Current action under the Doha Development Agenda in spite of the renewed activity at the WTO Secretariat which carries out administrative functions even in the provision of technical assistance is not moving as swiftly as it should especially with the protraction of the Doha Round.

In the Appendix, an in-depth study of one of the trade rules, in this instance the Agreement on Sanitary and Phytosanitary Measures, reveals that the development paradigm of a WTO rules throws up a significant number of challenges in their implementation by a developing country. Beyond the rules, judicial review of the development question still leaves room for improvement in the assessment and interpretation of both the special treatment provisions, and of the overall impact of the trade rules on developing countries' socio-economic circumstances.

We are of the view that the way forward is in the twin paths of multilateral co-operation, and internal reform. Whereas there has been an agreement to regulate trade, it is only legitimate that these regulations are founded on the expectation that there ought to be a benefit to both the individual and the society alongside the profits from trade. The WTO and its developing country members have achieved a lot in the area of addressing development goals by way of negotiations under the DDA and the recent Aid Initiatives. However, a lot still needs to be done.

At the 2006 WTO Public Forum 'What WTO for the XXIst Century?' the Prime Minister of Lesotho in his keynote address, noted the importance of trade to developing economies:

> Given low and unpredictable ODA, unresponsive FDI, and limited financial resources at the development financing institutions, resorting to the trade avenue offers more viable opportunities for stronger economic growth and development. Well designed and competently managed trade policies can trigger forward, backward and indeed lateral linkages that would entail wealth creation, improved employment and thus contribute to poverty reduction.[1]

The solution to the development anxiety of developing countries at the WTO does not lie in those exceptions to the trade rules which are regarded as 'special treatment' provisions. These are characteristically wordy and vague, without any real promise. Their only merit is in their ability to placate and soothe temporarily, much like a parent's misguided affection which solicits a child to keep quiet by promising to relieve it of doing its homework. SDT provisions may have provided some incentive for developing countries to participate in the WTO but they are not enough to build the trade capacity of these countries which is where special attention is needed.

This view was earlier pointed out by the 1985 Leutwiler Report. It noted that:

> Developing countries receive special treatment in the GATT rules. But such special treatment is of limited value. Far greater emphasis should be placed

on permitting and encouraging developing countries to take advantage of their competitive strengths and on integrating them more fully into the trading system, with all the appropriate rights and responsibilities this entails.[2]

Special treatment in our view ought to have arisen at the point of accession: by developing countries electing to undertake obligations only under those trade rules where they are able to do so. Accepting SDT provisions in consideration for agreeing to a single undertaking, appears in hindsight to be a very bad bargain. The devil has proved to be in the detail of the respective Agreements, and this particular devil resists the attempts at exorcism which are only a few ineffectual sprinkles of goodwill in the form of SDTs. In future, developing countries would be fare better if they harness their majority share towards blocking the adoption of rules in sectors where they consider their economies to be too vulnerable than where they expend time and effort pursuing the inclusion of further special treatment provisions.

That is not all. Greater action is required in the internal structure of domestic systems. Internal reform structures must also adopt 'well designed and competently managed trade policies' which can 'trigger forward, backward and indeed lateral linkages that would entail wealth creation, improved employment and thus contribute to poverty reduction'.[3]

Whereas the WTO is not a welfare system for national governments, it has development-related obligations to its Membership. Its trade-negotiating character must be balanced with its development character. Seeking fuller participation of developing country governments at the multilateral level must be balanced with the need to ensure that the citizens engaging in trade and other economic endeavour in these countries are also understood to be at the heart of the trade and development agenda. Trade rules must therefore not deprive policy making in the domestic environment of the flexibility needed for countries to adopt regulations suited to their level of development and their needs. The WTO mechanism must appreciate that there are limits to what a country can achieve at a particular time. While providing technical assistance towards building trade capacity and for fuller integration, it must bear in mind that trade liberalisation should take a second seat to more urgent development needs, whether they be institutional, infrastructural, social, or political reforms.

The Doha mandate has renewed the WTO commitment to economic development set out in the original GATT. The four pillars of the Doha Mandate are not in themselves new areas of interest at the international level. The fact that that they have received express mention at the international level is perhaps what gives them a renewed appeal. Will their elevation to the negotiating table of the world trading system yield any successes? Yes, and no.

Yes, because for instance, the TRTA and capacity building work undertaken by the WTO in conjunction with other international agencies is a step in the right direction though it is a step limited by circumstances. Targeting TRTA at government officials who are not the actual subjects of trade and economic endeavour in the domestic setting is risky. If they impart the information they gain to the stakeholders, it will be of benefit. If they don't, the knowledge gained is of no help to the local producer.

On the other hand, enhanced market access and balance in trade rules are determined by a multitude of factors many of which are not operative at the international level. There must be goods or services to trade which is more a question of trade capacity. There must be domestic policies which can trigger this improved capacity. There must be a well-regulated economy wherein new trade opportunities are constantly being identified. Support must be given to build trade capacity, to improve production, and to encourage innovation and diversification. Regulatory institutions which oversee many areas of trade and economic endeavour including corporate practice and governance, standards, quality of goods, etc, influence both imports and exports of goods and services. Developed economies thrive on these institutions and often, the lesson learnt in the domestic market is the instigation for trade rules and negotiations.[1]

Developing countries cannot boast of such institutions which derive from a long settled market economy and so particularly for the future, new rules such as rules on competition, must be introduced into the world trading system with caution. A balance in the rules will be a balance gained from putting aside subject areas which developing countries cannot effectively participate in, and concentrating on finding more practicable ways of addressing ways to build trade capacity, to address supply side constraints, and to give significant attention to the needs and circumstances of developing countries when they are involved in disputes at the DSB.

In any event, adopting a development agenda signifies that even at the multilateral trade level, the world is concerned about raising the living standards of the peoples, particularly those in the developing countries. For that alone the WTO deserves commendation.

Our review of the WTO's development obligation however shows that the Organisation continues to struggle in its attempt to satisfy all its members. It is an ambitious attempt because it is clearly difficult for such a large entity to satisfy *all* its Members, *all* the time, in *all* respects. For now, the needs and concerns of developing countries are priority. What gains their societies can make from trade will be determined by how long and how well their governments can hold the attention of the international community gathered under the WTO.

Ultimately, the test will be whether the richer countries can set aside their subjective economic interests in order to pursue a universal need – for the individuals and societies in the world's poorer countries to raise their living standards through an equitable and effective participation in the global trade environment. A lot also depends on how developing countries can individually and collectively internalise the gains from their majority position in the WTO and to what extent they can utilise the gains from this unique trade-negotiating arrangement in the realm of international relations, within their domestic environment.

Appendix (Selected Case Study)

OBLIGATIONS AND CHALLENGES UNDER THE WTO AGREEMENT ON SANITARY AND PHYTOSANITARY STANDARDS

Introduction

To fully appreciate the obligations and the impact of the rules-based system, one has to go beyond identifying that the WTO is a trade-negotiating body. It is in the detailed provisions of the respective Agreements that one may discern a true glimpse of the potential which trade has for development. In this selected study we opt for a more fundamental approach in assessing the dynamics of trade and economic development by taking a closer look at one such Agreement: the WTO Agreement on Sanitary and Phytosanitary Measures – *the SPS Agreement*.[1] The essence of the SPS Agreement lies in the demands for public health and safety which is a universal need, placed alongside the need to ensure that the protection of public health and safety does not constitute the basis of arbitrary restrictions on trade by national governments. Thus while the importance of public health and safety is acknowledged, the adoption of unfair restrictive trade measures lacking scientific basis is denied.

It is not too difficult to understand the reasoning behind this perspective. Regulating the international market and all trade and economic endeavour carried out therein must be seen to have a positive impact on not only producers, but also on consumers. This is because when a rule of international trade reaches into the domestic environment as they all inevitably do, its only justification must be that it is well balanced against the legitimate aims of the domestic regulations. Thus trade rules are negotiated with the objective of ensuring that the multilateral co-operation under the WTO takes into consideration those essential aspects of societal regulation which are for the common good. On the other hand, domestic trade policies and measures which have not been sufficiently backed by science cannot, riding on the need for public health and safety be allowed to restrict trade, a restriction which may only be a disguised form of protectionism.

This case study provides a more in depth and empirical study of the benefits and challenges which WTO Members face in exercise of their obligations as WTO Members. Particular emphasis will be on developing countries' capacity to execute their obligations under the Agreement. Our study will be in three broad parts. We will first examine the rules, and the interpretation of the fundamental provisions of the Agreement. Next we will consider the development paradigm of the Agreement including the SDT provisions, the scope of technical assistance offered, and the impact of private standards on developing countries. Finally, we will localise our study by focusing on work at domestic level, in this case in Nigeria. We will consider the work of the national enquiry point in the country and the relevance of SPS measures in the domestic environment.

1.1. The SPS Agreement: An Overview of the Rules and Interpretation

The *SPS Agreement* was signed into force with the other Agreements under the new WTO, on April 15 1994. It entered into force on the 1st of January 1995. An analogous Agreement is the Agreement on Technical Barriers to Trade, the *TBT Agreement*. The provisions of GATT 1947 had contained references to technical standards and regulations under Articles III, XI and XX. In 1979 after the Tokyo Round, a plurilateral Agreement on technical barriers known as 'the Standards Code' laid down the rules for the preparation, adoption, and application of technical regulations, standards, and conformity assessment procedures. Under the Uruguay Round, the *TBT Agreement* was formerly adopted as a multilateral agreement and became part of the WTO Agreement.

With Agreements such as the *SPS*, the DSB created for the purposes of interpreting WTO rules must also decide on disputes which juxtapose domestic policies against trade rules and which bear significantly on the former.[2] But this is not all. In the particular case of the SPS Agreement, the DSB must also have to consider scientific principles and procedures on which basis, domestic trade polices and measures relevant to the SPS Agreement are adopted by WTO Member States.

Challenges to developing countries with their limited financial and infrastructural capacity were anticipated in the provisions of the SPS Agreement. Apart from provisions on special and differential treatment, the Agreement also provides for technical assistance for developing country members. Under the Doha Round, the SDT provisions under the SPS Agreement receive the similar consideration of special treatment provisions across the respective WTO Agreements. Thus these provisions are also to be 'reviewed with a view to strengthening them and making them more precise, effective and operational'.[3]

In the first paragraph in its Preamble, the SPS Agreement defines the intent of the WTO rules on sanitary and phytosanitary measures. It states as follows:

> *Reaffirming* that no Member should be prevented from adopting or enforcing measures necessary to protect human, animal or plant life or health, subject to the requirement that these measures are not applied in a manner which would constitute a means of arbitrary or unjustifiable discrimination between Members where the same conditions prevail or a disguised restriction on international trade.

Since the SPS Agreement seeks to deter national governments from restricting the flow of international trade on unjustifiable grounds of public health, food, plant or animal safety, Article 2 of the Agreement grants Members 'the right to take sanitary and phytosanitary measures necessary for the protection of human, animal or plant life' in so far as any such measure adopted is 'based on scientific principles and is not maintained without sufficient scientific evidence'.[4] The exception to the need for sufficient scientific evidence is found in paragraph 7 of Article 5. That provision states that:

> In cases where relevant scientific evidence is insufficient, a Member may provisionally adopt sanitary or phytosanitary measures on the basis of available pertinent information, including that from the relevant international organizations as well as from sanitary or phytosanitary measures applied by other Members. In such circumstances, Members shall seek to obtain the additional information necessary for a more objective assessment of risk and review the sanitary or phytosanitary measure accordingly within a reasonable period of time.

It is important to bear in mind the exact objective of SPS measures to be adopted within the territory of a WTO member State which is where the provisions of the SPS Agreement find their application. Annex A of the Agreement defines an SPS measure to be any measure applied:

a) to protect animal or plant life or health from risks arising from the entry, establishment or spread of pests, diseases, disease carrying organisms or disease-causing organisms;

b) to protect human or animal life or health from risks arising form additives, contaminants, toxins or disease-causing organisms in foods, beverages or foodstuffs;

c) to protect human life or health within the territory of the Member from risks arising from diseases carried by animals, plants or products thereof, or from the entry, establishment or spread of insects; or

d) to prevent or limit other damage within the territory of the Member from the entry, establishment or spread of pests.

In such particular issues such as these concerning the adoption of domestic standards on health issues, standards adopted will vary amongst Members. In order to ensure that a measure of harmony is obtainable across the Members States, Article 3.1 of the Agreement requests Members to 'base their sanitary or phytosanitary measures on international standards, guidelines or recommendations where they exist' The harmonisation provisions of Article 3 in sub paragraph 4, go on to direct Members to participate "within the limits of their resources" in the relevant international organisations and their subsidiary bodies.' These bodies are the Codex Alimentarius Commission, the International Office of Epizootics and the international and regional organisations operating within the framework of the International Plant Protection Convention.

The Preamble to the Agreement affirms the intention of the WTO Membership that no Member shall be prevented from adopting or enforcing these measures of protection subject to the requirement that the measures 'would not constitute a means of arbitrary or unjustifiable discrimination between Members where the same conditions prevail or a disguised restriction on international trade'. To guard against this occurrence, Annex B of the Agreement makes provisions for the transparency of sanitary and phytosanitary regulations.[5] These provisions refer to:

1. Publication of regulations including laws, decrees or other applicable legal instruments on SPS measures. A reasonable length of time must be allowed between the time of publication and the entry into force of the measure in order to allow Members particularly developing country Members time to adapt to the requirements under these laws.
2. Each Member must ensure that it sets up "Enquiry Points" with the responsibility of providing answers and documents on adopted SPS measures.[6]
3. Every Member must notify others by their national notification authorities through the Secretariat at an early stage, of any new or changed SPS regulations adopted in the Member State.[7]

Annex C of the Agreement also provides for control, inspection and approval p[procedures. These procedures include procedures for sampling, testing and, certification which must be 'reasonable' and 'necessary'.[8] To provide a regular forum for consultations, assist in the monitoring of the process of international harmonisation, and to coordinate the work efforts with the relevant international organisations, a Committee on Sanitary and Phytosanitary Measures, the 'Committee' was established under Article 12 of the Agreement.

Therefore, pursuant to the Agreement, SPS measures must be:

- applied only to the extent that they protect human, animal or plant life or health;
- based on sufficient scientific principles;
- maintained with sufficient scientific evidence; and
- must be necessary to protect human, animal or plant life or health.

The use of the terms, 'necessary' and 'sufficient' with respect to the character of the scientific principles and evidence applicable under the Agreement is no doubt an 'innovation' in WTO law.[9] This 'innovation' also implies that SPS measures will be the subject of dispute complaints at the DSB as they have often been.[10]

1.1.1. Measures 'Based on' International Standards

In keeping with its theme of harmonising SPS standards across its Member States, the SPS Agreement requires that domestic SPS measures are based on international standards or at least conform to them. The findings of the AB in the *EC-Hormones* case lends some help to understanding this rule of the Agreement. The dispute was brought by United States who complained *inter alia*, that measures taken under EC Council Directives[11] restricted imports of meat and meat products from the US. At Panel level, the DSB found that the EU ban was inconsistent with the relevant provisions of Articles 3.1, 5.1 and 5.5 of the SPS Agreement.

Pertinent here are the provisions of the said Articles 3.1 and 5.5 which provide that members should base their SPS measures on international standards, and that to achieve consistency in the application of the concept of appropriate sanitary and phytosanitary protection, Members should avoid arbitrary or unjustifiable distinctions in the levels of SPS protection. With respect to Article 5.5, given that the objective is to achieve consistency in the application of appropriate levels of SPS protection, each Member should avoid arbitrary or unjustifiable distinctions if such distinctions are discriminatory, or are a disguised restriction on international trade.

In full, Article 3 states as follows:

To harmonize sanitary and phytosanitary measures on as wide a basis as possible, Members shall base their sanitary or phytosanitary measures on international standards, guidelines or recommendations, where they exist, except as otherwise provided for in this Agreement, and in particular in paragraph 3.

The Agreement however does not preclude maintenance of a higher level of SPS protection. Article 3.3 provides that:

> Members may introduce or maintain sanitary or phytosanitary measures which result in a higher level of sanitary or phytosanitary protection than would be achieved by measures based on the relevant international standards, guidelines or recommendations, if there is a scientific justification, or as a consequence of the level of sanitary or phytosanitary protection a Member determines to be appropriate in accordance with the relevant provisions of paragraphs 1 through 8 of Article 5.[12]

In full, Article 5.5 provides as follows:

> With the objective of achieving consistency in the application of the concept of appropriate level of sanitary or phytosanitary protection against risks to human life or health, or to animal and plant life or health, each Member shall avoid arbitrary or unjustifiable distinctions in the levels it considers to be appropriate in different situations, if such distinctions result in discrimination or a disguised restriction on international trade. Members shall cooperate in the Committee, in accordance with paragraphs 1, 2 and 3 of Article 12, to develop guidelines to further the practical implementation of this provision. In developing the guidelines, the Committee shall take into account all relevant factors, including the exceptional character of human health risks to which people voluntarily expose themselves.

The AB (reversing the finding of the Panel) held in respect of Articles 3.1 and 5.5, that the EC Directive was not inconsistent with the SPS Agreement. According to the AB, the requirement that the SPS measures adopted should be 'based on' international standards, guidelines or recommendations under Article 3.1 does not mean that SPS measures must conform to such standards. The AB noted that:

> To read Article 3.1 as requiring Members to harmonize their SPS measures *by conforming those measures with international standards,* guidelines and recommendations, *in the here and now,* is, in effect, to vest such international standards, guidelines and recommendations (which are by the terms of the Codex *recommendatory* in form and nature) with *obligatory* force and effect.

The Panel's interpretation of Article 3.1 would, in other words, transform those standards, guidelines and recommendations into binding *norms*. But, as already noted, the *SPS Agreement* itself sets out no indication of any intent on the part of the Members to do so. We cannot lightly assume that sovereign states intended to impose upon themselves the more onerous, rather than the less burdensome, obligation by mandating *conformity* or *compliance with* such standards, guidelines and recommendations. To sustain such an assumption and to warrant such a far-reaching interpretation, treaty language far more specific and compelling than that found in Article 3 of the *SPS Agreement* would be necessary.[13]

The AB was also of the opinion that the EC measures did not violate Article 5.5. It noted that there were three 'cumulative' elements present in the said Article:

> The first element is that the Member imposing the measure complained of has adopted its own appropriate levels of sanitary protection against risks to human life or health in several different situations. The second element to be shown is that those *levels of protection* exhibit arbitrary or unjustifiable differences ("distinctions" in the language of Article 5.5) in their treatment of different situations. The last element requires that the arbitrary or unjustifiable differences result in discrimination or a disguised restriction of international trade. We understand the last element to be referring to the *measure* embodying or implementing a particular level of protection as resulting, in its application, in discrimination or a disguised restriction on international trade.[14]

Considering these elements, the AB was of the opinion that the finding of the Panel that the "'arbitrary or unjustifiable" differences in the EC levels of protection across the Directives resulted in discrimination or were a disguised restriction of international trade, was "unjustified and erroneous as a matter of law" '.[15] In its view, this finding was not supported by the 'architecture and structure' of the EC Directives nor by the evidence produced by the Complainants. It therefore stated:

> We do not attribute the same importance as the Panel to the supposed multiple objectives of the European Communities in enacting the EC Directives that set forth the EC measures at issue. The documentation that preceded or accompanied the enactment of the prohibition of the use of hormones for growth promotion and that formed part of the record of the Panel makes clear the depth and extent of the anxieties experienced within the European Communities concerning the results of the general scientific

studies (showing the carcinogenicity of hormones), the dangers of abuse (highlighted by scandals relating to black-marketing and smuggling of prohibited veterinary drugs in the European Communities) of hormones and other substances used for growth promotion and the intense concern of consumers within the European Communities over the quality and drug-free character of the meat available in its internal market.[16] A major problem addressed in the legislative process of the European Communities related to the differences in the internal regulations of various Member States of the European Union (four or five of which permitted, while the rest prohibited, the use for growth promotion of certain hormones), the resulting distortions in competitive conditions in and the existence of barriers to intra-community trade. The necessity for harmonizing the internal regulations of its Member States was a consequence of the European Communities' mandate to establish a common (internal) market in beef.[17] Reduction of any beef surplus through an increase in the consumption of beef within the European Communities, is not only in the interests of EC farmers, but also of non-hormone using farmers in exporting countries. We are unable to share the inference that the Panel apparently draws that the import ban on treated meat and the Community-wide prohibition of the use of the hormones here in dispute for growth promotion purposes in the beef sector were not really designed to protect its population from the risk of cancer, but rather to keep out US and Canadian hormone-treated beef and thereby to protect the domestic beef producers in the European Communities.[18]

1.1.2. Basic Rights and Obligations

The crux of the SPS Agreement lies in the need for scientific justification; not in terms of whether the scientific process of assessing potential risk to public health and safety is the right one or even the only one, but that the demands for scientific-based assessment demanded by the Agreement is met in line with the procedure established under the Agreement.

Article 2.2, 5.1, and 5.1 of the Agreement set out the basic rights and exceptions of Member States in their adoption of SPS measures. Article 2.2 provides that:

Members shall ensure that any sanitary or phytosanitary measure is applied only to the extent necessary to protect human, animal or plant life or health, is based on scientific principles and is not maintained without sufficient scientific evidence, except as provided for in paragraph 7 of Article 5.

The referred Article 5.7 further provides that:

> In cases where relevant scientific evidence is insufficient, a Member may provisionally adopt sanitary or phytosanitary measures on the basis of available pertinent information, including that from the relevant international organizations as well as from sanitary or phytosanitary measures applied by other Members. In such circumstances, Members shall seek to obtain the additional information necessary for a more objective assessment of risk and review the sanitary or phytosanitary measure accordingly within a reasonable period of time.

It is important to note that Article 5.1 elaborates on Article 2.2 and directs Members as follows:

> Members shall ensure that their sanitary or phytosanitary measures are based on an assessment, as appropriate to the circumstances, of the risks to human, animal or plant life or health, taking into account risk assessment techniques developed by the relevant international organisations.

In *Japan-Apples*, the DSB had cause to consider whether a WTO Member could maintain SPS measures 'without sufficient scientific evidence' contrary to Article 2.2. The effect of Article 5.7 was also under consideration. The dispute had been brought by the United States. The US contended that Japan's maintenance of quarantine restrictions which Japan had adopted for the protection against the introduction of fire blight were contrary to certain provisions of the SPS Agreement. The AB upheld the Panel's finding that the measures were contrary to Articles 2.2, 5.7 and 5.1 of the SPS Agreement.

The Panel had found that scientific evidence suggested only a negligible risk of possible transmission of fire blight through apple fruit,[19] and that the same scientific evidence did not establish that apples are likely to serve as a pathway for the entry, establishment or spread of fire blight within Japan.[20] In its view, a measure is maintained 'without sufficient scientific evidence' within the meaning of Article 2.2 of the *SPS Agreement* if there is no 'rational or objective relationship' between the measure and the relevant scientific evidence.[21] The Panel was of the view that Japan's measure was clearly 'disproportionate' to the risk which the measures purported to contain.[22] Since such disproportion implied that a rational or objective relationship did not exist between the measure and the relevant scientific evidence, the Panel therefore concluded that Japan's measure was maintained 'without sufficient scientific evidence' within the meaning of Article 2.2 of the *SPS Agreement*.[23]

At appellate level, the AB referred to the decision in *Japan-Agricultural Products II* which had previously considered the application of the provisions of Article 5.7.[24] To this end, the AB reiterated that four elements had to be present to 'maintain a provisional phytosanitary measure':[25]

(i)   the measure is imposed in respect of a situation where "relevant scientific evidence is insufficient";
(ii) the measure is adopted "on the basis of available pertinent information";
(iii) the Member which adopted the measure "seek[s] to obtain the additional information necessary for a more objective assessment of risk"; and
(iv) the Member which adopted the measure "review[s] the ... measure accordingly within a reasonable period of time".[26]

The AB noted that these four requirements are 'clearly cumulative in nature'.[27] Referring to the AB in *Japan-Agricultural Products II*, it reiterated that 'whenever *one* of these four requirements is not met, the measure at issue is inconsistent with Article 5.7.'[28]

In addition, the AB noted that the particular methodology adopted for a determination of whether a measure is maintained without sufficient scientific evidence depends on the individual circumstances of a particular complaint. In its words,

> We emphasize, following the Appellate Body's statement in *Japan – Agricultural Products II*, that whether a given approach or methodology is appropriate in order to assess whether a measure is maintained "without sufficient scientific evidence", within the meaning of Article 2.2, depends on the "particular circumstances of the case", and must be "determined on a case-by-case basis". [29]

In its submissions on appeal, (in the instant case, *Japan-Apples*) Japan had argued that the Panel should have made its assessment under Article 2.2 in the light of Japan's approach to risk and scientific evidence. It was of the opinion that the Panel had erred by considering the view of the experts which the former had consulted in order to determine whether the US had established a *prima facie* case. Japan was of the view that deference ought to have been given to the Japanese scientific assessment of the risk involved in the imports.

The AB disagreed.[30] Recalling the *EC-Hormones case*, it noted that as regards fact-finding by panels and the assessment of scientific evidence, total deference to the findings of the national authorities would not ensure an objective assessment as required by Article 11 of the DSU. Other opinion including expert opinion by the Panel was also admissible in order to determine the scientific basis of an SPS measure.[31] This is to ensure that as the Panel in the *EC-Biotech* case reiterated following the AB in *EC-Hormones*, an SPS measure must be 'sufficiently warranted by', 'reasonably supported by', or 'rationally related to' the risk assessment.[32]

Whereas Article 5 of the Agreement requires all Members to ensure that their SPS measures are based on a risk assessment appropriate to the circumstances under which the measures were made, it must be noted that the risk assessment to be made must be in line with the requirements of paragraph 4 of Annex A in the SPS Agreement. In addition, a risk assessment must not necessarily be carried out by a Member State itself. It could be carried out by another Member State or by an international organisation.[33] In the EC-Hormones case, it was emphasised that a risk assessment could also 'set out both the prevailing view representing the "mainstream" of scientific opinion as well as the opinions of scientists taking a divergent view'.[34] Thus a risk assessment need not 'come to a monolithic conclusion that coincides with the scientific condition or view implicit in the SPS measure'.[35]

In Annex A, the SPS Agreement defines a risk assessment as follows:

> *Risk assessment-* The evaluation of the likelihood of entry, establishment or spread of a pest or disease within the territory of an importing Member according to the sanitary or phytosanitary measures which might be applied, and of the associated potential biological and economic consequences; or the evaluation of the potential for adverse effects on human or animal health arising from the presence of additives, contaminants, toxins or disease-causing organisms in food, beverages or feedstuffs.[36]

These factors were elaborated upon in *Australia-Salmon* where the AB identified certain factors necessary for a risk assessment. Accordingly, a risk assessment must:

(1) *identify* the diseases whose entry, establishment or spread a Member wants to prevent within its territory, as well as the potential biological and economic consequences associated with the entry, establishment or spread of these diseases;

(2) *evaluate the likelihood* of entry, establishment or spread of these diseases, as well as the associated potential biological and economic consequences; and

(3) evaluate the likelihood of entry, establishment or spread of these diseases *according to the SPS measures which might be applied.*[37]

Applying the principles laid down by the AB above, in *Japan-Apples*, the AB did not agree that Japan's 1999 Pest Risk Analysis under which the restrictions against apples were made satisfied the requirements of a risk assessment as above. According to the AB, Japan's Pest Risk Analysis: '(i) fails to "evaluate the likelihood of entry, establishment or spread of " the plant disease at issue, and (ii) fails to conduct such an evaluation "according to the SPS measures which might be applied" '.[38] Its risk assessment procedure was thus held to be contrary to the collective rights and obligations under Articles 2.2, 5.7, and 5.1 of the Agreement.

1.1.3. Adapting SPS Measures to Regional Conditions

Article 6 of the Agreement counsels Members to adapt their SPS measures to the SPS characteristics of the area, both of the area from which the product originates and the area to which the product is destined. Article 6.1 specifically provides that:

> Members shall ensure that their sanitary or phytosanitary measures are adapted to the sanitary or phytosanitary characteristics of the area – whether all of a country, part of a country, or all or parts of several countries – from which the product originated and to which the product is destined. In assessing the sanitary and phytosanitary characteristics of a region, Members shall take into account, *inter alia*, the prevalence of specific disease or pests, the existence of eradication or control programmes, and appropriate criteria or guidelines which may be developed by the relevant international organisations.

Members are however cautioned to recognise the concepts of pest-or disease-free areas and areas of low pest or disease prevalence,[39] and exporting members claiming that areas within their territories are compliant with this concept need to provide evidence to the demonstrate this.[40]

The implications for international trade are obvious. An exporting Member could insist without reasonable proof that its products are pest or disease free and have been produced in risk-free areas and conditions. On the other hand, an importing country could insist on an arbitrary list of requirements or for inspection and testing procedures which are merely designed to frustrate the export. The challenges posed by Article 6 have given rise to recurrent issues dealt with at Committee level. In a 2006 meeting of the Committee,[41] these issues were set out and rigorously debated with a view to addressing the difficulties faced by Members both as exporting and as importing countries in tackling SPS measures which are not adapted to regional conditions. Key issues raised at this meeting include the following points:

1. Difficulties posed by procedures and guidelines for the implementation of recognition of the concept of regionalisation including procedures for ensuring that areas in an exporting country are risk free. These will include eradication processes for diseases or pests, the emergency preparedness of a country to contain the speed of a disease or pest and contingency plans for outbreaks, surveillance and maintenance systems and, the need to involve producers, businesses, professionals and the public sector in action towards achieving risk free status.

2. The unpredictable element in obtaining a time frame for recognition of risk free areas by an importing country. This refers in some measure to the bureaucracy involved in obtaining approval from the relevant authorities in an importing country for products certified risk free to be exported, or to communicate that an importing country is not satisfied with the SPS protection in an exporting country so as to enable the exporter make necessary adjustments.

3. The adoption of new measures or a change in old ones demand transparency in both exporting and importing countries so that relevant information on procedures for recognising an area as risk free are immediately available.

4. The general difficulties faced in the recognition of regions by international setting standards bodies and by Members. This is especially significant for developing countries that have to meet up with long established standards which have been in practice in most developed countries. We agree with Finger and Schuler who note that:

> Although the SPS Agreement does not require that a country's *domestic standards* meet the agreements requirements, it does require that the standards the country applies *at the border* meet those requirements. In this regard, the agreement probably places a heavier burden on developing than on industrial countries because the standards already in place in industrial countries have more or less been established as the standard with which the developing countries must comply.[12]

These issues have been addressed by the SPS Committee in its *Guidelines to Further the Practical Implementation of Article 6 of the Agreement on the Application of Sanitary and Phytosanitary Measures*.[13] The document asks that Members should publish the basis for the recognition of risk free areas. It also directs Members to describe the processes used in the assessment, and to ensure that a contact point is in place to make the information available to other Member States. WTO Members are expected to provide a feedback on their experiences and to inform the Committee of such background information as is relevant. The Secretariat is in turn directed to prepare an Annual Report for the Committee based on the Members' experiences with the implementation of Article 6.

More recently, the Committee has set out non-binding guidelines on the concept of regionalisation which enhance and elaborate on the above.[44] These guidelines build on Members' proposals (particularly those by Chile and Australia) for the Committee to develop administrative guidelines, distinct from scientific guidelines to be clarified by the relevant international organisations, for the purpose of facilitating the implementation of Article 6.[45] In its Preamble, the Committee states that it has formulated the guidelines in collaboration with the IPPC and the OIE.

Under these guidelines, Members' States' decisions under Article 6 should consider the strength and credibility of the veterinary or phytosanitary infrastructure of the exporting Member in accordance with the importing Member's appropriate level of SPS protection (Sec.8). Initial discussions including general information on processes used by the importing Member should take place within a reasonable period of time (90 days), or as mutually decided, or as agreed in the event of a postponement (Secs.15/17).

Nine administrative steps are set out for a determination under Article 6 pursuant to Secs 20–31 of the Committee Guidelines:

A – Exporting Member requests information about procedure or recognitions. Requests for recognition of a pest- or disease-free area may be supported with scientific or technical information including reference to international recognition.

B – Importing Member explains requests.

C – Exporting Member provides documentation.

D – Importing Member evaluates the documentations and if necessary requests additional information.

E – Exporting Member responds to feedback.

F – Importing Member evaluates any additional information and if required seeks further clarification.

G – Importing Member conducts on-site verification.

H – Exporting Member responds to inspection request.

I – Importing Member makes a determination.

An Expedited Process can be undertaken under Sec. 32 where there has been official recognition of a free area; where an outbreak of pests or diseases has been previously recognised and suspended; where both importing and exporting members have similar veterinary or phytosanitary service; and where importing member agrees that there has been no previously notified occurrence of (the) pests or disease.

The Committee undertakes the responsibility of monitoring the implementation of these guidelines under Sec 33 even as it reminds Members in Sec 1 that:

> These guidelines are intended to provide assistance to Members in the practical implementation of Article 6 by improving transparency, exchange of information, predictability, confidence and credibility between importing and exporting Members. These guidelines are not intended to duplicate the technical and administrative guidance provided to Members by the IPPC and OIE.

1.1.4. Transparency

The SPS Agreement also demands that a Member State's adopted measures must be 'transparent'. Article 7 of the Agreement provides that 'Members shall notify changes in their sanitary or phytosanitary measures and shall provide information on their sanitary or phytosanitary measures in accordance with the provisions of Annex B'. The provisions of Annex B on *'Transparency of Sanitary and Phytosanitary Regulations'* request Members to publish all laws, decrees or ordinances which are applicable to SPS measures they have adopted.[46] 'Enquiry points' with the responsibility of providing answers to all reasonable questions from interested Members are also to be set up and relevant documents relating to such Members should be made available at the enquiry point.[47] Adopted SPS measures should also be notified to the Secretariat in English, French or Spanish and Members are to designate a 'single central government authority' as responsible for the implementation, at national levels, of the provisions concerning notification procedures under Annex B.[48]

The question of the scope of instruments which need to be published under the transparency provisions was considered in *Japan-Agricultural Products II*. In this respect, the focus was on Japan's SPS measures that established a testing requirement for the approval of additional varieties of certain agricultural products which were hitherto placed under import prohibition. The SPS measures served to avert the potential hosts of codling moths. The United States who brought the complaint alleged that Japan prohibited the importation of each variety of a product requiring quarantine treatment until the quarantine treatment had been tested for that variety, even if the treatment had proved to be effective for other varieties of the same product. The US contended that the testing requirement was not transparent in that no one Enquiry Point was responsible for the provision of answers to all reasonable questions from interested Members regarding the measure. Also, that there was no published source for the measure itself.[49] The Panel upheld the claims of the US.[50]

On appeal, Japan argued that the testing requirements were contained in its *Experimental Guide for Cultivar Comparison Test on Insect Mortality-Fumigation' (Experimental Guide)* which set out information requirements for varietal testing and which was not a legally enforceable instrument. It contended that the SPS regulations referred to in paragraph 1 of Annex B ought to mean laws, decrees and ordinances alone. The AB disagreed. In its opinion, the footnote to paragraph 1 of Annex B referred to SPS measures 'such as' laws, decrees or ordinances which are applicable generally. Therefore the list of instruments contained in the footnote to paragraph 1 of Annex B is 'as is indicated by the words "such as", not exhaustive in nature'.[51]

The AB noted as follows:

> The object and purpose of paragraph 1 of Annex B is "to enable interested Members to become acquainted with" the sanitary and phytosanitary regulations adopted or maintained by other Members and thus to enhance transparency regarding these measures. In our opinion, the scope of application of the publication requirement of paragraph 1 of Annex B should be interpreted in the light of the object and purpose of this provision.[52]

In light of this finding, the Agreement demands that any SPS regulation which is applicable generally, is mandatory, and is an import requirement of exporting countries, should be published.[53] The SPS Committee Decision, *Recommended Procedures for Implementing the Transparency Obligations of the SPS Agreement (Article 7)*[54] details certain requirements which Members should adopt in implementing the provisions of Article 7. The Recommendations have been adopted by the SPS Committee in the absence of objections by the prior agreed date of 30 May 2008.

The Recommendations in respect of the Transparency provisions of Article 7 again restate the importance of the transparency requirements for ease in ascertaining Members' SPS measures. However and commendably, a practical framework which harmonises the notification procedures is set out in the revised Recommendations effective from December 1, 2008.[55] Notifications on adopted SPS measures will therefore include such details as the notifying Member; the Agency responsible for promulgating the regulation; the tariff items and their numbers as contained in national schedules deposited with the WTO; the geographical regions or countries likely to be affected by the regulations; the title of the regulations; a summary of the SPS measures proposed or adopted clearly indicating the content and health protection objectives of the regulation. Members are also expected to indicate whether the regulations notified fall under the SPS or the TBT Agreement, respectively.

There must also be a clear statement of the objective and rationale of the regulation; whether the regulation conforms to a relevant international standard and in the alternative, the deviations from such international standards with the reasons for such deviations. Any other relevant documents including publications where the regulations appear or will appear should be indicated. Also website addresses or hyperlinks were the regulations will also be published or have been published should be indicated. Any charges for the supply of such material must also be included. Furthermore, the proposed date for the adoption and publication or the proposed date of entry into force is also requested on the Notification form. Final dates for comments from other WTO Members in line with the provisions of Annex B paragraph 5(b) of the SPS Agreement should be indicated. Members are encouraged to allow a period of at least sixty calendar days for comments although those Members who can comment on the notifications in less that sixty days are encouraged to do so.

For products of interest to developing country Members, a minimum of six months should be granted as time-exemption from the date of expected compliance with the regulations, where appropriate. There is however no reference to how this time exemption can be applied; whether the notifying authority would need to carry out inspections in the exporting country, or whether an importer can demand that a developing country producer or exporter should justify their need for time exemptions.

The proposals also demand identification of National Enquiry Points and of National Notification Authorities. Publication of SPS regulations on the internet is encouraged to reduce paper work and bureaucracy and make the documents more easily accessible to other Members. It also directs Members to international internet resources which could facilitate Members' access to SPS-related information.[56] Members are also encouraged to provide 'up-to-date information' on these international internet sites.[57] Furthermore, a format for emergency notifications is provided. In addition to the 'routine' notification procedure enumerated previously, a Member State must also indicate the underlying reasons for resorting to emergency action where this is relevant. Examples could be where a Member State experiences an incursion of pests associated with imports or where there is an outbreak of disease in supplying areas.

Procedures for the notification of determination of the recognition of equivalence of sanitary and phytosanitary measures are also indicated. These include a formal indication of the notifying Member; the title of the text stating the determination of equivalence and any associated procedures and regulations, and a mention of the parties involved. Other requirements include a statement of the products covered by the measures and a description of the measures recognised to be equivalent. The Member State using the procedure must also provide information as to where any further information pertaining to the notification on equivalence can be obtained. This could be from the National Enquiry Point or any other agency as indicated.

From the above, it is clear that the Committee places emphasis on the importance of national authorities concerned with SPS measures. Notification Authorities and Enquiry Points are necessary for the effective and practical implementation of the terms of the SPS Agreements. Not only for the information of foreign producers of goods and services, local manufacture and export of foods, pharmaceuticals, drugs, etc fall within the scope of influence of these agencies of national governments. We shall return to the work of national authorities later on in our study of the Nigerian experience.

1.1.5. Control, Approval and Inspection Procedures

Control, inspection, and approval procedures for SPS measures must satisfy the requirements of Annex C of the Agreement. Article 8 provides that:

> Members shall observe the provisions of Annex C in the operation of control, inspection and approval procedures, including national systems for approving the use of additives or for establishing tolerances for contaminants in foods, beverages or feedstuffs, and otherwise ensure that their procedures are not inconsistent with the provisions of this Agreement.[58]

Under Annex C, control, inspection and approval procedures include *inter alia*, procedures for sampling, testing and certification. Such procedures should not be discriminatory between imports and domestic products.[59] The standard processing period for each procedure should be published and undertaken without undue delay.[60] Information requirements are limited to what is necessary for appropriate control, approval and inspection procedures[61] Requirements for individual specimen of a product is limited to what is reasonable and necessary.[62] Members should also ensure that a procedure exists to review complaints concerning the operation of such procedures and to take corrective action when a complaint is justified.[63] Finally, where an SPS measure specifies control at the level of production, the Member in whose territory the production takes place shall provide the necessary assistance to facilitate such control and the work of the controlling authorities.[64]

1.1.6. Expert Opinion

Especially in this matter of public health, the relevance of expert opinion must be acknowledged. As the SPS Agreement demands scientific justification for measures undertaken pursuant to the Agreement, the opinion of experts is particularly relevant in the event of a dispute before the DSB. The Panel in the *Hormones case* sought such opinion pursuant to Articles 11.2 (SPS Agreement) and Article 13.2 and Appendix 4 DSU. Article 11.2 of the SPS Agreement provides that:

> In a dispute under this Agreement involving scientific or technical issues, a panel should seek advice from experts chosen by the panel in consultation with the parties to the dispute. To this end, the panel may, when it deems it appropriate, establish an advisory technical experts group, or consult the relevant international organizations, at the request of either party to the dispute or on its own initiative.

The relevant parts of Article 13.2 DSU provide as follows:

1. Each panel shall have the right to seek information and technical advice from any individual or body which it deems appropriate…
2. Panels may seek information from any relevant source and may consult experts to obtain their opinion on certain aspects of the matter. With respect to a factual issue concerning a scientific or other technical matter raised by a party to the dispute, a panel *may* request an advisory report in writing from an experts review group.

The Panel decided to request the opinion of experts on certain scientific and other technical matters raised by the Parties to the dispute. Rather than establishing an experts' review group, it considered it more useful to avail itself of the opinion of experts given in an individual capacity. According to the Panel,

> We considered, however, that neither Article 11.2 of the SPS Agreement nor Article 13.2 of the DSU limits our right to seek information from *individual* experts as provided for in Article 11.2, first sentence, of the SPS Agreement and Articles 13.1 and 13.2, first sentence, of the DSU.[65]

On appeal, the AB found nothing wrong with this practice. It stated as follows:

> We find that in disputes involving scientific or technical issues, neither Article 11.2 of the *SPS Agreement*, nor Article 13 of the DSU prevents

panels from consulting with individual experts. Rather, both the *SPS Agreement* and the DSU leave to the sound discretion of a panel the determination of whether the establishment of an expert review group is necessary or appropriate.[66]

Therefore, in its view, 'once the panel has decided to request the opinion of individual experts, there is no legal obstacle to the panel drawing up, in consultation with the parties to the dispute, ad hoc rules for those particular proceedings'.[67]

1.2. The Development Paradigm of the SPS Agreement

There is no doubt that developing countries stand to make welfare gains from effective implementation of SPS measures in their domestic legal framework; compliance with the respective SPS standards of their trading partners, and fulfilling their own obligations under the Agreement. Yet however logical and reasonable such advances may be for public health protection, the challenges of matching sophisticated R&D advances in food safety and environmental protection and of meeting the many standards both under the SPS Agreement and those set out by private bodies or importing countries, are only too real for developing countries particularly the least developed among them.[68]

The ability and capacity of developing countries to comply with their obligations under the Agreement appears at least on the surface, to be inversely proportional to their level of scientific and technological advancement. On closer observation, in the light of the limitations identified in Chapter Two in our discussions on Developing Country Integration, this view is not far from the truth. The requirement of a scientific justification which underlies the SPS Agreement is a requirement that developing countries given their level of social advancement cannot immediately satisfy. With agriculture in particular, the modern world has consistently been moving farther away from the dependence on staple goods and seasonal produce to increased consumption of new and improved varieties of food and agricultural produce sometimes giving rise to a decline in the market price obtainable for erstwhile staples.

Outbreaks of pests and diseases including those previously thought to have been eradicated demand stronger counter action both to eliminate the pests or diseases but also to contain the contamination of adjacent areas in places of infection. Countries face the further problem of proving that other foods, plants or animals including those offered for trade have not been contaminated. Where contamination has already occurred, these produce have to be recalled occasioning severe losses to the exporting countries' producers. Consumers likewise suffer in the face of a limited supply in the market.[69]

Implementation of the SPS Agreement in the domestic realm is thus doubly challenging for developing countries who struggle with the demands of technical and scientific know-how needed in order to make the gains from this Agreement. Nevertheless the SPS Committee notes that developing countries join other Members in raising 'Specific Trade Concerns' under the Agreement. It points out that over the thirteen years since the adoption of the SPS Agreement developing countries have been active participants in the workings of the Committee. Although their participation has not been on the same level as that of developed countries who have in the same period raised 179 trade concerns, supported 120, and have had 169 complaints on measures maintained by them; developing countries have raised 126 issues, supported 177, and have had 125 complaints on measures adopted by them.[70]

The real impact on developing Members on the application of the SPS Agreement can be assessed by the impact of the SDT provisions under the Agreement, and the extent to which technical assistance in response to their needs and concerns are provided to developing countries. The establishment and activities of both enquiry points and national notification authorities are also a measure of determining the compliance with the provisions of the Agreement in the domestic environment.

1.2.1. Special and Differential Treatment

Bearing in mind the importance of maintaining human, animal, and plant health and safety, the notion of special treatment for developing countries in this particular area of WTO rule making seems extremely accommodating. Why make exceptions on issues of universal importance? Surely food safety and the protection of animal and plant health ought to be more important than responding to political pressure to keep developing countries happy?

At the beginning of the Agreement, the Preamble notes that the WTO recognises:

> that developing country Members may encounter special difficulties in complying with the sanitary or phytosanitary measures of importing Members, and as a consequence in access to markets, and also in the formulation and application of sanitary or phytosanitary measures in their own territories, and desiring to assist them in their endeavours in this regard.

We may breakdown the promises of this statement to read that the WTO wishes to assist developing countries in:

(a) complying with SPS measures of importing Members;

(b) gaining access to markets further to (a) above;
(c) formulating and applying SPS measure in their own territories; and
(d) assisting them in their endeavours in respect of action above.

The special treatment in the WTO rules which ought to guide these four areas of special assistance under the SPS Agreement above, are set out in Article 10 of the Agreement. The Article provides:

1. In the preparation and application of sanitary or phytosanitary measures, Members shall take account of the special needs of developing country Members, and in particular of the least-developed country Members.
2. Where the appropriate level of sanitary or phytosanitary protection allows scope for the phased introduction of new sanitary or phytosanitary measures, longer time-frames for compliance should be accorded on products of interest to developing country Members so as to maintain opportunities for their exports.[71]
3. With a view to ensuring that developing country Members are able to comply with the provisions of this Agreement, the Committee is enabled to grant to such countries, upon request, specified, time-limited exceptions in whole or in part from obligations under this Agreement, taking into account their financial, trade and development needs.
4. Members should encourage and facilitate the active participation of developing country Members in the relevant international organizations.

The recommendations of the General Council under the Doha Work Programme that SDT measures be reviewed, including those under the SPS Agreement, have not brought any changes as yet to Article 10 of the SPS Agreement. However there have been some proposals referred to the Committee for the review of SDTs under the SPS Agreement. For instance, one proposal included a request that the phrase 'take account of the special needs of developing country Members, and in particular least developed country Members' under Article 10.1 should be interpreted to mean that members shall either withdraw measures that adversely affect any developing and least-developed country Members or which they find difficult to comply with, or shall provide the technical and financial resources necessary for the latter countries to enable them to comply with the measures.[72] Another proposal was that Members should initiate consultations whenever they decide to adopt any measures likely to affect developing countries and, establish whether these measures if justified by the Agreement, would be adverse to the interests of developing countries.[73]

In addition to the establishment of a facility to be established within the Global Trust Fund to assist developing countries in utilising the flexibilities under the SPS Agreement, the proposals also asked that technical and financial assistance to developing countries should be made cost free.[74] Article 10.4 was also to be made normative and not remain as an exhortatory provision.[75]

We find these proposals curious and yet enlightening. We have already commented on the vagueness and exhortatory nature of the SDT provisions across the WTO Agreements. We have also commented on the need for specific proposals to be made by developing countries: proposals which would be coherent and address practical areas of concern rather than general impracticable suggestions also reflected in the proposals enumerated above. We are therefore not surprised that the response by the Committee on these proposals was that it 'has to date been unable to develop any clear recommendations for a decision on the proposals on special and differential treatment referred to it by the General Council.'[76]

We consider that of the four SDT provisions in the SPS Agreement cited above, one is specific and has a clear direction: the SPS Committee powers to grant to developing countries 'upon request', time limited exceptions from the obligations of the Agreement. Respective developing countries, each according to his 'financial, trade and development needs' could seek exceptions to the Agreement. It would have been more illuminating to find how the Committee has exercised this flexibility for developing countries if the latter had made any use of it. Incidentally, to date, no such request has been received by the Committee.[77]

What is clear is that for developing countries to make any real gains under the SPS Agreement, assistance in their administrative and infrastructural environment is fundamental.[78] However, while the SDT provisions may not have recorded any significant successes, developing country needs and concerns have received better attention under the technical assistance provisions and the activities arising there from.

1.2.2. Technical Assistance

Article 9 of the SPS Agreement provides for the grant of technical assistance to developing Members. It states as follows:

1. Members agree to facilitate the provision of technical assistance to other Members, especially developing country Members, either bilaterally or through the appropriate international organizations. Such assistance may be, *inter alia*, in the areas of processing technologies, research and infrastructure, including in the establishment of national regulatory bodies, and may take the form of advice, credits, donations and grants, including for the purpose of seeking technical expertise, training and equipment to allow such countries

to adjust to, and comply with, sanitary or phytosanitary measures necessary to achieve the appropriate level of sanitary or phytosanitary protection in their export markets.

2. Where substantial investments are required in order for an exporting developing country Member to fulfil the sanitary or phytosanitary requirements of an importing Member, the latter shall consider providing such technical assistance as will permit the developing country Member to maintain and expand its market access opportunities for the product involved.

The above provisions confirm that Members agree to facilitate the provision of technical assistance to other Members, especially developing country Members. Such assistance may be bilateral, or through appropriate international organisations. The assistance may be in the area of research and infrastructure, processing technologies, technical expertise, training and equipment, and other measures to allow such countries adjust to, and comply with, sanitary or phytosanitary measures necessary to achieve the appropriate level of sanitary or phytosanitary protection in their export markets. In the event that a developing country Member would require substantial investments in order to fulfil the SPS requirements of an importing Member, 'the latter shall consider providing such technical assistance as will permit the developing country Member to maintain and expand its market access opportunities for the product involved'.[79]

Scott notes that Article 9 is 'conspicuously weak, though it is expressed in mandatory form'.[80] The weakness of this provision is better understood in the background of Article 13 of the Agreement which establishes the full responsibility of Members including the non-governmental entities within the domestic system and other government bodies apart from the central government itself. Article 13 provides:

Members are fully responsible under this Agreement for the observance of all obligations set forth herein. Members shall formulate and implement positive measures and mechanisms in support of the observance of the provisions of this Agreement by other than central government bodies. Members shall take such reasonable measures as may be available to them to ensure that non-governmental entities within their territories, as well as regional bodies in which relevant entities within their territories are members, comply with the relevant provisions of this Agreement. In addition, Members shall not take measures which have the effect of, directly or indirectly, requiring or encouraging such regional or non-governmental entities, or local governmental bodies, to act in a manner inconsistent with the provisions of this Agreement. Members shall ensure that they rely on the services of non-governmental entities for implementing sanitary or phytosanitary measures only if these entities comply with the provisions of this Agreement.

The obligations under the SPS Agreement for which Article 9 creates opportunities for technical assistance therefore do not stop with the responsibility of the government itself. Beyond its own activities, government must also intervene in potentially trade restrictive activities of non-governmental or regional bodies as they relate to SPS measures in order to ensure compliance with the SPS obligations. Such other bodies are not explicitly defined although Scott suggests that reference to the definitions under Annex 1 of the TBT Agreement ought to suffice.[81]

With neo-democratic institutions and indefinite political systems of developing countries which appear and disappear depending on the structure and focus of an incumbent head or party, there will of course be difficulties for a WTO Member State who has to both financially and institutionally, support the adoption and implementation of SPS measures across the various strata of institutions identified in Article 13. On the other hand of course, it may be easier for an autocratic government to insist on the observance of all obligations under the SPS Agreement within its domestic territory, though it may then alienate other actors in the domestic public health and safety arena. In any event, the extensive and interwoven dependency on the central government as it implements the SPS Agreement is one which iterates the necessity of technical assistance to developing country Members.

Unfortunately, neither developing countries nor their developed trading partners nor even the SPS Committee has been able to come to an agreement on what technical assistance (and the means of achieving this) is best suited to developing country problems. Certainly, the diverse circumstances of developing countries may be to blame, as one form of assistance may not be deemed suitable to another's circumstances. However, the problem is slightly more problematic that this. The proposals which have come from some developing countries, and ostensibly put forward in the background of their needs and concerns, have not been well received in the political negotiating atmosphere of the WTO. It is not difficult to see why.

Such proposals include that by the African Group below which focus on making Article 9.2 of the SPS Agreement mandatory,[82] and a request that developed countries should provide technical assistance for SPS requirements when needed by an exporting developing country in order to enable the latter to address 'specific problems of inadequate technology and infrastructure'.[83] The salient parts of this proposal are:

If an exporting developing country Member identifies specific problems of inadequate technology and infrastructure in fulfilling the sanitary or phytosanitary requirements of an importing developed country Member, the latter shall provide the former with relevant technology and technical facilities on preferential and non-commercial terms, preferably free of cost, keeping in view the development, financial and trade needs of the exporting developing country.

Where the importing Member does not actually provide such technical assistance, that Member shall withdraw the measures immediately and unconditionally; or the importing Member shall compensate the exporting developing country Members for loss resulting directly or indirectly from the measures.

It is understood that technical assistance shall be fully funded technical assistance and shall not entail financial obligations on the part of the exporting developing and least-developed country Members.

It is agreed that the WTO shall recommend that impact assessments shall be conducted to determine the likely effect on the trade of developing and least-developed country Members for any proposed standards before adoption, and if the impact would be adverse, the standards would not become applicable until it is established that developing and least-developed country Members that would be affected have acquired the capacity to beneficially comply with them.

It is no wonder that the SPS Committee noted in its conclusions in respect of these and other proposals by developing countries that:

these discussions have revealed an "expectations gap" between Members. All Members acknowledge that better-targeted and more effective technical assistance aimed at specific results will benefit developing country Members. This can, however, only be achieved by more successful communications and competent teamwork among involved Members. This commitment appears necessary to, at minimum, maintain the market access opportunities for products from developing country Members.[84]

Irrespective of the difficulties in identifying elements for a future discussion on technical assistance by the Committee, there have been important developments since the launch of the Doha Development Round.[85] In addition to various events including workshops, information sessions, technical assistance and capacity building seminars for developing country government officials organised by the WTO Secretariat, a joint initiative on coordination and funding mechanism operates at the international level. The Standards and Trade Development Facility (STDF) is a joint effort by the World Health Organisation (WHO), the World Bank, the World Organisation for Animal Health and, the Food and Agricultural Organisation (FAO). It was established in July 2002. The initiative asserts that 'in addition to facilitating international trade, SPS capacity building can result in improved human and agricultural health conditions for local markets and so favour economic and social development'.[86]

The value of the STDF as one of the mechanisms under the AFT Initiative in the current Doha Round has been reinforced by the WTO DG, Pascal Lamy. He points out that:

> completion of the Doha Development Agenda negotiations will further reduce obstacles to trade. We all know however, that the benefits of trade opening do not automatically flow to all. Various 'supply side constraints' can get in the way; compliance with sanitary and phytosanitary measures is one example. In this scientifically complex area, the STDF is a mechanism by which the promise of trade can be turned into reality. The STDF is an example of Aid For Trade in action.[87]

This view by the DG finds expression in the strategic aims of the STDF. These are:

• to assist developing countries enhance their expertise and capacity to analyze and to implement international sanitary and phytosanitary (SPS) standards, improving their human, animal and plant health situation, and thus ability to gain and maintain market access; and
• to act as a vehicle for co-ordination among technical co-operation providers, the mobilization of funds, the exchange of experience and the dissemination of good practice in relation to the provision and receipt of SPS-related technical co-operation.[88]

More recently, specific assistance measures have been proposed at the Committee which to a great extent has seen a lot of efforts aimed at bridging the gap between developing countries and their developed trading partners. An example is the recent proposal on the establishment of a 'mentoring system' to assist developing country Members in the operation of their SPS National Notification Authorities (NNA) and their National Enquiry Points (NEP).[89] The 'voluntary procedure' is established with the objective of assisting Members, and in particular developing country Members, 'to implement their obligations with respect to the transparency provisions of the SPS Agreement and to benefit as fully as possible from these provisions'.[90] The proposal offers a detailed reference to the available assistance including support through providing information and assistance via email or telephone on specific issues, legislative guidance, hands-on workshop and in-house training, amongst others.

Members are advised to be as specific as possible on the assistance to be given or received, whether they are volunteering as Mentors or, requesting assistance. Such specificity could be in respect of the development of an internal process to ensure that all relevant draft measures are notified in a timely manner; the preparation and submission of comments on notification; the establishment of a national web site; development of a training programme; and completion of notification formats. The duration of need of assistance, the regions from which Members would prefer to receive assistance, and any constraints on receiving assistance from specific Members are further details to be set out in the request.

With improved technical assistance procedures such as the new proposal mentioned above, challenges on the application and implementation of the SPS Agreement would gradually be reduced for developing country producers. However, there is no doubt that technical assistance for developing countries facing the challenges of fulfilling the SPS measures of importing countries is imperative particularly for the private sector who may not have first hand information of the operation of the SPS Agreement. A WTO case study on 'Nepal: Exports of Ayuverdic Herbal Remedies and SPS Issues'[91] highlights these challenges.

In August 2000, an order for processed medicinal herbs was cancelled by the Swedish importers of a Nepal based company producing ayuverdic herbal remedies. The cancellation was due to the fact that the company's product sample did not pass the 'satisfactory and sufficient' sanitary and quality standard tests for access to the Swedish market. The importer also required a certificate of good manufacturing practice (GMP)[92] for each consignment.

In October 2001, a Sydney based importer made an order for the same goods from the Nepalese company. However contrary to the Swedish importer, the Sydney-based firm requested only a general sample test for the products which were exported in the form of a single ingredient in powder form, before export to Sydney. The exporter could not reconcile these differences between the two importers. He therefore sought assistance from the relevant Enquiry and Notification offices in Nepal.

The main problem encountered by the Nepalese company here were in four respects. First, the company had no previous knowledge of the requirements for a specific test and a GMP certificate needed in order to export its products. Second, the Nepalese government drug quality control authority, the Royal Drug Research Laboratory (RDLR), and the Department of Food Technology and Quality Control (DFTQC), had no policy framework on SPS Standards relevant to the ayuverdic industry. Third, the sophisticated tests required by the Swedish importer were not easily available in Nepal.[93] Another problem which was even more directly inhibiting was the absence of private sector interaction with the national government. This meant that the needs and concerns of local businesses, both producers and exporters, were not being brought to the attention of the government even as the latter undertook the international obligations under the SPS Agreement on Nepal's accession to the WTO.

Some solutions to such problems for private sector participation can be found in the comments of the Nepalese business owner in respect of the application of the SPS rules:

> The private sector should also benefit from the technical assistance, as it had an immense role to play in the awareness and business advocacy on Nepal's entry into the WTO and its commitment to the SPS mechanism. Many stakeholders, including the business community, thought they did not have roles to play in the multilateral trading system. They need to be able to understand the possibility of unfavourable consequences in international business if trade rules are not well understood.
>
> There were two things to be done urgently in this regard. First of all there should have been regular government-private-sector interactions to exchange their views on the multilateral trading system. One of the objectives of the purpose should have been to listen to the voice and concerns of the Nepalese business community. However, that would not have been achieved until the private-sector associations came forward to lead in their respective fields.[94]

1.2.3. Private Standards

The difficulties posed by private organisations in contrast to the focus on national and international standards envisioned under the SPS Agreement, are increasingly prominent.[95] Such private bodies and organisations include supermarket chains and private groups who demand particular standards beyond those set by international multilateral organisations. Alerting to this fact, the World Organisation for Animal Health (OIE) state that 'some private standards relate to sanitary measures (plant health, animal health and food safety), some cover animal welfare, and others address issues such as protection of the environment and labour practices.'[96] The effect on developing countries of such private standards was set out as follows:

> Many studies have noted that the main problem with private standards is the relatively high cost of certification required, which is particularly burdensome for small producers and there are many more small producers in developing countries. Another concern is that many private standards tend to require the use of specific processing and testing techniques that are based on state-of-the-art technologies not available

(or too costly) for small producers. A further concern that has emerged from studies is that export consignments from many developing countries are consolidated from many small producers – and some of the private schemes require that the individual producer be certified, rather than accepting certification of exporters in aggregate.

In addition, developing countries are often less capable of mounting arguments against measures that are considered to be inconsistent with SPS obligations. Big companies in developed countries tend to be proactive in seeking market opportunities. Through intensive market research, such companies may find out about private standards and fairly quickly take steps to meet them or seek modifications that allow them to comply, while small enterprises and those in developing countries may be unaware of the existence of private standards, or learn about them long after their competitors, by which time both the opportunity to present alternative approaches and the potential market access have been lost.[97]

The introduction of private standards therefore include standards which may link imports with a producer's level of environmental activity, or a producer's corporate practices and labour standards, bringing in issues which fall outside the ambit of the SPS Agreement. For example, private bodies such as GLOBALGAP with its Good Agricultural Practice (GAP) standard, outlines several 'Terms of Reference' for its standards setting activities. It claims that its standard is primarily designed to reassure consumers about how food is produced on the farm 'by minimising detrimental environmental impacts of farming operations, reducing the use of chemical inputs and ensuring a responsible approach to worker health and safety as well as animal welfare'.[98] Membership is, 'open to any organization agreeing to the Terms of Reference'.[99]

The OIE'S argument against the rising reach of private standards is extremely important. International, science-based standards and guidelines are already accessible and pursuant to the SPS Agreement, should be applied by Member States whether as acceptable international guidelines (Article 3); as equivalent measures of other trading states which achieve an importing Member's appropriate level of sanitary and phytosanitary protection; or under the exception in Article 5.7 where a Member provisionally adopts an SPS measure on the basis of available pertinent information.

The introduction of new private standards will be inherently arbitrary as they will seek to apply restrictive measures to goods which do not fulfil the standards they set out. But, if the obligation of the WTO is to free trade as it is, it is difficult to determine the legality of any action attempting to limit these private standards-setting activities. Apart from the fact that private persons are not involved in the WTO dispute settlement procedures there is the further question of consumer choice. With the increased agitation on climate change and environmental protection including the activities of animal rights groups, insisting on WTO approved guidelines alone as the OIE submission intends, will essentially overreach to restricting the choice of consumers and their agents (here, we mean supermarket chains and shops) to decide what kind of goods they wish to purchase.

The OIE submission urges 'countries, regional organisations and international organisations to strongly support the OIE's standards, including its recommendations on animal welfare, as the appropriate references for the purposes of international trade'.[100] We are not entirely convinced of the purposes suggested for this submission which allegedly are for the harmonisation of, and continued reference to, international scientific guidelines as acknowledged by the WTO. There is no question that should private standards increase as they may well likely do, the impact will not only be on the developing countries per se, but on a declining reference to international organisations such as the OIE whose functions may well become redundant in the foreseeable future. Increased demand by consumers and the ability of producers and exporters to meet these demands will drive the market for any good including those which are covered by SPS measures in the international market.

Furthermore and speaking generally, private standards setting has not always proved harmful to developing country exports. We may examine the application of private standards under the TBT Agreement specifically, the impact of 'FAIRTRADE' labelled goods on international trade with respect to the enhancement of production activity in developing countries. Article 2 of the TBT Agreement on the *Preparation, Adoption and Application of Technical Regulations by Central Government Bodies* provides variously as follows:

2.2 Members shall ensure that technical regulations are not prepared, adopted or applied with a view to or with the effect of creating unnecessary obstacles to international trade. For this purpose, technical regulations shall not be more trade-restrictive than necessary to fulfil a legitimate objective, taking account of the risks non-fulfilment would create. Such legitimate objectives are, *inter alia*: national security requirements; the prevention of deceptive practices; protection of human health or safety, animal or plant life or health, or the environment. In assessing such risks, relevant elements of consideration are, *inter alia*: available scientific and technical information, related processing technology or intended end-uses of products.

2.5 A Member preparing, adopting or applying a technical regulation which may have a significant effect on trade of other Members shall, upon the request of another Member, explain the justification for that technical regulation in terms of the provisions of paragraphs 2 to 4. Whenever a technical regulation is prepared, adopted or applied for one of the legitimate objectives explicitly mentioned in paragraph 2, and is in accordance with relevant international standards, it shall be rebuttably presumed not to create an unnecessary obstacle to international trade.

2.6 With a view to harmonizing technical regulations on as wide a basis as possible, Members shall play a full part, within the limits of their resources, in the preparation by appropriate international standardizing bodies of international standards for products for which they either have adopted, or expect to adopt, technical regulations.

2.8 Wherever appropriate, Members shall specify technical regulations based on product requirements in terms of performance rather than design or descriptive characteristics.

It is necessary to address the distinction between the SPS and the TBT Agreements here. Whereas the SPS Agreement covers any measure whose purpose is to protect human, animal or plant life or health whether or not these are technical requirements, the TBT Agreement covers all technical regulations, voluntary standards and the procedures to ensure these are met, unless these regulations, standards or procedures are sanitary or phytosanitary measures as defined under the SPS Agreement. Thus, it is 'the "type" of measure which determines whether it is covered by the TBT Agreement, but the "purpose" of the measure which is relevant in determining whether a measure is subject to the SPS Agreement'.[101]

The Fairtrade Labelling Organisations (FLO) is a joint network of labelling initiatives working in twenty countries and representing fair-trade certified producers in the developing world across Latin America, Africa and Asia. Certification for products to carry the fair-trade mark is done by an independent organisation, FLO-Cert Gmbh. The standards for the Organisation centre around three objectives: the goods are produced by disadvantaged producers who may otherwise not have access to an international market; the goods must be produced in line with ethical standards including social security for the labour force employed and environmentally sound agricultures practices. Also, buyers of the goods must grant a reasonable share of the market price of the goods to the producers.

The success of such an approach is remarkable. The FLO Annual Report states that in 2007:

Global retail value surpassed 2.3 billion euros, meaning a growth of 47%. The sales volumes of bananas increased by 72% and reached a total of 233.791 metric tons; Coffee grew by 19%, reaching a total of 62.209 metric tons; The sales of sugar increased by 111% up to 15.074 metric tons; During 2007, Fairtrade cotton was introduced in five new markets and the sales of items made out of Fairtrade certified cotton, ranging from cotton buds to jeans and towels, surpassed 14 million.[102]

Granted, the fair-trade standards requirements fall in line with the 'voluntary' conformity requirements of TBT standards under the TBT Agreement. Had the guidelines adopted by the FLO been on technical regulations which affect Article 2.8 of the TBT Agreement mentioned previously, they may have been deemed a trade-restrictive measure and would be in breach of WTO obligations. However, the pertinent factor in our reference to the FAIR TRADE mark is that the affected parties i.e. consumers and developing country producers, are directly involved in the choice of goods consumed including in the adoption of private, independent ethical standards established by the FLO, a choice satisfied by the application of a single logo on a good. As the FLO notes in its 2007 Annual Report, 'the mission of the FLO [is] to connect consumers and producers through a FAIRTRADE Certification mark. It enables disadvantaged producers to combat poverty, strengthen their position and take more control over their futures'.[103]

Therefore, continuing with our expression of reservations on this reference to 'disproportionate effect of developing countries' on the application of private standards in submissions by the OIE at the SPS Committee level, our view is this: If on the other hand the interest is not merely in retaining such international standards-setting organisations but on meeting the needs and concerns of developing countries' producers for global market integration, the required action should be different from the OIE proposal. The WTO focus should be on directing practical assistance to these countries in respect of satisfying the SPS measures demanded by importing businesses across the Member States.

As it is, the OIE submission continues the limited perspective of more 'rule creation' demanding that Member States must comply with international standards. Rather, it would be beneficial for the Committee in particular and the WTO in general, to channel greater action towards building the capacity of developing countries to meet the demands of their importing partners. While reference to international standards is necessary for harmonisation, the reality of the increased adoption of private standards, and divergent consumer preferences cannot be ignored. The technical assistance needed here therefore is in R&D activities for developing country producers to enable them to produce goods which would be at the least, acceptable under international standards. Bilateral and regional co-operation in identifying scientific methods and processes which would satisfy these private standards would also be of more practical benefit.

1.3. Work at the Domestic Level: A Case Study on Nigeria

Concern over the safety of human, plant, animal and other environmental factors have also been the subject of other international agreements which countries have been party to.[104] However, the SPS Agreement dealing as it does with issues like public health and safety and the justifiability of a country's adopted measures for the protection of human, animal and plant life has had more considerable impact in developing countries not least the infrastructural and institutional activities which have been introduced in this area in the domestic arena. It is fair to say that whether one argues that the introduction of national agencies charged with the control, inspection, and approval procedures for the assessment of risk in determining SPS measures has been an entirely domestic initiative for WTO developing countries, the influence of the obligations under the SPS Agreement cannot be denied.

The implications for business and trade, whether WTO Member States applied SPS measures restricting imports or exports as the case may be, demanded greater infrastructural and institutional action. Thus, even developing countries could understand that this was an Agreement which though would present challenges to them, would also make it easier to ascertain what SPS measures were adopted by other countries and to oppose those which were trade restrictive. Therefore a harmonised system of SPS measures adopted according to international guidelines and recommendations under Article 3 was attractive.

Furthermore, provisions recognising that a country's SPS measures, while they may differ from others, may still be accepted so long as the exporting Member 'objectively demonstrates to the importing Member that its measures achieve the importing Member's appropriate level of sanitary or phytosanitary protection' meant that developing countries could develop their own (credible) scientific assessment procedures.[105] In addition, developing countries stood to benefit in their domestic environment, from the operation of the SPS Agreement. SPS measures could tackle the unchecked infiltration of sub-standard foods, fake drugs and cosmetics etc into developing country markets. Permits for the importation of such goods from erstwhile trading partners who are WTO Members could then be declined without the fear of undue political pressure.

Indeed the best prospect for developing countries has actually been domestic; an urgent and invaluable improvement in the quality and standards of goods locally manufactured for consumption. Also, the protection of plant and animal life and environmental safety which national governments may not have paid serious attention to has come under scrutiny as countries, including developing countries, have not only had to comply with international safety standards but also consider the domestic protection of their own environments. To ensure its benefits therefore, developing countries have also had to comply with the request for national offices and authorities established pursuant to the SPS Agreement.

In Nigeria, the National Notification Authority (NNA) for the SPS Agreement is the Federal Ministry of Commerce, Abuja.[106] Nigeria's trade representatives to the WTO are drawn from the Ministry. Recently, in order to ensure a stronger participation at the Organisation, a new enlarged and enhanced National Focal Point (NFP) has been established under the Federal Ministry to co-ordinate the country's activities in international trade (including at the WTO and other trade-related international organisations).[107] The body is expected to assist in Nigeria's negotiations at the international body including making available to the WTO, the country's notifications in respect of the various WTO Agreements.[108]

The aforementioned National Focal Point has recently been renamed as the *Enlarged National Focal Point* (ENFP) which is to be concerned with multilateral trade matters including at the WTO. The ENFP is to provide greater coherence in the nation's international trade affairs. It is set up under the multilateral trade division in the External Affairs section of the country's Federal Ministry of Commerce. A Trade Office to the WTO, in Geneva, is also established under the new division.

The ENFP is organised in three main committees with a number of sub committees:

A. Committee on Trade in Goods with sub committees on: Market Access; Agriculture; Standards; TRIMS; Customs Procedures; Trade Defence Measures; Plurilateral/New Issues.
B. Committee on Trade in Services with sub committees on: Transport Services; Trade in Professional Services; Financial Services; Movement of Natural Persons.
C. Committee on Trade-Related Aspects of Intellectual Property Rights with subcommittees on: Patents and Trade Marks; Copyright; Industrial Design and other Rights.

The ENFP main offices are in Nigeria's capital, Abuja. Not much can be said about the workings of this office given its new beginnings. However, the creation of a separate entity charged with multilateral trade affairs makes for an improved focus on Nigeria's obligations at the WTO. In respect of standards and SPS measures for instance, the country's activities in respect of public health and international trade can be easily accessible not only to other WTO Members but also to the citizens themselves who need such information in their trading endeavour. Given the difficulties in accessing information in the country including the threats of constant power failure and the inefficient telecommunications and transport network, it would be preferable if state liaison offices are also established in the near future to bring the initiative closer to the local industries and businesses enterprises. This would counter the constraints to information flow and readjustments occasioned by the absence of timely and up-to-date information on SPS measures adopted both in the domestic, and in the international trade arena.

Generally, the responsibility for regulation and monitoring of food safety standards and practices in Nigeria rest on the following agencies: the Federal Ministry of Health, National Agency for Food and Drug Administration and Control (NAFDAC), Standards Organisation of Nigeria (SON), National Codex Committee which is the SON working closely with NAFDAC, Federal Ministry of Agriculture and Water Resources, States and Local Governments. The Enquiry Point notified by the Nigerian government to the WTO SPS Committee is the National Agency for Food and Drug Administration and Control (NAFDAC), a parastatal of the Federal Ministry of Health.[109]

1.3.1. SPS Enquiry Point in Nigeria – NAFDAC

NAFDAC was established by *Decree No.15* of 1993 (as amended by Decree No.19, 1999) with the mandate to regulate and control quality standards for food, drugs, cosmetics, medical devices, chemicals, detergents, and packaged water imported, manufactured locally, and distributed in Nigeria.[110] Public health and restriction on importation and exportation of unsafe goods in the country is the central defining aim of NAFDAC.[111] Its functions include the following:[112]

- Regulate and control the importation, exportation, manufacture, advertisement, distribution, sale and use of drugs, cosmetics, medical devices, bottled water and chemicals.
- Conduct appropriate test and ensure compliance with standard specifications designated and approved by the council for the effective control of quality of food, drugs, cosmetics, medical devices, bottled water and chemicals and their raw materials as well as their production processes in factories and other establishments.
- Undertake appropriate investigation into the production premises and raw materials for food, drugs, cosmetics, medical devices, bottled water and chemicals and establish relevant quality assurance system, including certification of the production sites and of the regulated products.
- Undertake inspection of imported food, drugs, cosmetics, medical devices, bottled water and chemicals and establish relevant quality assurance system, including certification of the production sites and of the regulated products.
- Compile standard specifications and regulations and guidelines for the production, importation, exportation, sale and distribution of food, drugs, cosmetics, medical devices, bottled water and chemicals.
- Undertake the registration of food, drugs, medical devices, bottled water and chemicals.

- Control the exportation and issue quality certification of food, drugs, medical devices, bottled water and chemicals intended for export.
- Establish and maintain relevant laboratories or other institutions in strategic areas of Nigeria as may be necessary for the performance of its functions.
- Pronounce on the quality and safety of food, drugs, cosmetics, medical devices, bottled water and chemicals after appropriate analysis.
- Undertake measures to ensure that the use of narcotic drugs and psychotropic substances are limited to medical and scientific purposes.
- Grant authorization for the import and export of narcotic drugs and psychotropic substances as well as other controlled substances.
- Collaborate with National Drug Law Enforcement Agency in measures to eradicate drug abuse in Nigeria.
- Advise Federal, State and Local Governments, the Private sector and other interested bodies regarding the quality, safety and regulatory provisions on food, drugs, cosmetics, medical devices, bottled water and chemicals.
- Issue guidelines on, approve and monitor the advertisement of food, drugs, cosmetics, medical devices, bottled water and chemicals.
- Compile and publish relevant data resulting from the performance of the functions of the Agency or from other sources.
- Sponsor such national and international conference as it may consider appropriate.
- Liaise with relevant establishments within and outside Nigeria in pursuance of its functions.

The SPS Enquiry Point is defined in the WTO Glossary as 'an official or office in a member government designated to deal with enquiries from other WTO members and the public on a subject such as technical barriers to trade or sanitary and phytosanitary measures'.[113] NAFDAC's mandate to 'compile standard specifications and regulations and guidelines' and 'to liaise with relevant establishments within and outside Nigeria' in pursuance of its functions, puts it in good stead to fulfil the transparency obligations under the SPS Agreements. The regulations and procedure for imports and exports under NAFDAC are clearly stated on the organisation's web site and can be obtained by a visit to the agency's head office in Abuja, or at the Lagos office in Oshodi, Lagos State the country's former capital.[114]

According to NAFDAC, although there are some chemical substances which are Generally Regarded as Safe (GRAS), methods used in the production of regulated products for public use or consumption registration of regulated products must comply with primary guidelines of Good Manufacturing Practice (GMPs).[115] There is however no indication of the standards used in determining these GRAS, or the scientific justification for such standards. However, the Agency states that the NAFDAC assessment tests are carried out in specialised laboratories which have been accredited by various international organisations and bodies.[116]

We may briefly mention the other organisational activities regulating specific standards and regulations which impact on international trade. The Standards Organisation of Nigeria, (SON)[117] under its Conformity Assessment Programme (SONCAP) aims to ensure that Nigerian consumers 'are protected from unsafe and substandard goods as well as ensuring that Nigerian manufacturers are not subject to unfair competition from such goods'.[118] A comprehensive list of regulated products for these purposes include: toys, electrical and electronics, automotives, chemical products, mechanical materials and gas appliances, protective safety equipment, paper and stationery, mosquito nets.[119] The guidelines for exporters to Nigeria for products regulated by the SON are also available on the internet, in the SON country offices in the relevant exporting country or, at the nearest country office.[120]

1.3.2. The Relevance of SPS in the Domestic Environment

In Nigeria, the challenge of protecting human health is largely considered to be of more significance than regulations on plant health and safety hence the more visible action by NAFDAC owing to the significant rate of mortality arising from fake and substandard drugs and contaminated chemical products.[121] In addition, it must be noted that the cultural perception does not attach too much importance to animal and plant health and safety, as is the case in the West.[122] Thus dispute claims on food safety and environmental protection have not preoccupied the Nigerian government to the same extent as it has other WTO Member States. Nevertheless, some factors noticeably had significant impact on the country's ability to comply with, and to execute its SPS obligations.

A. Food and the Lack of Technological Expertise

The more urgent demand for food and the lack of technological expertise in determining scientifically acceptable measures for health safety in food production deserves mention at this point. In our consideration of the *EC-Biotech* case involving Argentina, we had mentioned that there are countries such as Argentina which is currently the largest developing country producer of GMO foods, and the US and Canada, with significant investment into biotechnology. On the other hand, there are developing countries such as

Nigeria who have not clearly determined in their domestic framework whether to reject or accept GMO foods.

Some African countries like Angola, Ethiopia, Kenya, Malawi, Mozambique, Lesotho and Zambia have restrictions on the importation of GMO foods, but Nigeria as yet has no conclusive policy on GMO foods.[123] In March 2004 however, the country signed a Memorandum of Understanding (MOU) with the United States government for the promotion of biotechnology and GMO products.[124] There is no evidence that this is due to an increased awareness of the benefits or risks of GMOs. Commenting on a proposed *Nigerian Bio-Safety Act,* it has been observed that the Act is 'an unimaginative legislation that mimics the standard fare: bio safety laws that adopt a permit system for the regulation of genetically modified organisms (GMOs).'[125]

This 'proposed' legislation has not been made public, if it exists at all.[126] In the absence of any legislation on bio-safety, it is safe to state that as yet, there is no national legislation on bio-safety or GMOs passed into law by the country's National Assembly. We note also that government directive(s) restricting imports of 'harmful foods' are usually arbitrary, and are not always transparent.[127]

B. Stakeholder Participation

Earlier we drew attention to the work of the STDF in assisting developing countries in respect of SPS capacity building. Nigeria is a beneficiary under the current project development activities of the STDF.[128] The focus of the current project is on 'Expanding Nigeria's Food Exports through Enhanced SPS capacity'.[129] Requested by NAFDAC in collaboration with the SON, the Federal Ministries of Agriculture and Rural Development, Health, and Commerce, the goal is to enhance human and institutional capacity in respect of SPS measures. Such assistance would include: training for key mid-level and senior government officials on the workings of the SPS Agreement, the workings of the SPS Committee, the practice of working bilaterally with other WTO members on SPS issues, and on developing closer working level relationships with international standard setting organisations.[130]

There will also be training for food inspectors to develop skill and expertise in HACCP and other food and safety systems required at all stages of production. Training on Good Agricultural Practices (GAP) would also be provided for food industry workers. The challenges of responding to trading partners' requirements is addressed under the proposals to sensitize food industry workers 'on the need for a traceability system which is an EU requirement, since the EU is a major trading partner'.[131]

Specific capacity building efforts under the scheme would target the following areas:

- Updating SPS-related legislation to reflect the official and commercial requirements of the current international trading regime.
- Seeking specific technical training from competent experts, especially through the Codex Alimentarius Commission (CAC), the World Organisation for Animal Health (OIE), and the International Plant Protection Convention (IPPC).
- Developing or modernizing data bases, e.g., for SPS pest and disease prevalence or surveillance.

The involvement of the private sector under this proposal is mentioned in what we consider to be a half-hearted attempt. The proposal states that 'the government will also conduct an outreach program to educate interested parties in the Nigerian private sector about SPS export requirements'. The response given to the invitation to provide in detail what role if any would be played by the private/public sector is also vague. The response states that, 'the Nigerian government will seek input from private sector exporter and producer interests for the preparation of the project proposal'.[132] Considering as we have pointed out throughout this work that it is people and businesses who engage in trade, the participation of the private sector surely deserves more detailed arrangements involving for instance the individuals, sector groups and organisations whose activities are relevant to the project.

Be that as it may, specific developing country technical assistance in respect of SPS measures such as by the STDF contributes to the necessary development dimension to the WTO which we have argued for in this work. The problem is the delay in beginning these projects and in their end results. The application for the STDF-SPS project initiative in Nigeria was approved in May 2007 with a small budget of $20,000. The project is still 'awaiting contracting'.[133] The outstanding task includes 'to conduct desk and field research on technical cooperation activities in the food safety area in order to ensure full synergy, identify key stakeholders and draft a sustainable project proposal in accordance with the STDF Operational Rules'.[134] A start date is yet to be confirmed and an implementing agency is still to be determined.[135]

Summary

It is interesting to observe that the development dimension for facilitating SPS capacity building in developing countries is mostly undertaken in the activities of the SPS Committee and in the programmes under the STDF mechanism, what the WTO DG admits is really an AfT initiative. The difficulties of implementing the SDT treatment provisions and the technical assistance provisions of the SPS Agreement have been temporarily sidestepped by looking beyond the trade rules on SPS measures themselves and focusing on areas for technical assistance.

Incidentally, the difficulties for developing countries in the implementation of the SPS Agreement and in meeting SPS requirements of importing countries have previously been summarised in a detailed study by Henson et al (2000).[136] In order of priority, these are: insufficient access to scientific/technical expertise; incompatibility of SPS requirements with domestic production/marketing methods; poor access to financial resources; insufficient time permitted for compliance; limitations in own country's administrative arrangements for SPS requirements; poor awareness of SPS requirements amongst government officials; poor awareness of SPS requirements within agriculture and food industry; and poor access to information on SPS requirements.

Henson et al, give suggested solutions to these general difficulties including for a review of notification procedures within the SPS Agreement and for a greater level of technical assistance, two areas where the SPS Committee has been particularly active. They also noted the need for longer periods of compliance with SPS requests for developing countries and recommended that developed countries should take greater account of the impact on developing countries in the setting of SPS requirements. A remarkable suggestion in our view was for greater regional co-operation between developing countries in SPS issues. We consider that just as we argued that greater market access for developing countries would be supported by closer regional trade activity, this suggestion for closer developing country co-operation will also be beneficial in the present respect.

Co-operation could be in the form of joint efforts at conducting risk assessments for SPS measures, R&D activities in food production, co-operative efforts in technical assistance and training in administrative and production processes, exchange of information and new initiatives on SPS matters both of WTO origin and of private standards, improving other supply side constraints such as transport networks, and more efficient bureaucratic methods of administration.

NOTES

Chapter One. The WTO and the Rules-Based System

1 Article II, para 1.

2 *Agreement Establishing the World Trade Organisation*, Article III para 1 (1994).

3 Id, para 2.

4 Id, para 3.

5 Id, para 4.

6 Matsushita et al, *op cit*, 5. The WTO is formally established by Article 1 of the WTO Agreement. No reservations may be made to the WTO Agreement. The WTO Agreement is registered in accordance with Article 102 of the UN Charter which provides that: (1) Every treaty and every international agreement entered into by any Member of the United Nations after the present Charter comes into force shall as soon as possible be registered with the Secretariat and published by it. (2) No party to any such treaty or international agreement which has not been registered in accordance with the provisions of paragraph 1 of this Article may invoke that treaty or agreement before any organ of the United Nations.

7 WTO Agreement Article 1 (1).

8 This was terminated at the end of 1997. See the WTO web page: [http://www.wto.org/english/docs_e/legal_e/legal_e.htm#wtoagreement]. See also, 'WTO Deletion of the International Dairy Agreement from Annex 4 of the WTO Agreement', *Decision of 10 Dec 1997, WT/L/251, 17 Dec 1997*.

9 This was also terminated at the end of 1997. See also 'WTO Deletion of the International Bovine Meat Agreement from Annex4 of the WTO Agreement', *Decision of 10 Dec 1997, WT/L/252, 16 Dec 1997*.

10 See the WTO structure chart available on the WTO web site at: [http://www.wto.org/english/thewto_e/whatis_e/tif_e/org2_e.htm].

11 Article IV(1–4).

12 Article IV(1).

13 Article IV(7) specifies the first three committees. The Committee on Trade and Environment was added by the Ministerial Conference meeting at Marrakesh April 1994, and the Committee on Regional Agreements was added by the Ministerial Conference meeting at Singapore in December 1996; See Schott Jefferey J & Buurman Johanna W. *The Uruguay Round: An Assessment* (1994), 137.

14 *See* WTO: 'Trading into the Future – the organisation – Whose WTO is it anyway? Online [http://www.wto.org/english/thewto_e/whatis_e/tif_e/org1_e.htm].

15 Article IV (5).

16 Agreement Establishing the World Trade Organisation Article IV(3); (4).

17 The General Agreement on Tariffs and Trade 1994 (GATT), General Agreement on Trade in Services (GATS) and the Agreement on Trade-Related Aspects of Intellectual Property Rights (TRIPS).

18 WTO: Annual Report 2003, Online: [http://www.wto.org/english/res_e/booksp_e/anrep_e/anrep03_e.pdf] p. 148.

19 See the Secretariat organisational chart online: [http://www.wto.org/english/thewto_e/whatis_e/tif_e/org4_e.htm].

20 Divisions include: the Council and Trade Negotiations Committee; Information and Media Relations; DDA Special Duties; Administration and General Services; Human Resources; Informatics; Language Services and Documentation; Trade and Environment; Trade Policies Review; Development; Economic Research and Statistics; Training and Technical Cooperation Institute; Technical Cooperation Audit; Accessions; Agriculture and Commodities; External Relations; Intellectual Property; Market Access; Legal Affairs; Rules; Trade and Finance; and Trade in Services Division.

21 When the General Council meets as the Dispute Settlement Body, decisions shall only be taken in accordance with the Understanding on Rules and Procedures Governing the Settlement of Disputes, Article 2(4) which also provides that the Body shall take a decision by consensus.

22 Id. See explanatory note 4 to Article IX(3).

23 WTO Agreement, Article IX(1).

24 Id; Article IX(1).

25 See Jefferey J Schott & Jayashree Watal, 'Decision Making in the WTO' *Policy Brief 00-2 Institute of International Economics March 2000*. Online: [http://www.iie.com/publications/pb/pb00–2.htm].

26 See WTO web page; [http://www.wto.org/english/thewto_e/whatis_e/tif_e/org6_e.htm]. With the exception of the Holy See (Vatican), countries must begin the accession process within five years of being observers.

27 Id.

28 See the UN website.

29 See Article 1.

30 See WTO web site at [http://www.wto.org/english/thewto_e/whatis_e/tif_e/org1_e.htm].

31 See Focus on the Global South; 'Internal Transparency and Decision-making processes at the WTO Critical Issues and Recommendations' WTO NGO Symposium, 1 May 2002; [http://www.wto.org/english/tratop_e/dda_e/summary_report_intern_transp.doc].

32 See Grainne Burca & Joanne Scott 'The Impact of the WTO on EU Decision Making', (Academy of European Law) 2000; Online [http://www.jeanmonnet program.org/papers/00/000601.html]. See generally the EU commitments to the WTO and the current Doha Development Agenda on its 'Trade Issues' web page: [http://ec.europa.eu/comm/trade/issues/newround/index_en.htm].

33 FN in original. A decision to grant a waiver in respect of any obligation subject to a transition period or a period for staged implementation that the requesting Member has not performed by the end of the relevant period shall be taken only by consensus.

34 A request for a waiver of the WTO Agreement shall be submitted to the Ministerial Conference which shall consider the request within 90 days. Where no consensus is reached, a decision can be taken by three-fourths of the Members. See para (a). A request for a waiver of the Agreements under Annex 1A, B or C, shall be submitted to the Council for Trade in Goods; Trade in Services or; TRIPS respectively who shall

consider it within 90 days and thereafter submit a report to the Ministerial Conference. See para (b).

35 The Ministerial Conference on the basis of an annual review may extend, modify or terminate the waiver.

36 See Understanding in Respect of Waivers of Obligations under GATT 1994, Article 1.

37 See *European Communities: Regime for the Importation, Sale and Distribution of Bananas, WT/DS27/AB/R* para 183.

38 *Op cit*, paras 184–7.

39 Id, para 184.

40 For a list of notified waivers past and present, see the WTO web page: [http://www.wto.org/english/res_e/booksp_e/analytic_index_e/wto_agree_03_e.htm#288].

41 Jackson, *The World Trading System op cit*, 94.

42 These provisions remain under GATT 1994.

43 See GATT 1947, Article XXII(1;2); see *Turkey – Consultation under Article XXII:2* 14S/59, Report of Working Party adopted March 28 1966 online: [http://www.worldtradelaw.net/reports/gattpanels/turkeytariffincrease.pdf].

44 '…If the application to any contracting party of any concession or other obligation is in fact suspended, that contracting party shall then be free, not later than sixty days after such action is taken, to give written notice to the Executive Secretary to the Contracting Parties of its intention to withdraw from this Agreement and such withdrawal shall take effect upon the sixtieth day following the day on which such notice is received by him.' See Article XXIII (2).

45 GATT BISD Vol 11, 188 (1952).

46 L/1923, 11S/95, adopted Nov 16, 1962.

47 See the Panel Report at p. 4. Online: [http://www.worldtradelaw.net/reports/gattpanels/uruguayrecoursea.pdf].

48 See Jackson, *The World Trading System* (1992) *op cit*, 95. See *US – Shirts and Blouses WT/DS33/AB/R* at p. 14, where the AB confirmed that 'the burden of proof rests upon the party, whether complaining or defending, who asserts the affirmative of a particular claim or defence'. The burden shifts to the other party who will fail unless it can rebut the evidence.

49 *See* Petersmann Ernst-Urich, "The Dispute Settlement System of the World Trade Organisation and the Evolution of GATT since 1948" 31 CMLR (1994), 1157; Hudec Robert .E *Enforcing International Trade Law: The Evolution of the Modern GATT Legal System*, (1993), 9. See generally Matsushita et al, *op cit*, 20.

50 Under GATT 1947, a defendant could block a request for a panel procedure by refusing a consensus adopting the decision to establish a panel, or block the adoption of a report by refusing to accept a consensus agreement. See generally John H. Jackson, 'Dispute Settlement in the WTO: Policy and Jurisprudential Considerations', *Discussion Paper No. 419 Research Seminar in International Economics School of Public Policy*, University of Michigan Feb 9 1998.

51 Matsushita et al, *op cit*, 20.

52 These include: The 1966 Decision on Procedures under Article XXIII 5 April 1966 GATT BISD (14th Supp) at 18 applying to disputes between a developing country contracting party and a developed country contracting party; Understanding Regarding Notification, Consultation, Dispute Settlement and Surveillance, 28 November 1979, GATT BISD (26th Supp) at 210; The 1982 Decision on Dispute Settlement Procedures, 29 November 1982, GATT BISD (29th Supp) at 9, 13–16; The 1984 Decision on

Dispute Settlement Procedures, 30 November 1984, GATT BISD (31st Supp) at 9–10); and The 1989 Decision on Improvements to the GATT Dispute Settlement Rules and Procedures, 12 April 1989, GATT (36th Supp) at 61. See Matsushita et al, *op cit*, 20.

53 Hereinafter referred to as the DSU (Dispute Settlement Understanding).

54 Article XVI (1) of the WTO Agreement also supports adherence to GATT decisions, procedures, and customary practices.

55 GATT Secretariat, *Multilateral Trade Negotiations Final Act Embodying the Results of the Uruguay Round of Trade Negotiations*, 33 Int'l Legal Materials_1125, 1227 (April 15, 1994) (noting that not only must the dispute settlement body ensure that the action brought before it is "fruitful", but its aim is also to provide a "solution mutually acceptable to the parties"). *See* Shin Susan H., 'Comparison of the Dispute Settlement Procedures of the World Trade Organisation for Trade Disputes and the Inter-American System for Human Rights Violations' 1, *16 New York Int'l Law Review 43* (Winter 2003) See also DSU Article 3(7).

56 The DSU makes general provisions on the suitability of any of these mechanisms: "Before bringing a case, a Member shall exercise its judgement as to whether action under these procedures would be fruitful. The aim of the dispute settlement mechanism is to secure a positive solution to a dispute. A solution mutually acceptable to the parties to a dispute and consistent with the covered agreements is clearly to be preferred. In the absence of a mutually agreed solution, the first objective of the dispute settlement mechanism is usually to secure the withdrawal of the measures concerned if these are found to be inconsistent with the provisions of any of the covered agreements. The provision of compensation should be resorted to only if the immediate withdrawal of the measure is impracticable and as a temporary measure pending the withdrawal of the measure which is inconsistent with a covered agreement. The last resort which this Understanding provides to the Member invoking the dispute settlement procedures is the possibility of suspending the application of concessions or other obligations under the covered agreements on a discriminatory basis vis-à-vis the other Member, subject to authorization by the DSB of such measures." See DSU Article 3(7).

57 See also DSU Article 4.

58 DSU Article 4(3); Requests for Panels must however comply with Article 6(2) – it should be in writing, and identify the specific measures at issue, amongst others. Failure to do so would negate such a request. *See United States v European Communities* (Appeal) from *European Communities – Customs Classification of Certain Computer Equipment* Appellate Body Report AB–1998–3 (1998).

59 DSU, Article 4(8).

60 Id, Article 4(4).

61 Id, Article 4(6).

62 Id, Article 5.

63 Id, Article 5(6). He will also do this upon request in dispute settlement cases involving a least-developed country. See Article 24(2).

64 Id, Articles 6–16.

65 Id, Article 7(1).

66 Id, Article 8(2). These will include well-qualified governmental and/or non-governmental individuals, teachers or authors on international trade law or policy, amongst others. See generally DSU, Article 8(1).

67 Id, Article 9.

68 Id, Article 10.

69 Id, Article 13; Appendix 4. The weight to be attached to expert advise was one of the issues raised in the *India-Quantitative Restrictions case* mentioned later herein.

70 Id, Article 8(5).

71 Id, Article 8(9).

72 This establishes that the Panel meets in a closed session and outlines the procedure which the Panel follows in resolving disputes.

73 Id, Article 12(9).

74 See generally DSU, Articles 17–19.

75 Id, Article 17(1). The current Working Procedure for Appellate Review is Document WT/AB/WP/5 of 4 January 2005. It is a consolidated, revised version, and reflects amendments to Rules 1, 18(5), 20, 21, 23, 27 and Annex I, as well as the addition of a new Rule 23bis and a new Annex III, as discussed in *WT/AB/WP/W/8* and *WT/AB/WP/W/9*. The Working Procedures for Appellate Review consolidated in this document will be applied to appeals initiated after 1 January 2005. See the document web page at: [http://www.wto.org/english/tratop_e/dispu_e/ab_e.htm].

76 Id, Article 17(5).

77 Id, Article 17(10;11), the same provision is made for panels under Article 14.

78 Id, Article 17(6).

79 Id, Article 17(3).

80 Id, Article 17(4). Third parties may not appeal. They may however make written submissions to and be heard by the Appellate Body.

81 Id, Article 20. It provides: "Unless otherwise agreed to by the parties to the dispute, the period from the date of establishment of the panel by the DSB until the date the DSB considers the panel or appellate report for adoption shall as a general rule not exceed nine months where the panel report is not appealed or 12 months where the report is appealed. Where either the panel or the Appellate Body has acted, pursuant to paragraph 9 of Article 12 or paragraph 5 of Article 17, to extend the time for providing its report, the additional time taken shall be added to the above periods".

82 Id, Article 25. This procedure is preferably 'expeditious' – see Article 25(1).

83 Id, Article 25(3).

84 Id, Article 25(4).

85 DSU, Article 16(4).

86 Id, Article 16(4).

87 Id, Article 17(4). The adoption procedure is without prejudice to the right of Members to express their views on an Appellate body report.

88 Id, Articles 21–26.

89 Id, Article 21(3) (a,b,c) provides that a reasonable period of time is: (**a**) the period of time proposed by the Member concerned, provided that such period is approved by the DSB; or, in the absence of such approval, (**b**) a period of time mutually agreed by the parties to the dispute within 45 days after the date of adoption of the recommendations and rulings; or, in the absence of such agreement, (**c**) a period of time determined through binding arbitration within 90 days after the date of adoption of the recommendations and rulings. In such arbitration, a guideline for the arbitrator should be that the reasonable period of time to implement panel or Appellate Body recommendations should not exceed 15 months from the date of adoption of a panel or Appellate Body report. However, that time may be shorter or longer, depending upon the particular circumstances.

90 Id, Article 21(4).
91 Id, See Articles 21(2; 8).
92 Id, Article 22(1).
93 See Article 22(2).
94 DSU, Article 3(2).
95 See John H. Jackson, "Global Economics and International Economic Law", *JIEL 1* (1998) pp 1–23 at p. 8.
96 Id.
97 Id.
98 John H. Jackson, *Sovereignty, the WTO and Changing Fundamental of International Law* Cambridge University Press (2006) at p. 3.
99 Article 3 (2) of the DSU makes this express reference: 'to clarify the existing provisions of those agreements in accordance with customary rules of interpretation of public international law.' See the first case under the WTO, *United States – Standards for Reformulated and Conventional Gasoline* (the Gasoline case) WT/DS2/AR/3 at p. 17 where it stated that the direction under Article 3(2) was "*a measure of recognition that the General Agreement is not to be read in clinical isolation from public international law*".
100 See 1961 Vienna Convention on the Law of Treaties, Article 31(1).
101 See Joost Pauwelyn, 'The Role of Public International Law in the WTO' 95 *AJIL* (2001) pp 535–578.
102 Vienna Convention, Article 31(3) (c).
103 See generally, Pauwelyn *op cit.*
104 AB Report (*EC-Poultry*) WT/DS69/AB/R.
105 Id para 172a.
106 See Joel P Trachtman. 'The Domain of WTO Dispute Resolution', *40 Harvard Int'l L.J.* 2 (Spring 1999); 333–377. See generally, Geping Rao, 'The Law Applied by World Trade Organisation Panels' 17 *Temple Int'l & Comp L. J.*, 125 (Spring 2003) pp 125–137.
107 See Rao *op cit*, 128.
108 Id.
109 WT/DS163/R, I May 2000.
110 Id, pp 190–191. The cases referred to were: (PCIJ) *Legal Status of Eastern Greenland* (1933) PCIJ Series A/B, No. 53, 22 at 71, the dissenting opinion of Judge Azilotti pp 91–92; (ICJ) Case concerning the *Temple of Preah Vihear* ICJ Reports 1962, 6 at pp 26–27.
111 Id.
112 See Martin Khor (Third World Network); 'DSU process becoming an outrage of law and justice, says critic' reporting the criticism by Chakravarthi Raghavan, Chief Editor of the South-North Development Monitor (SUNS), while making a presentation at a panel session on the WTO and its dispute settlement process at a seminar on: '*Current Developments in the WTO: Perspective of Developing Countries*', Online: [http://www.twnside.org.sg/title/twr123i.htm].
113 We are aware that such an attempt may be criticised as 'judicial activism' by the DSB. In our opinion however, considering the early stages of the DSB, the Panels and Appellate Bodies will have to lay the foundations for its rules of interpretations in instances where the Agreements have not made any provisions. See Elimma Ezeani, 'Trade Disputes Devoid of Judicial Activism: Too Much Too Soon for the WTO Dispute Settlement Body? *Journal of International Trade Law, Vol 3. Issue 2*, The Robert Gordon University Aberdeen, Dec 2004 pp 21–32.

Chapter Two. Development and the WTO Approach

1 See Catherine Soames, Alan Spooner and Sara Hawker (eds) *The Compact Oxford Dictionary Thesaurus and Word Power Guide* Oxford University Press (2002) p. 964. Words such as *barter, exchange, market* are derivatives of this term. See also, the Dictionary (id), at p. 964.

2 Id, p. 239.

3 Id.

4 See generally, WTO: *Understanding the WTO* Third Edition (May 2006).

5 Ray August, *International Business Law – Text, Cases, and Readings* Prentice Hall (3rd Ed.) (2000), p. 354.

6 See generally the history of the modern world trading system in August, *op cit*, p. 354; Matsushita M, Schoenbaum T & Mavroidis P.C, *The World Trade Organisation – Law, Practice, and Policy* Oxford University Press (2003) p. 1.

7 See August, *op cit*; See also, Richard Pomfret, *Trade Policy in Canada and Australia in the Twentieth Century*, Online [http://www.economics.adelaide.edu.au/contacts/archive/pomfret/cda_austradepolicy.pdf].

8 See *The Columbia Encyclopaedia Sixth Edition*; (2001–05) Online [http://www.bartleby.com/65/ha/HawleySm.html].

9 Participants at the Conference agreed that the world economy was crippled by monetary chaos (competitive devaluation, imposition of exchange controls) and trade wars (imposition of higher tariffs and quotas). In preparation for the conference, subcommittees were established to investigate each of these questions. The monetary committee reached the conclusion that nothing could be done to stabilise money as long as free trade principles did not prevail. The trade committee believed there was no point discussing trade liberalisation without a prior currency agreement. John Maynard Keynes wrote after the conference that it was inherently unlikely that 66 countries would agree on anything. See further, Harold James, *A Historical Perspective on International Monetary Arrangements*: Online [http://www.bos.frb.org/economic/conf/conf43/33p.pdf].

10 Text of the Atlantic Charter of August 12 1941; Online [http://usinfo.state.gov/usa/infousa/facts/democrac/53.html].

11 See the *United Nations Monetary and Financial Conference at Bretton Woods, Summary of Agreements*, July 22, 1944 online at [http://www.ibiblio.org/pha/policy/1944/440722a.html].

12 The IMF was established to promote international monetary cooperation, exchange stability, and orderly exchange arrangements; to foster economic growth and high levels of employment; and to provide temporary financial assistance to countries to help ease balance of payments adjustment. *See* the IMF website at *www.imf.org*

13 The IBRD is part of the World Bank Group which comprises of 5 closely associated development institutions – the International Bank for Reconstruction and Development (IBRD), the International Development Association (IDA), the International Finance Corporation (IFC), the Multilateral Investment Guarantee Agency (MIGA), the International Center for Settlement of Disputes (ICSID). *See* the World Bank Group website at www.worldbank.org

14 After the founding of the United Nations in 1945, multilateral trade negotiations were conducted within the framework of the United Nations Economic and Social Council, which in 1946 adopted a resolution in favour of forming an International Trade Organisation (ITO). See Matsushita et al, *op cit*, 1.

15 August suggests that President Truman uncertain of an endorsement of the Charter by an opposition Congress that had become conservative and protectionist did not submit the Charter for ratification. There were also fears that American policy would be

adversely affected. *See* August *op cit*, p. 356. Matsushita et al, more emphatically state that when the Republicans won the 1948 American elections for Congress, the Truman administration announced it would no longer seek congressional approval for the ITO. *See* Matsushita et al, *op cit*, 2.

16 See Phillipe Sands & Pierre Klein, *Bowett's Law of International Institutions* Sweet & Maxwell 5th Ed (2001) p. 116; See also John H. Jackson *The World Trading System – Law and Policy of International Economic Relations* MIT Press (1992) 37.

17 See the second paragraph, Preamble to GATT 1947.

18 See the third paragraph, Preamble to the WTO Agreement, 1994.

19 See the Preambles to the Agreement.

20 See Faizel Ismail, 'Mainstreaming Development into the World Trade Organisation', *JWT Vol 39. No. 1*, pp 11–21 at p. 13; See also V. Engammare & J.P. Lehmann, 'Does the Multilateral Trading System Promote the Interests of the Poor?' in CUTS: *From Cancun to Sao Paolo: The Role of the Civil Society in the International Trading System*' (2004).

21 See WTO Director General Pascal Lamy, 'The Doha Round at A Cross Road' *Speech to UN Economic and Social Council High-Level Dialogue*, 2 July 2007; [http://www.wto.org/english/news_e/sppl_e/sppl64_e.htm].

22 WTO Director General Pascal Lamy, Internet Chat 21 February 2006. Available online: [http://www.wto.org/english/forums_e/chat_e/chat_transcript_e.doc] accessed 23.02.06.

23 Debra P Steger, *Peace through Trade: Building the World Trade Organisation* (2004) Cameron May, p. 19.

24 There has been long interest in this area. See generally, Bulajic M, *Principles of International Development Law*, Martinus Nijhoff Pub 2nd Ed. (1998). See also the work at UNCTAD level beginning with the New International Economic order and the Charter of Economic Rights and Duties of States; the work of the International Law Commission. See also the International Development Law Organisation (IDLO) (*www.idlo.int*) which aims to increase awareness of the need for 'development law'.

25 Joseph Stiglitz, *Globalisation and its Discontents* (2002) Penguin Books pp 251–2.

26 Article 2; GA 41/128, 4 December 1986.

27 Faizel Ismail, 'Mainstreaming Development in the World Trade Organisation' *JWT* Vol 39. No.1 pp 11–21, at 2.

28 See Armatya Sen, *Development as Freedom* (1999) Oxford University Press p. 3.

29 Id, pp 3–4.

30 Id, p. 4.

31 See, Eugenio Diaz-Bonilla, Sherman Robinson, Marcelle Thomas Yukitsugu Yanona, "WTO, Agriculture, and Developing Countries: A Survey of Issues; *TMD Discussion Paper No. 81*, International Food Policy Research Institute (IFPRI) (Jan 2002), p. 5. Online: [http://www.ifpri.org/divs/tmd/dp/papers/tmdp81.pdf].

32 *Compact Oxford Dictionary Thesaurus and Word Power Guide, op cit*, p. 239.

33 See generally, Arze Glipo, Laura Carlsen, Azra Talat Sayeed, Jayson Cainglet and Rita Schwentesius, "*Agreement on Agriculture and Food Security: Perspectives from MesoAmerica and Asia*," Americas Policy, International Relations Centre, (September 2003) online: [http://americas.irc-online.org/wto/2003/0309aoa.html]; Aileen Kwa, "Agriculture in Developing Countries: Which Way Forward", T.R.A.D.E. Occasional Papers 4, South Centre (June 2001) online: [http://www.focusweb.org/publications/2001/agriculture_which_way_forward.html].

34 Support here refers to significant government or non-governmental support. Comparison can be made with the EC agriculture regime under its Common Agricultural Policy. The Policy, an agreement between the Member States entered into about fifty years ago with the prevalent food shortages of the period, was primarily for subsiding production of basic foodstuffs in the interests of self sufficiency. Emphasis in current years has shifted to direct payments to farmers. More recently, reforms which seek to simplify the CAP are underway. The reforms are geared predominantly towards a harmonisation of the policy rules under the various EU constituent markets. See generally the EU web page on Agriculture, online at: [http://europa.eu.int/comm/agriculture/index_en.htm].

35 See *International Trade – Unlocking the potential for Human Development*, "UN Human Development Report (2005)" Chapter 4, pp 111–148 at 115 online at: [http://hdr.undp.org/reportd/global/2005].

36 See generally, Sophia Murphy, '*Food Security and the WTO*' CAFOD Policy Papers (September 2001) online at [http://www.cafod.org.uk/archive/policy/wtofoodsecurity.shtml].

37 See generally WTO TPR (US): section on *Trade Policies by* Sector "Trade Policy Review – USA" (WTO Report) WT/TPR/S/160 (22 and 24 March 2006) p. 86.

38 See the EU web page *The Common Agricultural Policy (CAP) and the Lisbon Strategy – 'Agriculture – the heartbeat of rural areas'*, online at [http://europa.eu.int/comm/agriculture/lisbon/index_en.htm].

39 The United Nations *Human Development Report* (2005) *op cit*, refers.

40 See Edmund Goldsmith; *Development as Colonialism* (Eds, Edward Goldsmith and Jerry Mander) *The Case Against a Global Economy and For a Turn Towards Localisation*, (2001) Earthscan Publications Ltd p. 19. Prior to this public statement, there have been and continue to be political as well as economic based identifications of poorer countries, identified variously as 'The Third World'; The South.

41 See *A-Z of World Development* (Compiled by Andy Crump; Ed. Wayne Ellwood) New International Publications Ltd (1998) p. 78.

42 Much reliance in this regard is placed on the OECD List of countries determined to be Developing or Least Developing countries. See generally, *The DAC Journal Development Cooperation Report 2004*, Journal of the OECD Development Assessment Committee (DAC) Vol. 6. No. 1. 2005. See also '*Foreign Aid – An Introductory Overview of US Programs and Policy*', Updated April 15 2004 (US Congressional Research Service Report) Library of Congress Order Code 98–916, Online [http://usinfo.state.gov/usa/infousa/trade/files/98–916.pdf]; '*The European Consensus for Development*', Joint Statement by the Council and the Representatives of the Governments of the Member States Meeting Within the Council, The European Parliament and the Commission. Doc No. 14820/05 Annex 1 and Annex 11; DGE11Online[http://europa.eu.int/comm/development/body/development_policy_statement/index_en.htm]; *Japan's Medium-Term Policy on Official Development Assistance* [Provisional Translation] Government of Japan, Feb 4 2005 Online [http://www.mofa.go.jp/policy/oda/mid-term/policy.pdf]. Other independent groups include Non-Governmental Organisations (NGOs) who work actively in the development related sector. See for example: OXFAM, online at *www.oxfam.org*, and CAFOD at *www.cafod.org.uk*

43 See 'United Nations Standard Country or Area Code for Statistical Use'; Series M, No. 49, Rev. 4 (UN Publication, Sales No. M.98.XVII.9). See the UN Statistics Division web page [http://unstats.un.org/unsd/cdb/cdb_dict_xrxx.asp?def_code 5 491].

44 See Milan Bulajic, 'Subjects of International Development Law: Definitions of a Developing Country' in *Principles of International Development Law*, Martinus Nijhoff Pub 2nd Ed. (1998) pp 66–73 at 67.

45 The World Bank Group is made up of five organizations: the International Bank for Reconstruction and Development (IBRD), the International Development Association (IDA), the International Finance Corporation (IFC), the Multilateral Investment Guarantee Agency (MIGA), and the International Centre for Settlement of Investment Disputes (ICSID). [http://devdata.worldbank.org/wdi2005/UsersGuide.htm]. See *World Development Indicators* World Bank (2005).

46 See generally, the World Bank web site: www.worldbank.org

47 Id. The World Bank Group clarifies that: 'The term country, used interchangeably with economy, does not imply political independence, but refers to any territory for which authorities report separate social or economic statistics'.

48 The World Bank borrows from the UN statistics definition – The United Nations Statistics Division defines GNI as: 'The aggregate value of the gross balances of primary incomes for all sectors. GNI is equal to GDP less taxes (less subsidies) on production and imports, compensation of employees and property income payable to the rest of the world plus the corresponding items receivable from the rest of the world. Thus GNI at market prices is the sum of gross primary incomes receivable by resident institutional units/sectors. It is commonly denominated GNP. In contrast to GDP, GNI is not a concept of value added, but a concept of income.' ('United Nations, Commission of the European Communities, International Monetary Fund, Organisation for Economic Cooperation and Development and World Bank System of National Accounts 1993' (SNA 1993) Series F, No. 2 Rev. 4 (UN Publication Sales No. E. 94. XVII. 4 para 2.181 and para 7.16. [Online at http://unstats.un.org/unsd/cdb/cdb_dict_xrxx.asp?def_code=326].

49 For instance, Britain's GNI (like other countries') will include profits from British owned businesses located in other countries. See The Economist: *Guide to Economic Indicators – Making sense of economics* (The Economist) Fifth Ed. (2003) p. 28.

50 See n. 19 above.

51 Id.

52 The OECD is an organisation of countries which have ratified the Convention on Economic Co-operation and Development of 14 December 1960. They share a common aim of democratic governance and market economy. See the official website of the organisation: www.oecd.org

53 Id.

54 The List is compiled by the Development Assistance Committee of the OECD and sets out the countries for Aid-assistance by the 30–Member OECD. High income countries are not recipients of the organisation's Aid assistance. There is a 3 year review period for the Aid Assistance classification and the current one mentioned is for 2006, 2007, and 2008. See the OECD development data/statistics page [http://www.oecd.org/dataoecd/43/51/35832713.pdf].

55 This system of analysis has earlier been criticised. See Matsushita et al, *op cit*, at p. 373 where they argued that "there are anomalies in the method of classification. Certain Middle Eastern Countries have high per capita incomes because of oil resources that are not really industrialised. Other economies, such as Singapore and Israel are considered developing by some international organisations but have high per capita incomes. The economies of Eastern Europe including Russia are middle income economies but have many of the characteristics of industrialised countries."

56 See generally, the organisation's history on the UNCTAD website at www.unctad.org

57 Id.

58 See the UNCTAD Hand Book of Statistics 2005 Doc No. TD/STAT.30.

59 Id.

60 Id. p. 10.

61 Id. The UNCTAD Hand Book also covers a wider identification including distinguishing between 'major-petroleum exporting countries' and 'other developing economies', the latter subdivided into 'major exporters of manufactures and; remaining economies distributed by major geographical regions. The data also includes a list of LDCs.

62 See the UN website *op cit.*

63 E/2005/51/Rev. 1ˢᵗ/ESA/298, a publication of the United Nations Department for Economic and Social Affairs. The Report provides objective analysis of pressing long-term social and economic development issues, and discusses the positive and negative impact of corresponding policies. See the website at [http://www.un.org/esa/analysis/wess/index.html].

64 Renamed in 1998, formerly Committee for Development Planning. See the CDP background notes on its webpage at: [http://www.un.org/esa/analysis/devplan/cdp backgroundnote.pdf].

65 ECOSOC is the intergovernmental body which makes policy recommendations to the UN Member States and to the UN system on matters pertaining to development. See the CDP web page *op cit.*

66 Id.

67 Id.

68 Id. See generally, the CDP web page at http://www.un.org/esa/analysis/devplan/. See also the UN Human Development Report (2005) – 'International Cooperation at a Crossroads Aid Trade and Security in an Unequal World' online on the UNDP web page: [http://hdr.undp.org/reports/global/2005].

69 See the IMF webpage at http://www.imf.org/external/about.htm. See also the IMF Lending factsheet online: [http://www.imf.org/external/np/exr/facts/howlend.htm]. Any country can request financial assistance to make international debt payments under an 'arrangement' which requires the debtor country to adopt specific policies that will solve its debt problems. Criticism of this 'arrangement' requirement is mostly based on the severe crippling economic programmes developing countries have to implement to receive the loans. See for example Frances Stewart and Valpy Fitzgerald, 'The IMF and global economy: Implications for Developing Countries', *QEH Working Papers Series No. 3*, online: [http://www2.qeh.ox.ac.uk/RePEc/qeh/qehwps/qehwps03.pdf]; Dani Rodrik, 'The Limits of Trade Policy Reform in Developing Countries', Journal of Economic Perspectives Vol 6. No. 1 pp 87–105 at 89–91.

70 See the IMF web page, id.

71 See IMF World Economic Outlook, (May 1998) Statistical Appendix, available online at: [http://www.imf.org/external/pubs/ft/weo/weo0598/pdf/0598sta.pdf]. Country group composites for exchange rates, interest rates, and the growth rates of monetary aggregates are weighted by GDP converted to US dollars at market exchange rates (averaged over the preceding three years) as a share of world or group GDP Composites for other data relating to the domestic economy, whether growth rates or ratios, are weighted by GDP valued at purchasing power parities (PPPs) as a share of total world or group GDP.

72 See the BBC web page at [http://news.bbc.co.uk/1/hi/world/americas/country_profiles/3777557.stm].

73 As stated earlier the determination of which countries are 'developing countries' relies heavily on OECD recommendations. It appears on a close reading of the 2005 Summit Document that the reference to developing countries/territories weighed predominantly in favour of countries in Africa. See the G8 Summit 2005 Document–The Gleneagles Communiqué 2005 at: [http://www.fco.gov.uk/Files/kfile/PostG8_Gleneagles_Communique,0.pdf]. See also Oxfam: 'Zambia uses G8 debt cancellation to make health care free', 31 March 2006 online at: [http://www.oxfam.org.uk/press/releases/zambi_debt310306.htm].

74 This may become an issue in the accession process as was in the case with China. See generally Karen Halverson 'China's WTO Accession: Economic, Legal and Political Implications' *Boston College Int'l & Comp Law Review Vol 27. No.* 2, 2004; Frederick M Abbott (ed) *China in the World Trading System: Defining the Principles of Engagement* Kluwer Law International (1998); Jeremy Brooks Rosen 'China, Emerging Economies and the World Trade Order' *46 Duke L. J. No.* 5 April 1997 pp. 1519–1564.

75 See GATT Article XVIII:1.

76 With reference to the United Nations Committee for Development Planning earlier mentioned, FN 13, *above*. There are four criteria relied on in this regard: *per capita income; population size; quality of life index; and economic diversification.* See UNESCOR, 29 Session. Supp No. 2 at 64, 67; UN Doc E/1994/22 (1994).

77 WTO Agreement Article XI:2.

78 See the WTO web page: [http://www.wto.org/English/thewto_e/whatis_e/inbrief_e/inbr04_e.htm].

79 See Michael J. Trebilcock & Robert Howse, *The Regulation of International Trade* 2nd Ed. (Routledge 1999) p. 2.

80 Id p. 19.

81 The scholars note the exception of Britain in this regard.

82 See generally, Ha-Joon Chang, *Kicking Away The Ladder – Development Strategy in Historical Perspective* (2002) Anthem Press, London; Robert McGee, *The Moral Case for Free Trade* (1995) 29 Journal of World Trade, p. 69; Gilbert Winsham, *The Evolution of International Trade Agreements* (1992) University of Toronto Press, Chapter 1; P.Bairoch, *European Trade Policy 1815–1914* (Matthias & Pollard eds; The Cambridge Economic History of Europe Vol 8 – Cambridge MA: Cambridge University Press 1989) p. 103; Douglas Irwin, *Against the Tide: An Intellectual History of Free Trade* Princeton NJ: Princeton University Press, 1996.

83 See Ha-Joon Chang, *Trade Lessons for Developing Countries from the History Books*, Newsletter of the Economic Research Forum for the Arab Countries, Iran & Turkey, Vol. 10. No. 3, Autumn 2003. See also the Economic Research Form website at www.erf.org

84 See Joseph E. Stiglitz and Andrew Charlton, *Fair Trade for all – How Trade can Promote Development* (2005) Oxford University Press p. 16.

85 Id, p. 38.

89 Id.

87 Id, p. 17.

88 Joseph Stiglitz, *Addressing Developing Country Priorities and Needs in the Millennium Round*, R.Porter & P.Sauve (eds) "Seattle, The WTO and the Future of the Multilateral Trading System", Havard University Press (2000) 31–60 at pp 53–55.

89 Fifty six countries in total were involved. At this stage, many of these developing countries were either colonies or had just achieved independence from the developed Members. This link would have facilitated their involvement although they were not economically\

independent. Incidentally only one developing country, Liberia, ratified the ITO Charter. See Michael Hart and Bill Dymond, *op cit*, at 399.

90 GATT: Recital in Preamble, '*Trends in International Trade* GATT BISD (6th Supp) (1958).

91 (1958). It takes its title after the Panel Chairman.

92 See GATT, *Trends in International Trade, A Report by a Panel of Experts* (Geneva: GATT, 1958).

93 Id.

94 Michael Hart and Bill Dymond, *op cit*, at 400.

95 See *Uruguayan Recourse to Article XXIII* L/1923 (15 Nov 1962) GATT BISD (11th Supp) 95; L/2074 (30 Oct 1963) GATT BISD (13th Supp) 35; L/2278 (27 Oct 1964) GATT BISD (13th Supp) 45.

96 Austria, Belgium, Canada, Czechoslovakia, Denmark, Finland, France, Federal Republic of Germany, Italy, Japan, The Netherlands, Norway, Sweden, Switzerland and the United States.

97 Including edible oils, wheat , barley, patent leather, meats, amongst others.

98 See *General Observations* by the Panel, L/1923 (15 Nov 1962) *op cit*, at para 22.

99 L/1923, para 19.

100 See generally, the conclusions of the Panel Report.

101 See para 16–19 of the Report, id.

102 See Article XVIII: 2(a).

103 See Article XVIII: 2(b).

104 See Article XVIII:9.

105 Panel Report: (India Quantitative Restrictions) *WT/DS90/R* 6 April 1999.

106 Other Members joined in the complaint: Australia – WT/DS91/R; Canada – WT/DS92/R; New Zealand – WT/DS93/R; Switzerland – WT/DS94/R; European Communities – WT/DS96/R.

107 Annex - Part B of WT/BOP/N/24. 22 May 1997.

108 Article XVIII:11 allowed for the progressive relaxation of such restrictions until they were no longer necessary. A proviso states that '…no CONTRACTING PARTY shall be required to withdraw or modify restrictions on the grounds that a change in its development policy would render unnecessary, the restrictions which it is applying'.

109 Pursuant to Article 13 on the Right to Seek Information -See *Understanding on the Rules and Procedures Governing the Settlement of Disputes*, (Dispute Settlement Understanding– DSU) 1994.

110 See *Report on the Consultation with India*, WT/BOP/R/22, 3 March 1997, at para 8; *India-Quantitative Restrictions*, para 3.359–3.370.

111 See para 3.166–7, *India – Quantitative Restrictions, op cit*.

112 GATT Dispute: *BISD 8S/31*, 30 May 1959.

113 GATT Dispute: *BOP/R/63, 20 July 1973* adopted by GATT Council on 19 October 1973.

114 GATT: L/1088, 3 November 1959.

115 See para 3.165, *India – Quantitative Restrictions, op cit*. Italics for emphasis.

116 Ibid, para 5.174–5.176; 5.183; 5.219.

117 The Panel Report was adopted by the Appellate Body after an appeal by India in WT/DS90/AB/R, 23 August 1999.

118 In this regard, the Panel cited the Award of the Arbitrator in the case on *Indonesia – Certain Measures Affecting the Automobile Industry*, WT/DS54/15, WT/DS55/14, WT/DS59/13, WT/DS64/12, 7 December 1998, para 24. In the instant case, the

Panel had also earlier considered generally, the issues of special and differential treatment maintained under Article XVIII:B which allowed for the situations under which developing countries could adopt restrictions for balance of payment purposes – See generally paras 5.152–5.157 of the Panel Report. These situations had not been proved by India.

119 By 1 April 2001, India had complied with the recommendations. The Panel Report was adopted by the AB. See generally AB Report: *WT/DS90/AB/R* 23 August 1999 at paras 153–4.

120 See the Panel Report at para 3.205–8.

121 Id, para 5.154.

122 See the first sentence of Article XVIII:11.

123 See the Panel Report, *op cit*, para 5.221; See the AB Report *op cit*, para 130. It could be argued here that the Panel's reasoning here lends itself to the criticism that indeed it ought not to have assumed jurisdiction over the case. An evaluation of the propriety of the measures may have been better fulfilled under the BOP Committee and not pursuant to a judicial review. See further; Roessler F., '*The Institutional Balance Between the Judicial and the Political Organs of the WTO*', Conference on "Efficiency, Equity, and Legitimacy: The Multilateral Trading System at the Millennium June 1–2, 2000 Online: [http://www.ksg.harvard.edu/m-rcbg/Conferences/trade/roessler.htm].

124 See the Panel Report, *op cit*, para 3.210.

125 See the Panel Report *op cit*, paras 5.152–5.157; 5.221.

126 See generally, WTO: TPR Report of India–Report of the Secretariat, *WT/TPR/S/33* of 5 March 1998; Report of the Government of India, *WT/TPR/G/33* of 30 March 1998.

127 See *WT/TPR/G/33 op cit*, para 2.

128 See publication by the South Centre 'A Historical Note' *Special and Differential Treatment: Background and Policy Issues at Stake*, para 4, Online: [http:// www.southcentre.org/publications/snd/snd–03.htm#P295_44724]. See also Hesham Youssef, 'Special and Differential Treatment for Developing Countries in the WTO' South Centre T.R.A.D.E. Working Paper 2 (June 1999) p. 3.

129 At the same time some developing countries, seventy-seven (77) in number, formed the 'Group of Seventy-Seven'. With current Membership of over 130 countries, it retains its original name for historic reasons and is the largest gathering of developing countries' representation at the United Nations. It aims to provide the means for the developing world to articulate and promote its collective economic interests and enhance its joint negotiating capacity on all major international issues in the United Nations system, and promote economic and technical cooperation among developing countries. See the G–77 web site: www.g77.org

130 See 'About UNCTAD', at the organisation's website, *www.unctad.org, op cit.*

131 Id.

132 The Protocol amending the General Agreement on Tariffs and Trade to introduce a Part IV on Trade and Development adopted in February 1965, entered into force in June 1966. The time-limit for acceptance of the Protocol was extended annually until 1979, when the Protocol was accepted by all contracting parties to the GATT 1947. See the WTO website at: [http://www.wto.org/english/thewto_e/whatis_e/eol/e/wto02/wto2_12.htm#note2].

133 Article XXXVI: 1(a).

134 Article XXXVI:2.

135 See generally GATT Article XXXVIII.

136 Michael Hart and Bill Dymond, *op cit*, 401.

137 *European Communities – Refunds on Exports of Sugar Complaint by Brazil. 10 November 1980* GATT BISD (27th Supp), 69. Although decided in 1980, pre-WTO, this case is considered because it deals with the relevant application of Part IV GATT.

138 See *European Economic Community – Restrictions on Imports of Desert Apples – Complaint by Chile*, 22 June 1989, GATT BISD (36th Supp) at 93.

139 The Government of Brazil complained that the EEC was in breach of Articles XVI:1; 3. These provisions directed Contracting Parties to discuss the possibility of limiting the granting of a subsidy which would be a serious prejudice to the interests of any other contracting party and; where granted such subsidy should not result in the granting party having more than an equitable share of the world export trade in that product.

140 Part V (h) – *Conclusion*.

141 See para 12.32, id.

142 An UNCTAD initiative (1968) pursued with the co-operation of developed countries under the OECD. See the UNCTAD web page: [http://www.unctad.org/Templates/Page.asp?intItemID=3358&lang=1].

143 The waiver was on Article 1 of the General Agreement on the Most Favoured Nation (MFN) non-discriminatory rule which sought that the GATT Contracting Parties would accord the same treatment to goods originating from the territories of other contracting parties.

144 New Delhi, 1968.

145 See the UNCTAD-GSP web page: [http://www.unctad.org/Templates/Page.asp?intItemID=2309&lang=1]; See Decision of 25 June 1971, GATT BISD (18th Supp) p. 24 adopting the waiver under the GSP. The adoption of preferential tariff treatment for developing countries was adopted via: Decision of 26 November 1971, GATT BISD (18th Supp) p. 26.

146 There are 13 national GSP schemes currently notified to the UNCTAD Secretariat. The following countries grant GSP preferences: Australia, Belarus, Bulgaria, Canada, Estonia, the European Union, Japan, New Zealand, Norway, the Russian Federation, Switzerland, Turkey and the United States of America.

147 GATT Decision, L/4903, of 28 November 1979.

148 (FN in original). As described in the Decision of the CONTRACTING PARTIES of 25 June 1971, relating to the establishment of "generalized, non-reciprocal and non discriminatory preferences beneficial to the developing countries" (BISD 18S/24).

149 Id, para 2 (a–d).

150 *EC-Tariff Preferences* Panel Report *WT/DS246/R* 1 December 2003; AB Report *WT/DS246/AB/R*, 7 April 2004. In this case, India challenged the conditions under which the EC grants tariff preferential treatment to developing countries under its GSP scheme.

151 For an analysis of the requirement in the conditions for the grant of preferential treatment under EC-GSP scheme, see Lorand Bartles, 'The WTO Enabling Clause and Positive Conditionality in the European Community's GSP Programme' *6 JIEL* 2 (2003) pp 507–532; See also the analysis of the EU-ACP partnership and the development considerations in the trade arrangement, in Cosmas Ocheng; 'The EU-ACP Economic Partnership Agreements and the Development Question: Constraints and Opportunities Posed'; JIEL Online: [doi:10.1093/jiel/jgm009v1].

152 10 December 2001.

153 See the AB Report at para 173.

154 See para 175–6 of the AB Report.

155 See Tomer Bronde, *International Governance in the WTO: Judicial Boundaries and Political Capitulation* Cameron May (2004), p. 27.

156 See para 165 of the AB Report.

157 Id.

158 Para 167, AB Report.

159 *EC- Sugar cases* – Panel Reports: *WT/DS265/R (Australia); WT/DS266/R (Brazil); WT/283/R (Thailand)* of 15 October 2004; AB Reports WT/DS265/AB/R; WT/DS266/AB/R; WT/DS283/AB/R respectively, 28 April 2005. Third parties in support of the EC were Barbados, Belize, Congo, Côte d'Ivoire, Cuba, Fiji, Guyana, India, Jamaica, Kenya, Madagascar, Malawi, Mauritius, St. Kitts and Nevis, Swaziland and Zimbabwe. Thailand (subsequently joined as complainant) and the United States joined as third parties in support of the complainants.

160 19 June 2001.

161 See *WT/DS265/6*, para 7.366–7.374 at 7.373.

162 See *WT/DS265/AB/R* para 321–335. The AB reasoned that it was 'false judicial economy and legal error' not to make a finding on whether the export subsidies made contingent upon producers and exporters using domestic EC sugars were contrary to Article 3 of the SCM Agreement. In the AB's view, the findings under the Agreement on Agriculture were 'not sufficient to "fully resolve" the dispute'. See para 335.

163 See B. Balassa, '*Liberalising Trade between Developed and Developing Countries, The Importance of Trade for Developing Countries' New Directions in the World Economy* (1989) New York: NYU Press; See also, Caglar Ozden and Eric Reinhardt, 'The Perversity of Preferences: GSP and Developing Country Trade Preferences', *op cit*; See also, Tracking Developments in International Trade Disputes, The South Centre Quarterly on Trade Disputes Vol 1. Issue No. 4 (2005).

164 26 February 2001.

165 These products are subject to a gradual liberalisation process geared to setting zero duties for these products at specified times: bananas – January 2006; rice – September 2009; sugar – July 2009.

166 See Paul Brenton; 'Integrating the Least Developed Countries into the World Trading System: The Current Impact of European Union Preferences under 'Everything But Arms'' *Journal of World Trade* Vol 37. No. 3 (2003) pp 329–357.

167 Uruguay Round Agreement, 1994.

168 Id, para 2(i).

169 Id, para 2(ii).

170 Id, para 2(iv).

171 Id, para 2(iii).

172 Id, para 2(v).

173 Id, para 3.

174 *WT/L/304* of 17 June 1999. The waiver shall operate till 30 June 2009.

175 See, *Preferential Tariff Treatment for Least Developed Countries–'Decision on Waiver'* WT/L/304, adopted 15 June 1999.

176 See the WTO web page on developing countries: [http://www.wto.org/english/thewto_e/whatis_e/tif_e/dev1_e.htm]. See also the web page of the ACWL: *www.acwl.ch.* CF Chapter 3.

177 For a detailed analysis of the relevant provisions, see generally *Implementation of Special and Differential Treatment Provisions in WTO Agreements and Decisions' Committee*

on Trade and Development Doc No. WT/COMTD/W/77, 25 October 2000. Available online : [http://docsonline.wto.org/DDFDocuments/t/WT/COMTD/ W77.doc].

178 For a detailed summary of all SDT provisions, see *Guide to the Uruguay Round Agreements* Part 5 on Developing Countries in the WTO system *op cit*; See also *Annex 11: Summary of Provisions Contained in the Uruguay Round Agreements for the Differential and More Favourable Treatment of Developing and Least Developed Countries.* Available online: [http://www.wto.org/ english/tratop_e/devel_e/anexii_ e.doc].

179 See Constantinople Michalopoulos, "The Role of Special and Differential Treatment for Developing Countries in GATT and the World Trade Organisation" *Policy Research Working Paper WPS 2388*, World Bank Development Research Group Trade, (July 2000) at p. 15; See also, T. Ademola Oyejide; 'Special and Differential Treatment' in Hoekman et al (2002) 504–8.

180 See the Doha Ministerial Declaration *op cit* at para 44 where the Ministerial Conference stated: "We reaffirm that provisions for special and differential treatment are an integral part of the WTO Agreements."

181 See Thomas Fritz," Special and Differential Treatment for Developing Countries", *Global Issue Paper, No.18*, The Heinrich Boll Foundation (May 2005) at p. 13.

182 See "Implementation of Special and Differential Treatment Provisions in WTO Agreements and Decisions. Mandatory and Non-Mandatory Special and Differential Treatment Provisions, WT/COMTD/W/77/Rev. 1/Add. 1, 21 Dec 2001. Online on the WTO Documents webpage [http://docsonline.wto.org] hereinafter referred to as WTO 2001a. The document notes that provisions in Category (vi) all fall into one of the other five categories, but are distinctive insofar as their application relates exclusively to least-developed countries.

183 For a detailed analysis and presentation of the associated provisions for LDC's see WTO (COMTD): *Special and Differential Treatment for Least Developed Countries*, Committee on Trade and Development, Doc No. WT/COMTD/W/135, 5 October 2004. Many of the agreements provide LDCs flexibility in the implementation of certain rules and commitments including longer implementation periods. For example, the Agreement on Agriculture exempts LDCs from reduction commitments on domestic support, export subsidies and market access. The *SCM Agreement* exempts the least-developed Members and other poor developing countries from the prohibition on export subsidies. In many cases in which a transitional period has been allowed to developing country Members (e.g. TRIPS, TRIMS, SPS), the least-developed Members have been given a longer time-frame. Available online at: [http://docsonline.wto.org/DDFDocuments/t/ WT/COMTD/W135.doc].

184 Id, p. 1, para 3.

185 WTO 2001a *op cit*, p. 1, 3rd para.

186 See WTO2002a, 2nd para.

187 See 'Non-Mandatory Special and Differential Treatment Provisions in WTO Agreements and Decisions' WT/COMTD/W/77/Rev. 1/Add. 3; 4 February 2002 para 3, p. 2 hereinafter referred to as WTO 2002b *op cit*.

188 See paras 5–7 WTO 2002b.

189 See generally, Article X:1 – 10, WTO *Agreement*. Any Member may initiate a proposal for amendment which would need to be formally accepted by all the Members. The acceptance of any proposals for amendment depends on the provisions of the particular Agreement and the consensus by the required number of Members as set out in the respective Agreements needed to make the amendments of legal effect.

To date there has not been any recourse to amendment provisions of the WTO Agreement.

190 Article IX:2 WTO Agreement.

191 *Canada – Aircraft case*. An appeal from a complaint by Brazil, WT/DS70/AB/R, 20 August 1999.

192 See DSU, Article 13.1.

193 See para 187; *Canada – Aircraft case*. It is noted that the AB considered the *ordinary* dictionary meaning of the word 'should' finding that it implies no more than a moral obligation , thus distinguishing it (should) from the directly normative 'ought'. See FN 120 of the AB Report.

194 ("EC –Hormones"), WT/DS26/AB/R, WT/DS48/AB/R, 13 February 1998.

195 In the context of Article 11 DSU on the function of the panels; See para 33 of the AB Report.

196 See the Doha Declaration, para 44, *op cit.*

197 A corrigendum: "Implementation of Special and Differential Treatment Provisions in WTO Agreements and Decisions. Mandatory and Non-Mandatory Special and Differential Treatment Provisions, WT/COMTD/W/77/Rev.1/Add.1/Corr.1, 4 Feb 2002 hereinafter referred to as WTO 2002a.

198 Stanley E. Edwards, 'Drafting Fiscal Legislation' *32 Canadian Tax Journal (1984)* p. 727 at 728, quoted in Dennis R. Klinck, *The Word of the Law: Approaches to Legal Discourse*, Carleton University Press (1992) p. 220.

199 The full title is *"Implementation of Article VII of the General Agreement on Tariffs and Trade 1994"*.

200 Article 1 of the Customs Valuation Agreement is to be read together with Article 8. See General Introductory Commentary of the Agreement.

201 It had been analysed in 2001 that it would cost a typical developing country about 150m USD to implement Customs Valuation; SPS; TRIPS, about a year's development budget for LDCs – See J.M. Finger "Implementing the Uruguay Round Agreements: Problems for Developing Countries" The World Economy Vol 24. No. 9 at pp 1097–1098, cited in C. George and C. Kirkpatrick, *op cit*, at 323–4.

202 Asif H. Qureshi, *The World Trade Organisation – Implementing International Trade Norms*, Manchester University Press (1996) p. 139. Developing countries have often raised this issue of lack of capacity to administer the WTO Agreements and facilitate their reliance on the SDT provisions to their benefit in respective government reports under the Trade Policy Review Mechanism. See for example the Government Reports in the Trade Policy Reviews of the following: Angola, *WT/TPR/G/158* 14 & 16 February 2006 at p. 20; Trinidad and Tobago *WT/TPR/G/151* 14 & 16 September 2005 at p. 15; United Arab Emirates *WT/TPR/G/162* 24 & 26 April 2006 at p. 13.

203 Under this Agreement, four disputes have been raised but none reached judicial conclusion. See *Mexico – Certain Pricing Measures for Customs Valuation and other Purposes*, Complaint by Guatemala, *DS298*, 22 July 2003; *Romania – Measures on Minimum Import Prices* Complaint by US, *DS198*, 30 May 2000–both disputes reached a mutually satisfactory solution; *Brazil – Measures on Minimum Import Prices Complaint* by US, *DS197* 30 May 2000; *Mexico – Customs Valuation of Imports* Complaint by EU, *DS53* 27 August 1996 – in these two cases no Panels were established nor settlement notified.

204 The relevant provisions of Article 4 DSU are: **para 7** – "If the consultations fail to settle a dispute within 60 days after the date of receipt of the request for consultations, the complaining party may request the establishment of a panel. The complaining party may request a panel during the 60–day period if the consulting parties jointly

consider that consultations have failed to settle the dispute"; **para 8** – "In cases of urgency, including those which concern perishable goods, Members shall enter into consultations within a period of no more than 10 days after the date of receipt of the request. If the consultations have failed to settle the dispute within a period of 20 days after the date of receipt of the request, the complaining party may request the establishment of a panel".

205 *DS36*, 30 April 1996.

206 DSB Meeting, Held in the Centre William Rappard, Geneva, *WT/DSB/M/21*, 5 August 1996.

207 Pakistan also drew attention to the real difficulties faced by developing countries on the insistence by a developed country that consultations be held only in Geneva. At this point we suggest that issues such as these are properly addressed by the WTO in the area of technical assistance and capacity building where it has for instance provided for office space in Geneva for some Member States.

208 Both Parties eventually reached a mutually agreed solution notified to the DSB on 7 March 1997.

209 See Part 1, "*WT/COMTD/W/77/Rev. 1/Add. 2* of 21 Dec 2001 hereinafter referred to as WTO 2001b.

210 WTO 2001b; pp 34–36. The Annex sets out which provisions fall under each of the mentioned criteria and also distinguishes the provisions in line with the six general areas of special treatment identified by the WTO.

211 WTO 2001b, p. 1.

212 Id.

213 The WTO Secretariat has put in place a system whereby notifications of interest to developing and least developing countries are automatically sent to them. See Document *G/TBT/W/124* 22 December 1999.

214 The provision is also for the purpose of safeguarding the interests of developing country Members.

215 See the Committee web page at [http://www.wto.org/english/tratop_e/devel_e/d3ctte_e.htm]. Other Committees in related work include the Sub-Committee on LDCs, Working Group on Trade, Debt and Finance, Working Group on Trade and Transfer of Technology.

216 See para 51, Doha Declaration 4th WTO Ministerial Conference, Doha 14 Nov 2001, Doc No. *WT/MIN(01)/DEC/1*. See also "Doha Declaration Implementation-Related Issues and Concerns", *WT/MIN(01)/17* at para 12 which sets out COMTD responsibility in the area of SDTs.

217 See the CTD webpage *op cit*. See generally for example, "COMTD Work Programme for 2006", *WT/COMTD/56*, 10 March 2006.

218 Amrita Narlikar, *International Trade and Developing Countries: Bargaining Coalitions in the GATT and WTO* Routledge (2003) p. 14.

219 WTO; ERSD-2004–03 supra, at p. 9.

220 See also, the Joint Integrated Technical Assistance Programme (JITAP) website: *www.jitap.org*

221 The current Plan is for 2008/2009. See *WT/COMTD/W/160*, 2 Nov 2007.

222 See WTO: 'An Enhanced Integrated Framework'; Report of the Chairman of the Task Force on an Enhanced Integrated Framework Including Recommendations; *WT/IFSC/W/15* 29 June 2006.

223 Id.

224 Id.
225 See further, Julia Nielson, "Aid for Trade" in 'Trade, Doha and Development: A Window into the Issues" World Bank Papers, World Bank (2005) pp 323–332 at 329–330. The Secretariat of the Enhanced IF is at the WTO Headquarters in Geneva. The Task Force was set up after the Kong Kong Conference. See the WTO: Hong Kong Ministerial Conference: 'Doha Work Programme'; *WT/MIN(05)/DEC*, 22 December 2005 at para 57.
226 See the Hong Kong Declaration, *op cit*, at para 57. The AFT initiative is guided by the *Paris Declaration of Aid Effectiveness* 2 March 2005; a resolution of developed and developing countries, heads of bilateral and multilateral agencies. A full list of participants is available at: www.oecd.org/dac/effectiveness/parisdeclaration/members
227 WTO: 'Recommendations of the Task Force on Aid for Trade' *WT/AFT/1* 27 July 2006, at Section B.
228 Id, Section F.
229 Id, Section D.
230 Id.
231 See generally, the WTO Documents browse page ('Aid For Trade') for the respective AFT documents.
232 See the Hong Kong Declaration *op cit*, para 57.
233 See Helen Hughes, "Policy Forum: Economic Development: Trade or Aid? Trade, Aid and Development" *Australian Economic Review Vol 39, No. 1*, (March 2006) pp 63–68 at 65, where the author argues that "…it was already evident in the 1950's that development aid also had negative economic impacts in artificially appreciating a country's exchange rate, drawing resources from the private to the public sector, attracting incomes from rural to urban concentrations and, like unearned income, creating economic rents that spawned inefficiency and corruption." The author also cites the work of development economist Bauer P.T which drew "…attention to the negative impacts of development aid, in particular in keeping incompetent governments in power", concluding that "aid could thus serve to prevent institutional development."
234 See Carin Smaller, 'Can Aid fix trade?: Assessing the WTO's Aid for Trade Agenda', *Institute for Agriculture and Trade Policy* (IATP) Publication, (September 2006) pp 7–9.
235 Para 57, *op cit*.

Chapter Three. Developing Country Integration

1 Davey W.J, Jackson J.H & Sykes A.O.; *International Economic Relations* West Publishing Co. Third Ed. (1995) p.1206.
2 Id.
3 See Robert Hudec, *Developing Countries in the GATT* Gower, (1987) p. 228.
4 Id, 4.
5 Id. See particularly, pp 210–224.
6 Debra P. Steger, *Peace through Trade Building: Building the World Trade Organisation* Cameron May (2004) 19.
7 Constantine Michalopoulos; *Developing Countries in the WTO*, Palgrave Macmillan (2001) at p. 1.
8 See R. Samuelson, 'Persistent Poverty Defies the Wisdom on Globalisation' *International Herald Tribune* 21 Sep 2000.

9 We are not suggesting that this is a task for the WTO to undertake. Considerations such as these are properly within the field of social science and political economics and we would not presume to set the WTO beyond the scope of its work. However we consider that it is unwise to ignore the cultural influences in developing countries and the barriers these may place on a whole-sale adoption of the free market system.

10 (1987), p. xv.

11 See the World Bank Report, *op cit.*

12 See generally Oxfam Report; *Rigged Rules and Double Standards: Trade Globalisation and the Fight against Poverty* (2002); UNCTAD Trade and Development Report 2005 available on the UNCTAD website www.unctad.org; WTO International Trade Statistics 2005, 2006, 2007; all available on the WTO web site www.wto.org

13 UNCTAD Trade and Development Report 2005, *New Features of Global Interdependence* UN Publication (2005) p. III, online at [http://www.unctad.org/en/docs/tdr2005_en.pdf].

14 Id, p. VI.

15 B Hoekman and M Kostecki, *The Political Economy of the World Trading System* (2001) Oxford University Press, p. 9.

16 WTO (2005): World Trade in 2004 – Overview (Excel Charts): *Table 1.1 Growth in the volume of world merchandise exports and production 2000–04* Online: [http://www.wto.org/english/res_e/statis_e/its2005_e/its05_overview_e.pdf].

17 Id, *Table 1.5: Leading exporters and importers in world merchandise trade, 2004.*

18 Id, *Trade Volume and Output developments in 2004.*

19 See WTO (2007): 'World Trade Developments'; *International Trade Statistics 2006* Online [http://www.wto.org/english/res_e/statis_e/its2007_e/section1_e/its07_highlights1_e.pdf].

20 Id.

21 See WTO (2006): *Annual Report 2006,* p. III–IV. Online: [http://www.wto.org/english/res_e/booksp_e/anrep_e/anrep06_e.pdf].

22 See WTO (2007): 'Summary of Trade Developments in 2006–2007' *Annual Report 2007* p. 6 Online: [http://www.wto.org/english/res_e/booksp_e/anrep_e/anrep07_e.pdf].

23 See Joseph Stiglitz, *Globalisation and its Discontents op cit,* pp 6–8.

24 Silvia Ostry, *The Uruguay Round North-South Grand Bargain: Implications for future negotiations, The Political Economy of International Trade Law* Essays in Honour of Robert E. Hudec (Eds Daniel L.M Kennedy and James D. Southwick (2002) Cambridge University Press pp 285–300 at 287.

25 See further, Fred Bergsten, Director of the Institute for International Economics in Washington DC, *The Backlash against Globalisation,* Remarks made to the 2000 Annual Meeting of the Trilateral Commission Tokyo, 2000. He noted that developing countries seemed to be making these considerations after having acceded to the WTO, rather than before accession. Online at: [http:www.trilateral.org/annnmtgs/trialog/trlgtxts/t54/ber.htm].

26 Id, See J. Michael Finger, Comment: *The Uruguay Round North-South bargain: Will the WTO get over it?* Pp 301–310 at 308 commenting on Silvia Ostry, supra.

27 See generally Trade Policy Reviews of the US; EU *supra.* See also Neela Mukherjee, 'GATS and the Millennium Round of Multilateral Negotiations- Selected Issues from the Perspectives of the Developing Countries' *JWT Vol 33. No. 4* pp 87–102 at p. 93.

28 See Neela Mukherjee, 'GATS and the Millennium Round of Multilateral Negotiations – Selected Issues from the perspective of the developing countries'; JWT Vol 33. No. 4 (1999) pp 87–102, at 89.

29 Id.
30 See M.R. Narayana; '*ICT Sector and regional economic development: Evidence from Karnataka State*' (June 2005) ISEC-Cornell University Revised Conference Paper, September 2005. Available online [http://www.isec.ac.in/MRN].
31 See Kunal Kumar Kundu, '*India's underperforming industrial sector*' Asia Times Online (24 Dec 2004) Online at: [http://www.atimes.com/atimes/South_Asia/FL24Df01.html]. The author draws a comparison with Chinese industrial advancement which has placed China at the forefront of development achievement.
32 World Bank: *World Development Report 2005*, (Equity and Development (2005)) World Bank & Oxford University Press, p. 16.
33 Id.
34 Michael P Todaro, *Economic Development* (5th Ed) Longman Group UK Ltd p. 435. Emphasis in original.
35 Pascal Lamy in BBC 4 'Today Programme', (FM 93.90) Radio Interview, 31 January 2006.
36 The Seattle debacle, 2000 perfectly illustrates the conflicts of negotiating on issues of divergent interests and the conflicts of politics in negotiating strategies. See generally, John S. Odell, *The Seattle Impasse and its implications for the World Trade Organisation*, *The Political Economy of International Trade Law* Essays in Honour of Robert E. Hudec (Eds Daniel L.M Kennedy and James D. Southwick) *op cit*, pp 400–429.
37 Marc L. Busch and Eric Reinhardt, 'Developing Countries and General Agreement on Tariffs and Trade/World Trade Organisation Dispute Settlement' *JWT Vol 37. No. 4* (2003) pp 719–735 at 734.
38 See the WTO web page on developing countries.
39 P. Samuelson, *Economics* (10th Ed) (1976), p. 692.
40 Id.
41 P. Samuleson & W.D.Nordhaus, *op cit*, p. 673.
42 Adam Smith, *An Inquiry into the Nature and Causes of the Wealth of the Nations* (1776) (E. Canaan (ed.) University of Chicago Press, (1976) Vol 1. 478–9).
43 See P. Samuelson & W.D.Nordhaus, *op cit*, p. 689.
44 Id.
45 See the WTO web page, *Understanding the WTO: The case for open trade, op cit*. For a modern exposition of the concept, see Alan Sykes, 'Comparative Advantage and the Normative Economics of International Trade Policy' *JIEL* 1 (1998), 49–82.
46 See the WTO web page *Case for Open Trade* Ibid. (Emphasis in original).
47 *Op cit*, (3rd Edition) p. 3–4.
48 See Report of the De Beers Group: 'From Natural Resources to Shared Wealth: Diamonds and Development – the story of Botswana" – [http://www.debeersgroup.com/en/Media-centre/Videos/2008/From-Natural-Resources-to-Shared-National-Wealth/].
49 See the Republic of Botswana Government information on Economic growth in the country online at [http://www.gov.bw/index.php?option=com_content&task=view&id=63&Itemid=74].
50 In this respect, the income from diamonds and the contribution to the economy is not unlike the income from crude oil operations in other African countries.
51 See TPR Botswana W/TPR/S/35, 1 April 1998.
52 See *W/TPR/G/35*, 15 April 1998.
53 See the Republic of Botswana web page *op cit*.
54 See the DeBeers Annual Report: 'Living up to Diamonds – From Natural Resources to Shared Wealth' *Report to Society 2007*, pp 29.

55 See Kennedy K. Mbekeani (BIDPA) 'Inter-Agency Policy Co-ordination in Botswana' WTO Case Study available online: [http://www.wto.org/english/res_e/booksp_e/casestudies_e/case6_e.htm].

56 Per Jay Salkin, Id.

57 By this we mean exemptions such as under the Enabling Clause (waiver of Article 1 GATT).

58 See generally, Alan Deardoff, 'How Robust is Comparative Advantage?' *Research Seminar in International Economics Discussion Paper No. 537 (University of Michigan)* May 16 2005 particularly at p. 7.

59 Both economic and political studies have emphasised the influence on political considerations on trade policy making and trade activity. See for example, Dani Rodrik, Political Economy of Trade Policy, in Grossman Gene and Kenneth Rogoff (eds) *Handbook in International Economics* Elsevier (19950, Chapter 28; Andrew G. Long and Brett A. Leeds, 'Trading for Security: Military Alliances and Economic Agreements' Journal of Peace Research 7 2006 Vol 43. pp 433–451.

60 Yong-Shik Lee, *Reclaiming Development in the World Traing System* (CUP) 2006, pp 149–150.

61 Dani Rodrik, *Industrial Policy for the 21ˢᵗ Century*, Paper prepared for UNIDO (September 2004) p. 7.

62 Philip I. Levy, 'Do We Need an Undertaker for the Single Undertaking? Considering the Angles of Variable Geometry' in Simon J. Evenett & Bernard M. Hoekman (eds) *Economic Development and Multilateral Trade Cooperation* Palgrave Macmillan (2006) pp 417–437 at 417.

63 See Article II:1 *WTO Agreement, op cit.*

64 Jeffery J. Schott and Jayashree Watal, *op cit.*

65 See WTO: See 'Non-Mandatory Special and Differential Treatment Provisions in WTO Agreements and Decisions', WT/COMTD/W/77/Rev.1/Add.3, 4 February 2002, Part 1, para 6. Hereinafter referred to as WTO 2002b.

66 *Op cit.*

67 See generally, Alexander Keck & Patrick Low, 'Special and Differential Treatment in the WTO: Why, When, and How? in Simon J. Evenett & Bernard M. Hoekman (eds) (2006) *op cit*, pp 147–188.

68 John H Jackson *The World Trading System – Law and Policy of International Economic Relations* MIT Press (1997/2000) 2nd Ed. p. 111.

69 Judith Goldstein & Lisa L. Martin, 'Legalisation, Trade Liberalisation, and Domestic Policies', *54 Int'l Org* (2000) 603, at 603–4.

70 VanGrasstek C & Sauvé P, 'The Consistency of WTO Rules: Can the Single Undertaking be Squared with Variable Geometry?' *J. Int Ec Law 2006 Vol 9*; pp 837–864 at 863. The article presents an interesting analysis of the single undertaking from the perspectives of the US (which by virtue of a federal central governing authority is partial to the consistency of the single undertaking; the EU which is more amenable to the practice of 'code reciprocity' in line with its policy for integration across its membership and; the developing countries who demand for greater flexibility in the WTO Agreements to allow them meet their domestic social and economic demands.

71 Kal Raustiala, 'Form and Substance in International Agreements', *AJIL Vol. 99 No. 3*, (July 2005) pp 581–614 at p. 613.

72 WTO; *Understanding the WTO op cit*, 2.

73 Philip I. Levy in Simon J. Evenett & Bernard Hoekman *op cit* suggests that rather than basing WTO obligations on an acceptance of a broad range of trade agreements under a

single undertaking or even on single sector negotiations and undertakings, a middle ground for cross-sectoral negotiations would be beneficial to both developing and developed countries. He considers that such a middle ground is to be found not in the range of undertakings but with respect to the flexibility allowed in the 'amount of time allocated for developing countries to phase in reforms' p. 429. In our view, such a flexibility would have to be considerably more extensive than the present time frames in the current Agreements.

74 See the WTO web page on building trade capacity: [http://www.wto.org/english/tratop_e/devel_e/build_tr_capa_e.htm].

75 Id. Emphasis in original.

76 See, Hon Chibudom Nwuche, Deputy Speaker Nigeria House of Representatives, 'Nigeria and the World Trade Organisation' (Speech) *The Guardian* Newspapers (Nigeria), 6 March 2002, p. 70.

77 Id.

78 See Dr Adeboye Adeyemo, 'Should Nigeria pull out of WTO?' *Nigerian Tribune* 8 October 2005, p. 12.

79 Id.

80 See Walter Odhiambo, Paul Kamau & Dorothy McCormick, 'Kenya's Participation in the WTO: Lessons Learned' WTO Case Study: [http://www.wto.org/english/res_e/booksp_e/casestudies_e/case20_e.htm].

81 See for e.g, Ademola Oyejide, A Ogunkola and A Bankole; 'Import Prohibition as Trade Policy Instrument: The Nigerian Experience'; Case Study 32: *Managing the Challenges of WTO Participation*: [http://www.wto.org/english/res_e/booksp_e/casestudies_e/case32_e.htm].

82 See Tonia Kandero: 'Malawi in the Multilateral Trading System' WTO Case Study: [http://www.wto.org/english/res_e/booksp_e/casestudies_e/case23_e.htm].

83 See in particular Faizel Ismail, *op cit*; Constantinople Michalopoulos "The Role of Special and Differential Treatment for Developing Countries in GATT and the World Trade Organisation" *op cit*.

84 Pascal Lamy, "The Perspectives of the Multilateral Trading System", Speech at Lima, 31 January 2006, available online at: [http://www.wto/English/news_e/ppl_e/spp117_e.htm].

85 See The Economist: "More pain than gain", A *Survey of the World Economy*, September 16 2006.

86 See the WTO GATS page: [http://www.wto.org/english/tratop_e/serv_e/gats_factfiction1_e.htm].

87 The objective of the considerations under the WPDR is to ensure that measures relating to licensing requirements and procedures, qualification requirements and procedures, and technical standards do not constitute unnecessary barriers to trade in services. See the WTO WPDR Document: 'Disciplines on Domestic Regulation Pursuant to GATS Article VI:4' *JOB(06)/225*; July 2006. [http://www.tradeobservatory.org/library.cfm?refID= 88479] visited 25.10.07; See also the WPDR Document April 18 2007. See further, Elisabeth Tuerk, 'Domestic Regulation: Transparency, Proportionality, Harmonisation and Regulatory Capacity: A Development Perspective' UNCTAD Presentation – GATS and Financial Services Seminar; BIICL, 21 May 2007 See also See Mina Mashayekhi, 'Regionalism, Doha Negotiations and the Way Forward – PTAs, Institutions, Sustainability and Convergence with GATS Norms: A Development Perspective', UNCTAD Presentation – GATS and Financial Services Seminar; BIICL, 21 May 2007.

88 See also, Rupa Chanda, 'Movement of Natural Persons and the GATS – Major Trade Policy Impediments' in Hoekman et al (2002) 304–314.

89 See generally, Parts II (Scope and Use) and III (Enforcement) of the TRIPS Agreement. See also, Jayashree Watal; 'The TRIPS Agreement' in Hoekman et al 92002) 359–368; Arvind Subramanian; 'Proprietary Protection of Genetic Resources and Traditional Knowledge'; id, 382–9

90 See for example, *Brazil – Measures Affecting Patent Protection WT/DS199* 30 May 2000, a complaint by the US against provisions of Brazil's 1996 industrial property law and other related measures requiring a 'local working' requirement for granting patent rights. A mutually satisfactory solution was reached by both parties; *India – Patent Protection for Pharmaceutical and Agricultural Chemical Products (India-Patents (EC)) WT/DS79/R* 24 August 1998, where the DSB recommended that India bring its disputed patent laws in line with its obligations under Article 70: 8(a); 9 of the TRIPS Agreement which provides that a country provide patent protection and exclusive marketing rights for such products upon the country's entry into the WTO. See also, *Canada – Patent Protection of Pharmaceutical Products (Canada – Pharmaceutical Patents)* WT/DS114/R 17 March 2000.

91 See WTO: 'Declaration on the TRIPS agreement and Public Health' *WT/MIN(01)/DEC/2,* 14 Nov 2001.

92 Id.

93 *WT/L/540,* 1 Sep 2003.

94 See generally for example; Liu Deming, 'Now the Wolf has indeed come! Perspective on the Patent Protection of Biotechnology Inventions in China', *53 AJCL 1* (Winter 2005) pp 207–260.

95 Vol V Cap 68 Laws of the Federation of Nigeria (LFN) 1990.

96 Decree No. 48 1992.

97 Decree No. 42 1999.

98 Cap 436 LFN 1990.

99 Cap 344 LFN 1990.

100 Note: Fn to Article 1:3 in WTO TRIPS: When "nationals" are referred to in this Agreement, they shall be deemed, in the case of a separate customs territory Member of the WTO, to mean persons, natural or legal, who are domiciled or who have a real and effective industrial or commercial establishment in that customs territory.

101 See generally, the *Nigerian Patents and Design Act, op cit.*

102 See the application history of the patent No. 5663484 at the US Patents and Trademarks Office web site: www.uspto.gov

103 See generally, the *National Office of Industrial Property Act Vol XVII Cap 268 LFN 1990.* The Office also recognises IP protection for any rights granted under the WTO legal framework.

104 See *WT/COMTD/W/145, op cit* at para 21.

105 See Ajit Singh; 'Elements for a New Paradigm on Special and Differential Treatment: Special and Differential Treatment, the Multilateral Trading System and Economic Development in the 21st Century'; A joint publication of UNCTAD, ICTSD, UNDP; (April 2003). Online [www.ictsd.org/dlogue/2003–05–06/**Singh**_S&DT_final.pdf].

106 See C. George and C. Kirkpatrick, *op cit,* at p. 323.

107 See Joseph E. Stiglitz and Andrew Charlton, *Fair Trade for all – How Trade can Promote Development* (2005) Oxford University Press (OUP) p. 42. The table is an adaptation from this work.

108 About 142 countries were part of the Round at the start. The number has since increased to 154 countries as at July 2008.

109 The 'triangular' impasse is reviewed thus: 'Side A is the EU's apparent inability to move further on market access for agricultural products; Side B is America's reluctance to

offer further cuts in domestic subsidies for agriculture; and Side C is the unwillingness of the more powerful developing countries to open their industrial markets to competition, seemingly preferring "policy space" to global cooperation'. See R.K Morris (The Global Business Dialogue), *The Global Positions Note Book* Vol 5, No. 9, The Global Business Dialogue Inc, August 11, 2006; p. 1.

110   The Hong Kong Ministerial Declaration restates this commitment: "We emphasise the central importance of the development dimension in every aspect of the Doha Work Programme and recommit ourselves to making it a meaningful reality, in terms both of the results of the negotiations on market access and rule making and of the specific development-related issues ..." Hong Kong Ministerial Declaration: Doha Work Programme *WT/MIN(05)/DEC,* 22 December 2005. Online: [http://www.wto.org/english/thewto_e/minist_e/min05_e/final_text_e.htm].

111   Para 2 Doha Ministerial Declaration, *op cit.*

112   See generally, the Doha Declaration, *op cit.*

113   UN (1997), cited in Clive George and Colin Kirkpatrick; "Putting the Doha Principles into Practice: The Role of Sustainability Impact Assessment" in Honi Katrak and Roger Strange (eds) *The WTO and Developing Countries* Palgrave Macmillan (2004) pp 315–338.

114   Italics for emphasis.

115   Id.

116   Para 2 of the Doha Declaration, *op cit.*

117   First proposed to the WTO by 11 WTO Members – Cuba, Dominican Republic, Honduras, Pakistan, Haiti, Nicaragua, Kenya, Uganda, Zimbabwe, Sri Lanka, and El Salvador on 23 June 2000, see generally, WTO document *G/AG/NG/W/13.*

118   Roberts et al; 2002; Ruffer et al, 2002 reproduced in: Alan Matthews, 'Special and Differential Treatment in the WTO Agricultural Negotiations' *IIIS Discussion Paper No. 61/January 2005* p. 9. Online: [http://www.tcd.ie/iiis/documents/discussion/pdfs/iiisdp63.pdf].

119   See para 2.1 of the document, *op cit.*

120   Para 1, Hong Kong Ministerial Declaration *WT/MIN(05)/W/3/Rev. 2.* See also, Simon J. Evenett, "The World Trade Organisation Ministerial Conference in Hong Kong: What Next?" for a review of the Hong Kong Declaration *40(2) J.W.T* (2006) pp 221–238. Evenett is of the view that 'the Declaration contained a number of agreements on specific matters, the binding nature of which is not immediately apparent', at p. 222.

121   See WTO: "July Package – Post Cancun Decision" *WT/L/579* adopted 1 August 2004 at paras 41 and 42. See also, ICTSD: 'Special Products and the Special Safeguard Mechanism: Strategic Options for Developing Countries' *ICTSD Issue Paper No. 6* December 2005.

122   Some of the issues include an insistence by the developed countries such as the EU that the new SSM ought not to replace the Safeguard provisions of the existing WTO Agreements.

123   See Peter Sutherland, 'The Doha Debacle' *Wall Street Journal (New York)* August 2, 2006; p. A10.

124   See Peter Sutherland, 'The Doha Debacle' *Wall Street Journal (New York)* August 2, 2006; p. A10. The argument of the SDT provisions as an anti-development agenda insists that SDT allowances to developing countries limits the potential for their industries to be open to global competition and for their markets to operate in accordance with the non-discriminatory principle of the WTO.

125 See Alan Matthews, *op cit*, p. 12.

126 Id.

127 *WT/COMTD/W/145*, 1 December 2005.

128 See Communication from Zambia on behalf of LDCs (Committee on Agriculture Negotiation Group on Market Access) – *TN/CTD/W/30; TN/MA/W/74; TN/AG/GEN/20*; 12 June 2006. Annex F of the Hong Kong Ministerial is on special and differential treatment for developing countries and includes provisions on reduction of duties and removal of quotas on goods from LDCs.

129 See for e.g the *Dakar Declaration of Third Least Developed Countries Trade Ministers Meeting*: online at [http://www.enda.sn/English/dakardec.htm]; See also the Sectoral *Initiative on Cotton*: "Proposed initially by Benin, Burkina Faso, Chad and Mali, this later became a document of the Cancun Ministerial Conference (10–14 Sep 2003) – "Poverty Reduction – Sectoral Initiative in Favour of Cotton" *WT/MIN(03)/2* 15 August 2003; *WT/MIN(03)/W/2/Add. 1* 3 September 2003. A cotton sub committee under the Agriculture negotiations was formed on 19 November 2004 and it addresses the development related issues of market access, domestic support and export competition. See the WTO web page: [http://www.wto.org/english/tratop_e/agric_e/negs_bkgrnd20_cotton_e.htm].

130 See generally Dani Rodrik, *Industrial Policy for the 21ˢᵗ Century*, See also, p. 1.

131 Id, p. 2.

132 See further: the WTO web page on RTAs about 180 of which are believed to be operational as at June 2005. RTAs notified to the WTO include: the European Union (EU); North American Free Trade Area (NAFTA); Southern Common Market (MERCOSUR); Association of Southeast Asians (ASEAN) Free Trade Area (AFTA); The Common Market of Eastern and Southern Africa (COMESA) Caribbean Community and Common Market (CARICOM); Generalised System of Trade Preferences among developing countries (GSTP); West African Economic and Monetary Union (WAEMU).

133 Jagdish Bhagwati, "The Agenda of the WTO" in Pitou van Dijck and Gerrit Faber (eds) supra, pp 27–59 at 27. Hudec, was also not in favour of preferential arrangements particularly those ostensibly offering special treatment to developing countries. *Op cit*, 210–224.

134 See for e.g Article 3 of the Treaty Establishing the European Community which sets out the areas of common policy of the EU Member States.

135 For instance, regional groupings such as the African Union (AU) have strong political overtones; the Economic Community of West African States (ECOWAS) has not exerted a viable influence on the economy of the West African region, which has long seen political instability.

136 See generally for e.g, the North American Free Trade Agreement (NAFTA) between USSA, Canada and Mexico.

137 See GATT Article 24; GATS Article 5. An RTA Committee was formed on 6 February 1996 to oversee RTA activities.

138 See Constantine Michalopoulos, *Developing Countries in the WTO op cit*, at p. 87.

139 Paul Demaret et al, *op cit* at p. 842. The late MIT economist, Prof Rudi Dornbusch, who also held this view, in 1991 argued that the Uruguay Round expansion of the trade sectors to come under GATT rules – agriculture, services, IP, etc, was too ambitious and that there was no rush. In his view, world free trade could be introduced at some later date when regional free trade had settled down. See "Dornbusch on Trade", *The Economist* (London) 4 May 1991 at p. 89.

140 The principle makes the provisions of the EU Treaty directly enforceable in national courts and so could be the basis of a claim by private persons – first considered in *Van Gend en Loos*, *C26/62*, 1963.

141 See Robert Wade; "The Doha talks must fail for the sake of the world's poor", (Comment); *The Guardian* (London) 3 July 2006, p. 28.

142 See the reply by the EU Commission trade spokesman, Peter Power: "Poor countries will gain from Doha" (Reply) *The Guardian* (London) 5 July 2006, p. 33.

143 See also United States – *Anti-Dumping Measure on Shrimp from Ecuador WT/DS35/R* 30 January 2007; *US-Continued Dumping and Subsidy Offset Act (US-Offset Act-Byrd Amendment)* Panel Report *WT/DS17/R*; AB Report *WT.DS17/AB/R*; Restrictions under Article XI GATT – *Canada – Certain Measures Concerning Periodicals WT/DS31/R*; Ban on GM/biotech products – *EC – Measures Affecting the Approval and Marketing of Biotech Products* Complaint by US – *WT/DS/291/R*; Complaint by Canada – *WT/DS292/R*; Complaint by Argentina *WT/DS/293/R*; See also, *US-Shrimp WT/DS58/R*.

144 *US:DS291, Canada: DS292, Argentina:DS293*. In the Complaint by Argentina, third Parties included: Australia, Brazil, Canada, Chile, China, Chinese Taipei, Colombia, El Salvador, Honduras, Mexico, New Zealand, Norway, Paraguay, Peru, Thailand, Uruguay, US. See the *South Centre Quarterly on Trade Disputes, Vol 1 No. 4, op cit* at pp 12–14.

145 For a full background of the case, see IATP: Backgrounder on WTO Dispute: 'US vs EC Biotech Products Case [www.iatp.org/global]. Sep 2005.

146 Id p. 9. The US has always claimed that bio-tech products can help address hunger issues in developing countries particularly Africa. See IATP *op cit*, pp 5–6.

147 See 'Tracking Development in International Trade Disputes' *South Centre Quarterly on Trade Disputes, Vol 1 No. 4*, at pp 12–14.

148 See Panel Report WT/DS293/R 29 Sep 2006.

149 See AB: *EC-Hormones* para 98; 109.

150 Id.

151 See further, *AB: Japan Agricultural Products II*, para 133; See also T. Christoforu, 'The Regulation of Genetically Modified Organisms in the EU: The Interplay of Science, Law and Politics' *C.M.L.R 41.3* (2002); V.R. Walker, 'Keeping the WTO from becoming the "World Trans-Science Organisation": Scientific Uncertainty, Science Policy, and Fact Finding in the Growth Hormones Dispute' *31 Cornell Int'l LJ* (1998).

152 See WTO: *Understanding the WTO* Geneva (2005) p. 101.

153 The 'triangular' impasse is reviewed thus: 'Side A is the EU's apparent inability to move further on market access for agricultural products; Side B is America's reluctance to offer further cuts in domestic subsidies for agriculture; and Side C is the unwillingness of the more powerful developing countries to open their industrial markets to competition, seemingly preferring "policy space" to global cooperation'. See R.K Morris (The Global Business Dialogue), *The Global Positions Note Book* Vol 5. No. 9, The Global Business Dialogue Inc, August 11, 2006; p. 1.

154 See generally, Yong-Shik Lee (2006). Although outside the specific ambit of the WTO rules, Lee also considers the capacity of regional agreements and FDI to influence development. He argues that the proliferation of FTAs including RTAs also places barriers to developing countries who are not members of the arrangement. Furthermore, he is of the view that the potential of FDI to positively influence development in developing economies is limited to those few countries with substantial market potential and those who possessing essential natural resources, can have a real negotiating power with foreign investors. See pp 141–155.

155 Id, p. 43.

156 Id, pp 62–140.

157 Id, pp 43–8.

158 Id.

159 See Bernard Hoekman, Constantine Michalopoulos, Alan Winters, 'More Favourable and Differential Treatment of Developing Countries: Towards a New Approach in the World Trade Organisation' *World Bank Policy Research Working Paper No. 3107*, 1 August, 2003; See generally, RIS *World Trade and Development Report 2006 op cit* which highlights developing countries' perspectives towards making the WTO a 'development friendly organisation'; See also, Bernard Hoekman, 'Operationalising the concept of policy space in the WTO: Beyond Special and Differential Treatment' *JIEL Vol 8. No. 2* (2005) 405–424.

160 See The Economist: Country Profile Australia (9 July 2008); New Zealand (5 June 2008): [http://www.economist.com/countries/]. See also the TPR OF Australia *WT/TPR/S/178/Rev. 1* 1 May 2007; New Zealand *WT/TPR/S/115* 14 April 2005: [http://www.wto.org/english/tratop_e/tpr_e/tp_rep_e.htm].

161 Id, p. 26.

162 See Trebilcock and Howse, *op cit* (3rd Ed) p. 8.

163 Id.

164 See for instance, Philip Sauré, 'Revisiting the Infant Industry Argument' *Journal of Development Economics* Vol 84 (1) Sep 2007 pp 104–117; Mitsuhiro Kaneda, 'Policy Designs in a Dynamic Model of Infant industry Protection', *Journal of Development Economics* Vol 72 (1) Oct 2003 pp 91–115.

165 See Jean Imbs and Romain Wacziarg, 'Stages of Diversification' *American Economic Review* 93:1 (2003) 63–86, at 64.

166 Rodrik, *Industrial Policy in the 21st Century*, p. 6.

167 See Klinger, Bailey and Lederman, 'Discovery and Development: An Empirical Exploration of "New" Products, World Bank Research Working Paper 3450 (2004).

168 See Klinger, Bailey and Lederman, 'Innovation and Export Portfolios' World Bank Research Working Paper 3983 (2006).

169 Rodrik, *op cit*, 4. See also, Mari Pangestu; 'Industrial Policy and Developing Countries', in Hoekman et al 92002) 149–159.

170 Id. See also Klinger et al, *op cit* (2004).

171 Alan Winters, 'Trade Policies for Poverty Alleviation' in Hoekman et al (2002) 28–37.

172 See Peter Van Den Bossche, *op cit*, p. 677.

173 See generally, Lee, *op cit*, pp 49–81.

174 See, Annex 1, *Notes and Supplementary Provisions to the GATT, Ad Article XVIII*.

175 See Peter Van den Bossche, *op cit*, p. 678; See also WTO COMTD; 'Information on the Utilisation of Special and Differential Treatment Provisions' Note by the Secretariat, Addendum; *WT/COMTD/W/77/Rev.1/Add.4*, 7 February 2002, although Article XVIII has been invoked in a number of complaints by developing countries. See the GATT Analytical Index on Article XVIII: [http://www.wto.org/English/res_e/booksp_e/analytic_index_e/gatt1994_06_e.htm#article18].

176 We note the adjacent provisions in the WTO Agreements aimed at protecting the goods of Member Countries including the *Agreement on Safeguards, the SCM Agreement and the Antidumping Agreement* and to records of disputes brought under these Agreements. A review of the dispute cases under the DSB reveals that of the two thirds developing country membership, it is mainly India, China and Brazil, together with Argentina

that have recorded the most participation at the DSB in respect of these complaints, a fact which confirms that industrial production generally across the developing world is not substantial.

177 See Article 8.2 SCM Agreement. See also Article 9.

178 A special meeting of the SCM Committee in December 1999 failed to reach a consensus on the extension of Article 8 (and others – Article 6.1; Article 9). Developing countries sought a review of Article 8 the sub provisions of which they considered too restrictive citing amongst others, a lack of experience in the application of subsidies; the limits imposed by the thresholds for the grant of subsidies. They also considered the range of programmes for which subsidies were allowed to be limited. See generally, *G/SCM/22*.

179 *WT/MIN(01)/17* 14 Nov 2001; See also Para 12 of the Doha Ministerial.

180 Id para 10.2.

181 See, Prof Robert Wade, *op cit*.

182 See the (UN) 'Technical Report of the High Level Panel on Financing for Development' under the chairmanship of Ernesto Zedillo (2001) 9.

183 Development tools referred to as the Development-Facilitation Tariff (DFT); Development-Facilitation Subsidy (DFS). See Lee *op cit*, 65–80.

184 See generally Doha Declaration at paras 38–41 and the specific commitments in paras 16, 21, 24, 26, 27, 33, 38–40, 42, 43. Technical assistance is paired with capacity building and these provisions will also refer under our discussions on capacity building programmes hereafter.

185 See SPS Agreement Article 9; TBT Agreement Articles 11.2–6, 12.3, 12.7; Customs Valuation Agreement Article 20.3; TRIPS Agreement Article 67.

186 See the WTO web page on Technical Cooperation at: [http://www.wto.org/english/tratop_e/devel_e/teccop_e/s_and_d_eg_e.htm].

187 See Constantine Michalopoulos; *Developing Countries in the WTO*, Palgrave Macmillan (2001) at p. 1.

188 World Bank: Human Development Report, Chapter 4 on International Trade *op cit*, pp146–7.

189 See, WTO: 'Irregularities Identified in the Negotiation and Decision Making Process at the Sixth WTO Ministerial Conference', (Communication from Venezuela and Cuba) 7 February 2006: *TN/C/7 WT/GC/105* 9 February 2006.

190 Id, p. 3.

191 Established 26 October 2000.

192 The challenges envisioned by those involved in the Shanghai Centre are reflected in this discussion of the work of the body: "The objective of the Centre was clearly described as taking active measures to cope with the opportunities and challenges that Shanghai would face after accession to the WTO. It was decided at the start that, constitutionally, the Centre's main functions would be to provide training, information, study, information and legal aid services which are related to WTO affairs; to assist governments, enterprises and public institutions to familiarize themselves with and to adopt practices that are in accordance with the relevant WTO rules; and to expand trade and economic co-operation with other countries around the world." See Gong Baihua, 'Shanghai's WTO Affairs Consultation Centre: Working Together to Take Advantage of WTO Membership; (Peter Gallagher, Patrick Low & Andrew Stoler (eds) *Managing the Challenges of WTO Participation*, WTO (2006) Case Study II; online at [http://www.wto.org/english/res_e/booksp_e/casestudies_e/case11_e.htm].

193 See para 40 of the Doha Declaration. Here, emphasis is placed on the need for technical assistance to benefit from "secure and predictable funding." The WTO income for its annual budget comes from Members' Contributions based on share of international trade. It also manages funds contributed by Members which are used in technical cooperation projects and training programmes for developing countries. See the WTO web page on budgets.

194 See the DSU Articles 3.12, 4.10, 8.10, 12.10, 12.11, 21.2, 21.7, 21.8; (24.1 and 24.2 both of which specially address LDCs); 27.2.

195 See generally, Marc l. Busch and Eric Reinhardt, *op cit*.

196 See generally, Jose Luis Perez Gabilondo, "Developing Countries in the WTO Dispute Settlement Procedures: Improving their Participation" 35 *J.W.T.4 (2001)* pp 663–689.

197 See further DSU Article 27.

198 See DSU Article 3.10.

199 See the Doha Declaration, para 38.

200 Id, para 16.

201 Id, para 21.

202 Id, para 24.

203 Id, para 26.

204 Id, para 27.

205 Id, para 33.

206 Id, paras 42–3.

207 See J.P. Singh: *Services Commitments: Case Studies from Belize and Costa Rica* (WTO Case Study 5): [http://www.wto.org/english/res_e/booksp_e/casestudies_e/case5_e.htm].

208 See generally the WTO Agreement particularly Article VI which provides for the WTO Secretariat. There is no definition of responsibilities for the Director-General and the other staff of the Secretariat save that their responsibilities shall be 'exclusively international in character'.

209 Doha Declaration, *op cit*, para 38.

210 Neela Murkherjee, *op cit*, p. 97.

Chapter Four. Judicial Review of the Development Question

1 Zambia on behalf of the LDC group, (*TN/DS/W/17*, 9 October 2002) cited in Asif H. Qureshi, "Interpreting World Trade Organisation Agreements for the Development Objective" 37 *J.W.T.5* (2003) pp 847–882 at p. 848.

2 Qureshi; id, p. 852.

3 *Agreement Establishing the Advisory Centre on WTO Law*.

4 Busch & Reinhardt *op cit*, p. 732.

5 *EC-Bed Linen*; WT/DS141/R, 30 October 2000.

6 EC Regulation No 2398/97, 28 November 1997.

7 Agreement on Implementation of the General Agreement on Tariffs and Trade, 1994.

8 *EC-Bed Linen supra*, para 6.219.

9 Id, para 6.221. Japan, a third party, was of the opinion that there was no obligation on developed countries under the Article, while the US was of the opinion that the provision was only a procedural safeguard and does not require any substantive outcome or any specific accommodation to be made on the basis of developing country status – See para 6.225 of the judgement.

10 Id, para 6.227 at fn 85.

11 Id, para 6.229.

12 Id, para 6.219. The Panel noted that its reasoning was in line with the earlier case of *EC-Imposition of Cotton Yarn from Brazil*, Panel Report ADP/137 of 30 October 1995, where the earlier Panel at para 584, held the same opinion on a consideration of Article 13, Tokyo Round Anti-dumping Code, a precursor of Article 15 of the Anti-dumping Agreement.

13 Id, para 6.238.

14 See WT/DS141/AB/R, 1 March 2001.

15 Notably, this issue was not revisited on appeal.

16 Under its terms of reference pursuant to Article 7 of the DSU (*Understanding on Rules and Procedures Governing the Settlement of Disputes* (Annex 2 to the WTO Agreement)).

17 *Indonesia – Automobile; Complaints by the European Communities – WT/DS54; Japan – WT/DS64; the United States – WT/DS59.*

18 Italics for emphasis. See para 12.11 of the Panel Report, *op cit.*

19 See BBC News Archive 'Indonesia wins IMF Bail Out', BBC News Saturday Nov 1, 1997; Online [http://news.bbc.co.uk/1/hi/events/indonesia/archive/19565.stm]; India Express Newspapers 'Indonesia signs revised IMF package deal' 16 January 1998; Online http://www.indianexpress.com/fe/daily/19980116/01655524.html]. See also: Bello Walden, 'Finance: What is the IMF's agenda for Asia?; who appraised the recourse to the IMF loans as follows: '...in the most recent renegotiation of the IMF Accord with Indonesia, the most prominent feature is the virtual abandonment of Indonesia's attempts at strategic industrial policy: the "national car project" that has upset Detroit and Tokyo and the plan to manufacture indigenously designed passenger jets that has worried Boeing'; Online [http://www.southcentre.org/southletter/sl30/South%20Letter%2030trans-02.htm#TopOfPage].

20 *Supra.*

21 See para 8.50(f) of the Panel's Report.

22 See para 8.53 (b); k; l of the Panel Report *op cit.*

23 The Argentinean allegations centred on the SPS Agreement – Articles 2, 5, 7, 8, 10, Annex B, Annex C; Agriculture Agreement – Article 4; GATT – Articles I, III, X, XI; and the TBT Agreement – Articles 2, 5, 12.

24 Argentina –Hides and Leather *WT/DS155/R*, 19 December 2000.

25 Article XX(D) GATT.

26 See Panel Report para 8.302.

27 Id, para 8.303.

28 Id. The Panel suggested that such features include '(e.g. an informal economy, inflation, an inequitable tax system, tolerance of failure to comply with regulations, lack of simple and precise rules, inefficient tax administration, corruption, low levels of education, a disregard for tax-paying obligations, etc.)'.

29 Id, para 12.1–12.7.

30 *Brazil – Aircraft* Panel Report *WT/DS/46/R*, 14 April 1999; AB Report *WT/D46/AB/R.*

31 See para 7.89, of the Panel Report, *op cit.*

32 Id, para 2.1–2.6.

33 See particularly, para 163 AB Report. Other cases where a country's state of development has been raised include: *India – Quantitative Restrictions on Imports of Agricultural, Textiles and Industrial Products, WT/DS90/R* 6 April 1999, para 3.54 where India explained in that it did not announce its quotas as required by GATT Article XIII:2a since as 'a developing country with a low standard of living, India simply did

not have the financial and administrative resources to identify and administer the quotas for nearly 2,300 tariff lines'.

34 See particularly para 160–163 of the AB Report.

35 We note that the Doha negotiations have considered time extensions under a review of Article 27.4 of the SCM Agreement See WTO (Doha Development Agenda): *Procedures for extension under Article 27.4 for certain developing country members; G/SCM/39* 20 November 2001.

36 The following reference is a footnote in the original statement of the Panel: It may be noted that under Article 27.14, "[t]he Committee [on Subsidies and Countervailing Measures] shall, upon request by an interested Member, undertake a review of a specific export subsidy practice of a developing country Member to examine whether the practice is in conformity with its development needs." In our view, a body such as the Committee is far better equipped to perform this type of examination than is a panel.

37 See DSU Article 7(1).

38 See the WTO web page on TPR. Article III (4) of the WTO Agreement cites the TPRM as one of the Organisation's basic functions. Annex 3 to that Agreement lists the objectives of TPRM, principal to which is to ensure transparency of the trade policies in Member States.

39 WTO Agreement Annex 3 A(i).

40 Id.

41 See the TPRM document – Annex 3 to the *WTO Agreement*, para A (ii).

42 Id.

43 Para 7.89 Panel Report.

44 See Bernard Hoekman; 'The WTO: Functions and Basic Principles' in Hoekman et al (2002) 41–9.

45 Id, p. 45.

46 Id.

47 DSU Article 13(2).

48 *US – Upland Cotton*; WT/DS267/R, 8 Sep 2004 supra. Third parties included Argentina, Australia, Benin, Canada, Chad, China, Chinese Taipei, European Communities, India, New Zealand, Pakistan, Paraguay, Venezuela. The Appellate Body adopted the Panel Report on 3 March 2005–WT/DS267/AB/R.

49 Brazil based its submissions on the following: Articles 5(c), 6.3(b), (c) and (d), 3.1(a) (including item (j) of the Illustrative List of Export Subsidies in Annex I), 3.1(b), and 3.2 of the SCM Agreement; Articles 3.3, 7.1, 8, 9.1 and 10.1 of the Agreement on Agriculture; and Article III:4 of GATT 1994.

50 See Article 13, *Agreement on Agriculture* which defines certain domestic measure as non-actionable or exempt. See generally Article 13: (a), (b), (c) of the Agreement. Note that the Peace Clause under the Agriculture Agreement was for a period of 10 years, ending in 2005.

51 See generally Part VIII of the Panel Report, para 8.1 (a–h); Article 3.8 *DSU* on nullification and impairment.

52 Para 8.2, p. 350 of the Panel Report. The Panel did not base its findings on all of Brazil's claims per se preferring to examine the parties' submissions where relevant. See para 7.1510 of the Panel Report where it justifies its subjective application of judicial economy: "The Panel recalls that it need not examine all legal claims before it. Rather, we need only address those claims that must be addressed in order to resolve the matter in issue in the dispute. This is the case provided that we address those claims on which a finding is necessary to enable the DSB to make sufficiently precise recommendations and rulings so

as to allow for prompt compliance by a Member in order to ensure effective resolution of disputes to the benefit of all Members."

53 The DSB is bound by the principle of judicial economy not to dwell on matters which are not raised in the complaints brought by the parties. Although not expressly stated in the provisions of the DSU, Articles 3.7 which direct the DSB to secure a positive solution to disputes and, Article 3.4 which instruct that recommendations or rulings of the DSB should be tailored to the provisions of the DSU and the covered Agreement will immediately preclude the consideration of matters not raised in a complaint.

54 See AB Report, *US–Safeguard Measure on Imports of Fresh, Chilled or Frozen Lamb from Australia – WT/DS178/AB/R; New Zealand WT/DS177/AB/R; (US-Lamb)*; 1 May 2001, at para 191. The quotations in the instant citation are references to the following disputes where the principle of judicial economy was considered: AB Report, *US – Measures Affecting Imports of Woven Wool Shirts and Blouses from India – WT/DS33/AB/R, (US – Shirts and Blouses)* 23 May 1997, para 340; AB Report, *India Patent Protection for Pharmaceutical and Agricultural Chemical Products – WT/DS50/AB/R, (India – Patents)* 16 Jan 1998, para 87; AB Report, *Australia – Measures Affecting Importation of Salmon – WT/DS18/AB/R*, 6 Nov 1998, para 223.

55 See Christophe Larouer *op cit*, at pp 113–119.

56 See *Japan – Measures Affecting Consumer Photographic Film and Paper (Japan-Film) WT/DS44/R.; European Communities – Measures Affecting Asbestos and Asbestos-containing Products (EC-Asbestos) WT/DS35/R.* See also AB Report: *EC-Asbestos, WT/DS35/AB/R.* Also, *Korea – GPA* supra; *India – Patents*, supra.

57 Christophe Larouer *op cit*, p. 112.

58 Id, p. 125.

59 See the WTO publication, *A Handbook on the WTO Dispute Settlement System* Cambridge, (2004).

60 Id p. 32. See also, Christophe Larouer, 'WTO Non-Violation Complaints: A Misunderstood Remedy in the WTO Dispute Settlement System', *NILR LIII 2006* pp 97–126 at p. 100.

61 As Article 26 DSU.

62 See Christophe Larouer, *op cit*, p. 99.

63 See Frieder Roessler, 'Should Principles of Competition Policy be incorporated into WTO Law Through Non-Violation Complaints? *2 JIEL (1999)* at p. 418 where he suggested that: 'The negotiators of the GATT thus regarded the concept of non-violation nullification or impairment as a benchmark guiding consultations, negotiations and multilateral decision-making...'

64 The first part of Article 26(1) refers to Article XXIII:1(b) GATT complaints brought under a covered agreement; Article 26(2) refers to Article XXIII:1(c) GATT complaints also under a covered agreement.

65 See for instance, Article 64.2 TRIPS Agreement.

66 See: Article 19 Agreement on Agriculture; Article 11 SPS Agreement; Article 14 TBT Agreement; Article 8 TRIMS Agreement; Article 17 Antidumping Agreement; Article 19 Customs Valuation Agreement; Article 8 Agreement on Pre-Shipment Inspection; Article 8 Agreement on Rules of Origin; Article 6 Agreement on Import Licensing Procedures; Article 5 SCM Agreement; Article 14 Agreement on Safeguards; Article XXIII GATS; Article 64 TRIPS; Article XXII Agreement on Government Procurement.

67 See the WTO TRIPS web page on the non-violation complaint: [http://www.wto.org/english/tratop_e/trips_e/nonviolation_background_e.htm].

68 The 'impediment to the attainment of an objective' claim was raised in the GATT disputes – *European Communities – Refunds on Exports of Sugar*, BISD 26S/290, 6 November 1979; *Japan – Nullification or Impairment of the Benefits Accruing to the EEC and Impediment to the Attainment of GATT Objectives*, L/5479, 1983; the claims were however not successfully pursued.

69 Article 3(2) DSU.

70 See Peter Sutherland (ed) The Future of the WTO: Addressing Institutional Challenges in the New Millennium', (Report by the Consultative Board to the WTO Director-General) Chapter VI; pp 49–60; WTO, Geneva (2005). The Report considered amongst others, the problems of implementing dispute settlements between rich and poor countries.

71 WTO Agreements are silent on this point save Article 17.6 AD Agreement which provides for a *deferential* standard to be applied in anti-dumping procedures: Article 17.6(1) states: "...in its assessment of the facts of the matter, the panel shall determine whether the authorities' establishment of the facts was proper and whether their evaluation of those facts was unbiased and objective" Article 17.6(2) provides further; "...Where the panel finds that a relevant provision of the Agreement admits of more than one permissible interpretation, the panel shall find the authorities' measure to be in conformity with the Agreement if it rests upon one of those permissible interpretations".

72 For a general discourse on the concept of Standard of Review in WTO Law, see Stefan Zleptnig, 'The Standard of Review in WTO Law: An Analysis of Law, Legitimacy and the Distribution of Legal and Political Authority' *European Integration Online Papers (EIoP) Vol 6* (2002) No. 17 online at [http://eiop.or.at/eiop/texte/2002–017a.htm].

73 *European Communities – Measures Affecting Meat and Meat Products (US Hormones)* WT/DS26/AB/R; *Canada Hormones – WT/DS48/AB/R*, 16 Jan 1998. The EC had banned imports of growth-hormone treated beef. The US and Canada alleged a violation of the SPS Agreement challenging the ban on the grounds that the EU provided no scientific evidence for the danger resulting from the consumption of hormone treated beef.

74 Id, para 13.

75 See Stefan Zleptnig, *op cit*, 3.

76 Id. 'De novo' review here refers to the Panel imposing its own (new) judgement of the (scientific) evidence in question. See AB Report para 13–15.

77 *United States-Restrictions on Imports of Cotton and Man-made Fibre Underwear - Costa Rica*, WT/DS24/AB/R.

78 See also the AB Report in *Argentina-Safeguard Measure on Imports of Footwear (Argentina-Footwear EC)* WT/DS121/AB/R para 121–122; *United States-Definitive Safeguard Measures on Imports of Wheat Gluten from the European Communities* WT/DS166/AB/R para 162.

79 See *US-Underwear* panel report supra; para 7.13.

80 AB Report, *Hormones case* supra; para 115.

81 See generally, Roessler Frieder, '*The Institutional Balance Between the Judicial and the Political Organs of the WTO*', Conference on Efficiency, Equity, and Legitimacy: The Multilateral Trading System at the Millennium June 1–2, 2000: Online [http://www.ksg.harvard.edu/m-rcbg/Conferences/trade/roessler.htm].

82 Steven P Croley & J.H Jackson 'WTO Dispute Panel Deference to National Government Decisions. The Misplaced Analogy to the US Chevron Standard-of-Review Doctrine,

International Trade Law and the GATT/WTO Dispute Settlement System (ed. Petersmann Ernst-Ulrich) Kluwer Academic Publishers (1997) p. 209.

83 DSU Article 11, *op cit*.

84 See *Report of the Consultative Board (2005)*, *op cit*, at p. 53. The Report states that: 'Under GATT and now WTO rules, compensatory measures have traditionally not been monetary payments ("cheque in the mail"). On the contrary, such measures have generally been additional market access measures by the party called upon to correct its failure to fulfil its WTO obligations'.

85 Article 22(2).

86 See the Report of the Consultative Board, *op cit*, p. 53.

87 In the earlier cited Report of the Consultative Board (2004), the report states that as at 17 September 2004, there have been 12 cases of a sequencing agreement, including in the followings disputes: *US-Shrimp; EC-Bed-Linen, supra; US-Tax Treatment for "Foreign Sales Corporations" US-FSC WT/DS108/12* a dispute brought 18 November 1997 (last report circulated – Appellate Body Report on Second Recourse to Article 21.5 dated 13 February 2006.) In these cases, the prior sequencing arrangement agreed to by the parties stalled the operation of Article 22 DSU pending a determination of the outcome of recourse to Article 21(5). The Report is of the view that the difficulties with the text of the DSU become more apparent with the need to address the question of 'sequencing'. The Report suggests that the matter of stalling retaliatory measures under Article 22 may be addressed by determining clearly '…how a challenge on whether the response of a losing party has been adequate and can operate consistently with the provisions allowing the winning party to take counter measures.' See the Report, *op cit*, at p. 53.

88 Article 22(6) provides that the DSB may authorise suspension of concessions within 30 days of the expiry of a reasonable period unless the DSB rejects the request. The matter may also be referred to arbitration if the Member concerned objects to the level of the suspension, or to suspensions in the same sector or under another covered Agreement. See also *EC-Bananas III WT/DS27/ARB* para 8.1.

89 Article 22(8) DSU.

90 Article 22(4) DSU.

91 Article 22(3)a.

92 Article 22(3)b.

93 Article 22(3)c.

94 The provision actually uses the word 'shall', which though it may imply a duty, actually refers to an exhortation given the expected result it qualifies: It asks that a party seeking to suspend concessions 'shall take *into account*'. Nothing more than an appeal to the disputing party to consider the importance of trade in the sector brought under the dispute.

95 See also, John H Jackson, 'International Law Status of WTO Dispute Settlement Reports: Obligation to Comply or Option to 'Buy Out'?' (Editorial Comment), *AJIL 98 January 2004*: pp 109–125.

96 *US- DS320; Canada – DS321*.

97 See *US-Continued Suspension* DS320 paras 7.206–7.215.

98 Id para 7.856.

99 Id para 7.857. An appeal by the EC to the AB has been notified.

100 See p. 64 of the Report. Emphasis in original. The Report suggests that this may 'diminish the extent to which companies, trading and investing, can rely on the rules to provide market predictability'.

101 See the Report at p. 54.

102 See Ngangjoh H. Yemkong, 'World Trade Organisation Dispute Settlement Retaliatory Regime at the Tenth Anniversary of the Organisation: Reshaping the "Last Resort" Against Non-Compliance', JWT *Vol 40. No.* 2, pp 365–384.

103 See Robert Hudec, 'The Adequacy of WTO Dispute Settlement Remedies: A Developing Country Perspective' in Hoekman et al (2002) 81–91.

104 Id.

105 See generally, *EC-Bananas III: Recourse to Arbitration by the EC under Article 22.6 of the DSU,* WT/DS27/ARB/ECU. *US-Gambling* DS285 – Antigua was granted approval to seek authorisation to suspend the application to the US of concessions and related obligations under the GATS and TRIPS; See also *US-Upland Cotton,* although Brazil subsequently suspended its request for authorisation. No developing country has applied these authorisations. See also IATP: 'Strengthening Compliance at the WTO: Cross-Retaliation in WTO Disputes' Online: [http://www.iatp.org/iatp/publications. cfm?accountID=451&refID=89107].

106 See paras 70–3; 93–4 of the Arbitration Report. See also Hudec in Hoekman et al, (2002)88–90.

107 Id, p. 90.

108 Id. He also noted the potential discomfort to developed countries in cross-retaliation under the TRIPS Agreement – 'the denial of IPRs of foreign owners results in assets being made available to developing countries at cheaper prices and would cause more political discomfort than the usual small-scale trade retaliation'. Id. He however cautioned (as did the Panel, paras 130–165) that TRIPS retaliation will involve a number of distinctive legal, practical and economic problems for the retaliating State.

109 Id.

110 See the IATP: 'Strengthening Compliance at the WTO: Cross-Retaliation in WTO Disputes' *op cit.*

111 See paras 130–165 of the Arbitration Report, *op cit.*

112 DSU Article 22(4).

113 Id, p. 55.

114 Similar to the Advisory Opinion rendered by the ICJ under Article 65 Statute of the International Court of Justice; See the opinion of the court in *Reservations to the Genocide Conventions Case 18 ILR 364* to the effect that the advisory opinion sought in this case was 'to guide the UN in respect of its own action'. See also Article 96 UN Charter.

Chapter Five. The Way Forward: Multilateral Co-Operation and Internal Reform

1 See Ronald A. Cass & John R. Haring, referring to the arguments of Stolper & Samuelson, 1941; Samuelson, 1948; Samuelson 1949: 'Domestic Regulation and International Trade: Where's the Race? Lessons from Telecommunication and Export Controls' in Kennedy & Southwick *op cit,* pp 111–154 at 111.

2 Id, referring to arguments by Murphy & Welch, 1991; Borjas, Freeman, & Katz, 1992.

3 See the views on free trade and the impact on the American workers/market prior to the 2008 American presidential elections, 'Free Trade and the US Election' 18 Oct 2007, BBC Business web page: [http://news.bbc.co.uk/1/hi/business/7048568.stm].

4 They also refer to Bhagwati, 1968 and Deardoff, 1986 who argue respectively, that 'trade-linked welfare reduction, like growth-linked welfare reduction, traces to underlying welfare-distorting policy, not independently to trade or growth' and, that the conditions from which factor price equalization was deduced seldom occur; p. 111. See also pp 134–141.

5 Id, p. 113; See also pp 134–141.

6 *WTO Agreement*, *op cit*.

7 Ortino, *op cit*, p. 3.

8 See Pitou van Dijck and Gerry Faber (eds) *Challenges to the New World Trade Organisation* Kluwer Law Intnl (1996) pp 77–91 at p. 80.

9 See Zdenek Tomes and Monika Jandova, *'Political Economy of Trade Policy'* European Trade Study Group Conference Paper (Eight Conference) Vienna 2006, online at [http://www.etsg.org/ETSG2006/papers/Jandova.pdf] p. 1. The paper sets out the contrast between international trade theory and the reality of trade policy. The authors find that in real terms, trade policies remain protectionist even amongst the richer countries: in the EU (under the CAP); in the US (via antidumping legislation); in Japan (by the application of non-tariff barriers, and in many developing countries whose trade policies is openly protectionist.

10 In Hoekman et al, *Development, Trade and the WTO: A Handbook* World Bank (2002) pp 3–10 at 3–4.

11 Id.

12 Joseph Stiglitz, in R.Porter & P.Sauve (eds) *op cit*, pp 53–55.

13 Deborah Cass, *The Constitutionalisation of the World Trade Organisation: Legitimacy, Democracy, and Community in the International Trading System* OUP (2005) p. 244.

14 Id.

15 Id.

16 UNCTAD: 'The Least Developed Countries Report; Developing Productive Capacities' (2006) Online: [http://www.unctad.org/en/docs/ldc2006_en.pdf].

17 Id.

18 These suggestions were well received at the Evian Group Session: *Trade and Development post-non Doha: Let's get real*; WTO Public Forum 2006, 26 September 2006. Transcripts at: [http://www.wto.org/english/forms_e/public_forum_e/session_26_num17_e.htm].

19 WTO; *ERSD-2004-03 op cit*. p. 9.

20 By this we mean the interests aroused by joint developing country proposals.

21 See the guidelines for appointment of officers to WTO Bodies in these WTO Documents: *PC/IPL/14* of 9 December 1994; revised in *WT/L/31* of 7 February 1995.

22 Id.

23 See Susan Prowse, '"Aid for Trade": A Proposal for Increasing Support for Trade Adjustment and Integration'; in Simon J. Evenett & Bernard Hoekman (eds) *Economic Development and Multilateral Trade Cooperation* Palgrave Macmillan & IBRD (2006) pp 229–267 at 241. See also ICFTU: 'Trade, Employment and Development in the Peoples' Republic of China' *Report to the WTO General Council Review of the Trade Policies of China'* (4th & 6th April 2006) [http://www.icftu.org/www/pdf/chinatradeemploymentanddevelopment.pdf]; Oxfam: 'Harnessing Trade for Development', *Oxfam Briefing Paper August 2001* Online at: [http://www.oxfam.org/en/files/pp0108_Harnessing_trade_for_development.pdf?searchterm=globalisation]; See generally, Thomas Hertel & Alan Winters (eds) *Poverty and the WTO: Impacts of the Doha Development Agenda* Palgrave Macmillan (2006); Also, Kym Anderson & Will Martin (eds) *Agricultural Trade Reform & the Doha Development Agenda* Palgrave Macmillan (2006).

24 See J. Stiglitz *Globalisation and its Discontents op cit*, p. 45; Stiglitz and Charlton *op cit*, 1.

25 Piet Eeckhout, 'The Domestic Legal Status of the WTO Agreements; Interconnecting Legal Systems', *Common Market Law Review* Vol 34 pp 11–58.

26 See Hudec, *op cit* (1987), p. 233–4. In this respect however, Hudec was of the view that the move towards integrating developing countries into a reciprocal trade system at the time of the GATT would be assisted by developing countries working through the Trade and Development Committee to readdress what he considered to be the disadvantages of the non-reciprocal trade regime of the GATT.

27 See the observation of Hudec, *op cit*, 229 where he notes that 'a government's own trade policy decisions are really the most important determinants of its economic gains form trade'.

28 The WTO because it is the international spokesman for the free trade ideology at present, appears to be the altar of trade liberalisation. But countries can indeed adopt trade liberalisation measures without even being part of the WTO – membership of the WTO is not mandatory. The appeal as with all things international in nature is that countries 'belong' and are secure in the knowledge that they share predictable responsibilities and rewards with others.

29 Id, p. 10.

30 See *This Day* Newspapers (Nigeria) 'Reviewing the WTO Treaty (Editorial); 28 October 2004, p. 11 quoting the then Information Minister, Prof Jerry Gana.

31 Article XVI:4 WTO Agreement.

32 Franklin Delano Roosevelt (US President 1933–1945); 'The Only Thing We Have to Fear is Fear Itself' *Presidential Inaugural Speech* March 4 1933.

33 See John Madeley and Jon Barnes, "Setting the Scene"; 'Making or Missing the Links? The Politics of Trade Reform and Poverty Reduction', *Panos Media Tool Kit on PRSPs* No.3, Panos, London (August 2006) p. 2.

34 See, Hon Chibudom Nwuche, Deputy Speaker Nigeria House of Representatives, 'Nigeria and the World Trade Organisation' (Speech) *The Guardian* Newspapers (Nigeria), 6 March 2002, p. 70, *op cit*.

35 Id.

Conclusion

1 H.E Mr Pakalitha Mosisili, 'What WTO for the 21st Century?', Keynote Address at the 2006 WTO Public Forum, Geneva, Switzerland; 25 September 2006. See the address at [http://www.wto.org/english/forums_e/public_forum_e/forum06_e.htm].

2 See Hudec (1987) p. 130.

3 See H.E Mr Pakalitha Mosisili *op cit*.

4 The newer interests in subjects like government procurement, services, Intellectual Property, competition, etc are obviously offshoots of concerns raised in the domestic markets.

Appendix: Obligations and Challenges Under the WTO Agreement on Sanitary and Phytosanitary Standards

1 See further: Joanne Scott: *The WTO Agreement on Sanitary and Phytosanitary Measures* OUP (2006); G. Bermann & P.C. Mavroidis (eds) *Trade and Human Health and Safety* CUP (2006); Lukasz Gruszynski, 'Science in the Process of Risk Regulation under the WTO

Agreement on Sanitary and Phytosanitary Measures', *7 German Law Journal No. 4* (2006) [http://www.germanlawjournal.com/article.php?id=718]; Van den Bossche & D. Prevost, 'The Agreement on the Application of Sanitary and Phytosanitary Measures' in P. Macrory et al (edS) *The World Trade Organisation – Legal, Political and Economic Analysis* Vol. 1 Springer (2005) 231–370. G. Marceau & J.P.Trachtman, 'The TBT,SPS and GATT: A Map of the WTO Law of Domestic Regulation' 36 JWT (2002) 811–881; Alan Sykes, 'Domestic Regulation, Sovereignty and Scientific Evidence Requirements;' A Pessimistic View' *3 Chi J. Int'l Law* (2002) 353; Christoforou T., "Settlement of Science-Based Trade Disputes in the WTO: A Critical Review of the Developing Case Law in the face of Scientific Uncertainty".*NYU Envt LJ No. 8* (2000) 622–648.

2 See generally, Joanna Scott: 'European Regulation of GMOs: Thinking about Judicial Review in the WTO'; Jean Monnet Working Paper 04/04; New York University School of Law (2004).

3 See the Doha Declaration, *op cit*, para 44.

4 See Articles 2.1; 2.2.

5 See also Article 7 of the Agreement.

6 The Committee has a list of Enquiry Points of WTO Members States: *G/SPS/ENQ/23* of 27 March 2008.

7 The List of National Notification Authorities is in the Committee Document *G/SPS/NNNA/13* of 27 March 2008.

8 See generally, Annex C, Articles 1–3. See also Article 8 of the Agreement.

9 See Frederico Ortino, *Basic Legal Instruments for the Liberalisation of Trade* A Comparative Analysis of EC and WTO Law (Hart Publishing) 2004, where he examines the introduction of the test of 'reasonableness' under the SPS and TBT Agreements, comparing it to the 'rule of reason' in EU jurisprudence, pp 434–469.

10 Main disputes under the SPS include: *EC-Biotech, op cit; EC-Measures Concerning Meat and Meat Products (EC-Hormones) WT/DS26; WT/DS48; United States/Canada – Continued Suspension of Obligations in the EC-Hormones Dispute (Hormones II) WT/DS320, WT/DS321 respectively; Japan – Measures Affecting the Importation of Apples (Japan-Apples) (WT/DS245); Japan – Measures Affecting Agricultural Products (Japan-Agricultural Products II) WT/DS76; Australia – Measures Affecting the Importation of Salmon (Australia – Salmon) WT/DS18.* Altogether, there have been about 32 consultations on the SPS Agreement. Seven of the disputes were instigated by developing countries. LDC's have to date not raised complaints in this area. See www.worldtradelaw.net for a list of disputes.

11 Council Directives 81/602, 31 July 1981; 88/146, 7 March 1988; 88/299, 17 May 1988. Although the Directives were in force before the adoption of the SPS Agreement in 1995, they were still deemed to be covered by the SPS Agreement. Note that Article 2.4 of the SPS Agreement provides that: 'Sanitary or phytosanitary measures which conform to the relevant provisions of this Agreement shall be presumed to be in accordance with the obligations of the Members under the provisions of GATT 1994 which relate to the use of sanitary or phytosanitary measures, in particular the provisions of Article XX(b).'

12 (FN in original) For the purposes of paragraph 3 of Article 3, there is a scientific justification if, on the basis of an examination and evaluation of available scientific information in conformity with the relevant provisions of this Agreement, a Member determines that the relevant international standards, guidelines or recommendations are not sufficient to achieve its appropriate level of sanitary or phytosanitary protection.

13 AB: EC-Hormones, para 165. Emphasis in original.

14 Id. See para 214–5.

15 EC-Hormones id, para 246.

16 (FN in original) See, for example: Opinion of the Economic and Social Committee of 13 December 1984 on the proposal for a Council Directive amending Directive 81/602/EEC concerning the prohibition of certain substances having a hormonal action and of any substances having a thyrostatic action, Official Journal, No. C 44, 15 February 1985, p. 14; Resolution of the European Parliament of 11 October 1985 on the proposal for a Council Directive amending Directive 81/602/EEC concerning the prohibition of certain substances having a hormonal action and of any substances having a thyrostatic action, Official Journal No. C 288, 11 November 1985, p. 158; Resolution of the European Parliament of 16 September 1988 on the use of hormones in meat production, Official Journal, No. C 262, 10 October 1988, p. 167; and Resolution of the European Parliament of 14 April 1989 on the USA's refusal to comply with Community legislation on slaughterhouses and hormones, and the consequences of this refusal, Official Journal, No. C 120, 16 May 1989, p. 356. The latter Resolution was based on, *inter alia*, the Pimenta Report, Parts A and B.

17 (FN in original). Article 7a of the Treaty Establishing the European Community stipulates:

The Community shall adopt measures with the aim of progressively establishing the internal market over a period expiring on 31 December 1992 ...

The internal market shall comprise an area without internal frontiers in which the free movement of goods, persons, services and capital is ensured in accordance with the provisions of this Treaty.

18 See para 245.

19 Panel Report, para 8.169.

20 Id, para 8.176.

21 Id, paras 8.101–8.103 and 8.180. See AB: *Japan – Agricultural Products II*, paras 73–74, 82, and 84.

22 Id, para 8.198.

23 Id, para 8.199.

24 AB: Japan-Apples, para 176; See also Panel Report *EC-Biotech* para 7.2939.

25 See Japan-Agricultural Products II, para 89.

26 AB Report: *Japan – Agricultural Products II*, para 89. The third and fourth requirements relate to the *maintenance* of a provisional phytosanitary measure and highlight the provisional nature of measures adopted pursuant to Article 5.7. See AB: Japan-Apples, para 175.

27 AB Report, *Japan – Agricultural Products II*, para 89.

28 Id. (original italics). See AB-Japan Apples, para 176.

29 Id para 164. See Appellate Body Report, *Japan – Agricultural Products II* para 84.

30 Id See para 167–8. The AB stated that a Panel is not obliged to give precedence to the importing Member's approach to scientific evidence and risk when analysing and assessing scientific evidence.

31 Id, para 165. See EC-Hormones AB Report, para 117. See also the further deliberations on DSU Article 11 in the instant case in Part X of the AB Report in *Japan-Apples* para 217–231.

32 See the Panel Report: *EC-Biotech* para 7.3067; AB in *EC-Hormones*, para 193.

33 See AB Report *EC-Hormones*, para 165; See also AB Report: *Australia-Salmon* para 122 and footnotes.

34 *EC-Hormones, ibid*, para 194.
35 Id.
36 Emphasis in original.
37 AB Report: *Australia-Salmon*, para 121.
38 See AB Report: Japan-Apples, para 243 (d). See also the Panel Report, para 8.291, 9.1 (c).
39 Article 6.2.
40 Article 6.3.
41 See the SPS Committee: 'Issues in the Application of Article 6 of the Agreement in the Application of Sanitary and Phytosanitary Measures' *G/SPS/GEN/640/Rev.1*, of 14 Sep 2006.
42 J. Michael Finger and Philip Schuler, 'Implementation of WTO Commitments: The Development Challenge', in Hoekman et al (2002) 493–503 at 496. See also, John S. Wilson; 'Standards, Regulations and Trade: WTO Rules and Developing Country Concerns' id, 428–438.
43 SPS Committee: *G/SPS/W/218, 25* Feb 2008.
44 SPS Committee: *G/SPS/48*, 16 May 2008.
45 Chile (*G/SPS/W171*); Australia(*G/SPS/W/172*); Submissions at the Committee meeting *G/SPS/R/36/Rev.1*, 14 June 2005.
46 SPS Agreement, Annex B, para 1, 2.
47 Id, para 3,4.
48 Id, para 10; See para 5–8.
49 See Panel Report Japan-Agricultural Products II, para 3.1 (f).
50 Id, para 8.111; 8.116.
51 AB Report, para 105.
52 Id,para 106.
53 Id para 107–8.
54 SPS Committee: *G/SPS/W/215/Rev.2*, of 22 April 2008.
55 See the revised Proposals on Transparency – *G/SPS/7/Rev.3* of 20 June 2008, effective as from 1st December 2008.
56 Internet sites mentioned are the WTO Secretariat's Document Online Facility and SPS Information Management System (SPSIMS) http://spsims.wto.org and the FAO's International Portal on Food Safety, Animal and Plant Health, http://www.ipfsaph.org
57 Id.
58 The US in *Japan-Agricultural Products* II, had asked the AB that in the event it finds that the Japan's testing requirement was consistent with Article 7 and Annex B of the SPS Agreement, it should make a determination as to whether the SPS measure fulfilled the conditions of Article 8 and Annex C. Since the AB did not make such a finding, it did not dwell on the said Article 8 and Annex C. See the AB Report Part F; See also the Panel Report, para 8.117.
59 See generally para 1 (a; f; g) of Annex C.
60 Id para 1(b).
61 Id para 1(c).
62 Id para 1(e)
63 Id, para 1(i)
64 Id, para 2.
65 US Panel Report, para 8.7; Canada Panel Report, para 8.7.
66 AB Report para 147.
67 Ibid, para 148.

68 There have been a number of works discussing the issue of developing country challenges in meeting SPS measures and, the current challenges of private standards as well. See for e.g, Grace Chia-Hua Lee, 'Private Food Standards and their Impacts on Developing Countries': [http://trade.ec.europa.eu/doclib/docs/2006/november/tradoc_127969. pdf]; Henson, Spencer and Jaffee; 'Understanding Developing Country Strategic Responses to the Enhancement of Food Safety Standards' 31 (4) *World Economy* (2008) 548–568; Scott, (2006) *op cit*, pp 302–6; World Bank Report: The Impact of Food Safety and Agricultural Health Standards on Developing Country Exports *Poverty Reduction and Management* (2005); P. Athukorala and S. Jayasuriya, *Food Safety Issues, Trade and WTO Rules: A Developing Country Perspective*, Blackwell Publishing (3003); S.J Henson & R.J. Loader, 'Barriers to Agricultural Exports from Developing Countries: The Role of Sanitary and Phytosanitary Requirements *World Development* 29 (2001) 85–102; S.Henson, R.Loader, A.Swinbank, M.Bredhal & N.Lux, 'Impact of Sanitary Phytosanitary Measures on Developing Countries, University of Reading (2000) at: [http://www.reading.ac.uk/ nmsruntime/saveasdialog.asp?lID=17696&sID=72895]; Ellen Mangus, 'Developing Countries and the SPS Agreement at: [http://www.nodai.ac.jp/campuslife/oversea/iss/ en/full%20paper%20English/2006/2-2-4%20WU%20Netherlands%20re% 20fp%20Oct12.htm].

69 The losses by farmers, governments, and consumers in importing countries in the recent outbreaks of the foot and mouth disease (Britain); avian flu (some parts of Asia and Africa) are demonstrative.

70 See the SPS Committee Notes on 'Specific Trade Concerns', *G/SPS/GEN/204/Rev.8* of 27 March 2008. LDCs have raised only two concerns and supported one. There have been no trade concerns regarding measures maintained by LDCs raised at the Committee.

71 Where the appropriate level of protection allows scope for the phased introduction of SPS measures, the longer time frame here shall mean a period not less than six months. See the Doha Ministerial Conference document: *WT/MIN(01)17*, para 3.1.

72 See SPS Committee: Report on Proposals for Special and Differential Treatment, *G/SPS/35*, 30 June 2005, para 15.

73 Id, para 16.

74 Id, paras 17;18.

75 Id, para 19.

76 Id, para 41.

77 See 'Review of the Operation and Implementation of the Agreement on the Application of Sanitary and Phytosanitary Measures, *G/SPS/12*, of 11 March 1999, para 13; See generally, also *G/SPS/35 op cit*.

78 See Graham Mayeda; Developing Disharmony? The SPS and TBT Agreements and the Impact of Harmonisation on Developing Countries; JIEL 7(4) 2004, pp 737–764; The International Trade Centre: 'Technical Assistance for SPS Measures: Protect Health not Trade' A Joint Study of six developing countries by the ITC/Commonwealth Secretariat; *International Trade Forum, Issue 3/2002.* Online: [http://www.tradeforum.org/news/ fullstory.php/aid/460/Technical_Assistance_for_SPS_Measures:_Protect_Health,_Not_ Trade.html]; E Boutrif & M. Pineiro, 'The New International Trade Context for Developing Countries: The Impact of SPS and TBT Agreements; Online at: [http://wwww.cirad.fr/colloque/fao/pdf/2–pineiro.pdf].

79 See Article 9.2 of the Agreement.

80 Joanne Scott; The *WTO Agreement on Sanitary and Phytosanitary Measures: A Commentary op cit*, p. 296.

81 See Scott, id, p. 32. See also Annex 1 of the TBT Agreement wherein the terms, 'regional body or system', 'central government body', 'local government body' and, 'non-governmental body, are defined.

82 By changing the phrase 'shall consider providing' in Article 9.2 to 'shall provide'; Also that the phrase 'substantial investments' shall be construed as follows: that 'any changes that would require additional resources to existing levels of current expenditure or their restructuring, or additional training or staffing, shall be construed to amount to "substantial investments" See SPS Committee: *G/SPS/35, op cit*, para 10.

83 Id.

84 Id. The disparity in expectations and the actual technical assistance rendered had earlier been noted in the World Bank Report: *Food, Safety and Agricultural Health Standards: Challenges and Opportunities for Developing Country Exports* World Bank Report No. 31207, 10 Jan 2005.

85 See Scott, *op cit*, p. 299.

86 See the STDF site: [http://www.standardsfacility.org/].

87 See the STDF Newsletter Vol 1 Issue 1, March 2008. Available via the WTO SPS web page, *op cit*.

88 Id.

89 The proposal was by New Zealand in October 2007.

90 See *G/SPS/W/217* of 20 February 2008.

91 By Bijendra Shakya. See the WTO SPS web page: [http://www.wto.org/english/tratop_e/sps_e/sps_e.htm#work].

92 The GMP is recognised under different jurisdictions as a system of quality assurance and quality control for the production of food and pharmaceutical products. Different countries apply this GMP some more highly sophisticated than others although that recognised under the WHO is adopted by most developing countries.

93 These three problems have to some extent been addressed, first with Nepal's adoption of the SPS obligations under the WTO since it acceded to the Organisation in 2003, and also with technical assistance funding fro national SPS capacity building. See Bijendra Shakya, *op cit*.

94 In Bijendra Shakya, *op cit*. To address this question of private sector involvement, Nepalese business owner formed the Ayuverdic Medicine Producers of Nepal. (AMPAN).

95 See further, Grace Chia-Hua Lee, *op cit*; Henson, Spencer and Jaffee, Steven; 'Understanding Developing Country Strategic Responses to the Enhancement of Food Safety Standards' 31 (4) *World Economy* (2008) 548–568; Scott, (2006) *op cit*, pp 302–6.

96 See the submission by the OIE: 'Considerations relevant to Private Standards in the Field of Animal Health, Food Safety and Animal Welfare', *G/SPS/GEN/822*, of 25 Feb 2008, p. 2.

97 Id.

98 See the GLOBALGAP website: www.globalgap.org

99 Id.

100 See the OIE Submissions to the SPS Committee, *op cit*, p. 3.

101 See the WTO: *Understanding the WTO Agreement on Sanitary and Phytosanitary Measures*, on the WTO web page: [http://www.wto.org/English/tratop_e/sps_e/spsund_e.htm]

102 Id, p. 6.

103 See the FLO Annual Report 2007: *An Inspiration for Change*. Available online: [http://www.fairtrade.net/uploads/media/FLO_AR2007_low_res_01.pdf].

104 For e.g the Convention on Biological Diversity (1993); the Cartegana Protocol on Biosafety (2003).

105 Article 4, 'Equivalence' provisions.

106 See the List of National Notification Authorities in: *G/SPS/NNA/13*, of 27 March 2007.

107 Inaugurated 16 August 2001, the body had been previously established in 1994 but was largely inactive. See Nneoma Ukeje Eloagu, 'Professionals to head new WTO units in Ministries' *This Day* Newspapers 16 November 2004. See the webpage of the Ministry on WTO affairs at: [http://www.commerceng.org/departments/external%20trade/wto_branch.htm].

108 See: http://www.wto.org/english/thewto_e/countries_e/nigeria_e.htm.

109 See the List of Enquiry Points in respect of the SPS Agreement: *G/SPS/ENQ/23*, of 27 March 2008.

110 See generally, S.5 of the Decree.

111 See the NAFDAC web site: www.nafdacnigeria.org

112 See the Organisation's website, id.

113 See also, the online Glossary at: [http://www.wto.org/english/thewto_e/glossary_e/enquiry_point_e.htm].

114 Product registration at NAFDAC entails administrative, evaluative and analytical processes as well as post market surveillance. There is available a list of tariffs; the requirements for registration including the labelling requirements for foods, drugs, cosmetics. Guidelines for prospective exporters of regulated products and also, guidelines for prospective importers are also clearly listed.

115 See the NAFDAC webpage: [http://www.nafdacnigeria.org/regulation.html].

116 For instance, the Agency states that its seafood laboratories have EU accreditation for food and shrimp export, while its Central Vaccine Control Laboratory is recognised by the WHO. Its Pesticide Residue, Pesticide Formulation and Mycotoxin laboratories are affiliated with the International Atomic Energy Agency (IAEA) and its Vitamin Analysis laboratory is affiliated with UNICEF. See the NAFDAC website above.

117 SON is a body corporate established by Act No. 56 1971 (amended in 1976, 1984, 1990) with the responsibility of national policies on standards, standard specification, quality control and metrology. It is a member of the Codex Alimentarius Commission and of the International Standards Organisation (ISO).

118 See the SONCAP web site: www.soncap.com

119 The list of regulated products is available online: [http://www.soncap.com/pdfs/products.pdf]. It must be pointed out that that these regulated products are subject to constant change and indeed exporters are always advised to ensure they have up-to-date information on regulated products.

120 See the guidelines at [http://www.soncap.com/pdfs/guidelines.pdf].

121 See the statistics available on the NAFDAC web site above.

122 A personal observation.

123 See the Report of the Environmental Rights Action (ERA) *'Genetically Modified Crops: The African Challenge'* Lagos, Nigeria, March 2005. Online at: [http://www.eraction.org/publications/eragmoreport.pdf].

124 Id. See also the Resolution of the African Conference on GMOs and the response of the Nigerian consumer groups condemning the MOU; Lagos, Nigeria, 21–23 March 2005. Online: [http://www.connectotel.com/gmfood/an160305.txt].

125 See Maryam Mayet, *'Comments on Nigerian Bio-Safety Act 2006'* African Centre for Bio-Safety' February 2007. Online at: [http://www.biosafetyafrica.net/portal/DOCS/Nigerian_Safety_Act_2006_Comments.pdf].

126 There is no mention of the Act on the National Assembly List.

127 The Nigerian government makes media announcements on restricted imports of products. Other countries also ban food exports from Nigeria. See for example: 'Angola, Mali and Guinea join Nigeria Poultry Ban': [http://nm.onlinenigeria.com/templates/ ?a=6931&z=7]. In either case, there has been no dispute brought to the WTO.

128 See the STDF Newsletter, *op cit*.

129 See also the Report by the WTO Secretariat: 'Activities of the SPS Committee and Other Relevant WTO Activities from 2006 to the Present'; Joint FAO/WHO Food Standard Programme, Codex Alimetarius Commission, *CAC/30/INF/5 Thirtieth Session* Rome, Italy, 2–7 July 2007. See also, the project proposal on the STDF web page at: [http://www.standardsfacility.org/files/Project_documents/Project_Preparation_ Grants/STDF_172_Application_form.pdf].

130 STDF project proposal, id.

131 Id.

132 Id.

133 Id.

134 Id.

135 See the STDF web site, *op cit*.

136 Although the authors assessed EU SPS requirements, we consider that these difficulties are also general to developing countries.

BIBLIOGRAPHY*

Books/Papers

Abbott F.M. (ed) *China in the World Trading System: Defining the Principles of Engagement* Kluwer Law International 1998

Achime N. "A Case against SAP", *National Concord* (Nigeria) 15 March 1989: 3

Adeyemo A. "Should Nigeria pull out of WTO?" *Nigerian Tribune* 8 October 2005: 12

Afeikhena J. "Institutional Framework and the Process of Trade Policy Making in Africa: The Case of Nigeria" *Conference Paper-African Economic Research Institutions and Policy Development: Opportunities and Challenges*: Dakar, Jan 28–9, 2005. Online: [http://www.idrc.ca/uploads/userS/11085711371Institutional_Framework_of_Trade_Policy.pdf]

Alegimenlen O.A.O. "Structural Adjustment and Nigerian Development; A Third World Angle" *Nigerian Current Legal Problems* (Ayua I.A. ed) *Vols 4 & 5*; 1996–98, NIALS (2000): 28–48

Analogbei F.C.O. "Trade Reforms and Productivity in Nigeria" *Central Bank of Nigeria Papers* 9th ACZRU Paper 9 31 Dec 2000

Anderson K & Martin W. (eds) *Agricultural Trade Reform & the Doha Development Agenda* Palgrave Macmillan 2006

Bairoch P. European Trade Policy 1815–1914 (Matthias & Pollard eds) *The Cambridge Economic History of Europe Vol 8 – Cambridge MA*: CUP: 1989

Baihua G. "Shanghai's WTO Affairs Consultation Centre: Working Together to Take Advantage of WTO Membership" in Peter Gallagher, Patrick Low & Andrew Stoler (eds) *Managing the Challenges of WTO Participation*, _WTO: 2006 Case Study II; Online: [http://www.wto.org/english/res_e/booksp_e/casestudies_e/case11_e.htm]

Balassa B. *New Directions in the World Economy* New York: NYU Press 1989

Bartles L. "The WTO Enabling Clause and Positive Conditionality in the European Community's GSP Programme" *6 JIEL 6 no. 2* (2003) 507–532

BBC News Archive: '*Indonesia wins IMF Bail Out*', BBC News Saturday Nov 1, 1997 [http://news.bbc.co.uk/1/hi/events/indonesia/archive/19565.stm] visited 08.06.06

Bello W., '*Finance: What is the IMF's agenda for Asia?* http://www.southcentre.org/southletter/sl30/South%20Letter%2030trans-02.htm#TopOfPage

Bergsten F., (Director of the Institute for International Economics in Washington DC), *The Backlash against Globalisation*, Remarks made to the 2000 Annual Meeting of the Trilateral Commission Tokyo, May 9, 2000. Online: http://www.petersoninstitute.org/publications/papers/paper.cfm?ResearchID=377

---

* Except where expressly indicated, all online sources were re-accessed and verified live as of 1 February 2009.

Bermann G. & Mavroidis P.C. (eds) *Trade and Human Health and Safety* CUP 2006

Bhagwati J. *In Defence of Globalisation* Oxford 2004

Brenton P. "Integrating the Least Developed Countries into the World Trading System: The Current Impact of European Union Preferences under 'Everything But Arms'" *JWT Vol 37, No. 3* (2003):329–357

Bronde T. *International Governance in the WTO: Judicial Boundaries and Political Capitulation* Cameron May 2004

Bulajic M. *Principles of International Development Law* Martinus Nijhoff Pub 2nd Ed. 1998

Burca G. and Scott J. "The Impact of the WTO on EU Decision Making" *Academy of European Law* 2000. Online [http://www.jeanmonnetprogram.org/papers/00/000601.html]

Busch M.L., and Reinhardt E., "Developing Countries and General Agreement on Tariffs and Trade/World Trade Organisation Dispute Settlement" *JWT Vol 37, No. 4* (2003): 719–735

Cass D. *The Constitutionalisation of the World Trade Organisation: Legitimacy, Democracy, and Community in the International Trading System* OUP 2005

Chang H. *Kicking Away The Ladder: Development Strategy in Historical Perspective* London: Anthem Press 2002

Chang H. "Trade Lessons for Developing Countries from the History Books" *Newsletter of the Economic Research Forum for the Arab Countries, Iran & Turkey* 10, no. 3, Autumn 2003

Christoforou T. "Settlement of Science-Based Trade Disputes in the WTO: A Critical Review of the Developing Case Law in the face of Scientific Uncertainty" *NYU Envt LJ No. 8* (2000):622–648

Cogan J.K. 'Noncompliance and the International Rule of Law', *Yale Journal of International Law Vol 31*, (2006):189–210

Croley S.P. & Jackson J.H. 'WTO Dispute Panel Deference to National Government Decisions. The Misplaced Analogy to the US Chevron Standard-of-Review Doctrine" in Petersmann Ernst-Ulrich *International Trade Law and the GATT/WTO Dispute Settlement System* (ed.) Kluwer Academic Publishers (1997) 209

Crump A and Ellwood W.E. *A–Z of World Development* New International Publications Ltd (1998)

Das D.K., "The Doha Round of Multilateral Trade Negotiations and Trade in Agriculture" *JWT 40 no. 2* (April 2006) 259–290

Davey W.J, Jackson J.H & Sykes A.O. *International Economic Relations* West Publishing Co. Third Ed. 1995

Demaret P., Bellis J.F., Jimenez G.C. *Regionalism and Multilateralism after the Uruguay Round: Convergence, Divergence and Interaction,* EIP Series European Policy 1997

Deming Liu, "Now the Wolf has indeed come! Perspective on the Patent Protection of Biotechnology Inventions in China", *53 AJCL 1* (Winter 2005): 207–260

Diaz-Bonilla E., Robinson S., Thomas M., and Yanona Y. "WTO, Agriculture, and Developing Countries: A Survey of Issues; *TMD Discussion Paper No. 81,* International Food Policy Research Institute (IFPRI) (Jan 2002)

Dijck Pv. and Faber G. (eds) *Challenges to the New World Trade Organisation* Kluwer Law Intnl 1996)

Dillon T.J. (Jr) 'The World Trade Organisation: A New Legal Order for World Trade', *Michigan Journal of Int'l Law,* 16 (1995):349 at 355

Dornbusch R. "Economic Focus" *The Economist,* 4 May 1991

Edwards S.E. "Drafting Fiscal Legislation" *32 Canadian Tax Journal (1984)* p. 727 at 728

Eeckhout P. 'The Domestic Legal Status of the WTO Agreements; Interconnecting Legal Systems' *CMLR* Vol 34 no. 1 (1997): 11–58

Eloagu N.U. 'Professionals to head new WTO units in Ministries' *ThisDay Newspapers* Online Archives 16 November 2004

Engammare V. and Lehmann J.P, 'Does the Multilateral Trading System Promote the Interests of the Poor?' in *From Cancun to Sao Paolo: The Role of Civil Society in the International Trading System* CUTS (2004)

Epstein M.J. and Schnietz K.E. 'Measuring the Cost of Environmental and Labour Protests to Globalisation: An Event Study of the Failed 1999 Seattle WTO Talks', *International Trade Journal* XVI no. 2 Texas A&M International University (Summer 2002):133–136

Evenett S.J. "The World Trade Organisation Ministerial Conference in Hong Kong: What Next?" *JWT 40 no. 2* (2006):221–238

Evenett S. and Hoekman B. (eds), *Economic Development and Multilateral Trade Cooperation* Palgrave Macmillan & IBRD 2006

Eze O.C. *Nigeria and the World Trade Organisation* Nigerian Institute of International Affairs 2004

Ezeani E.C. "Trade Disputes Devoid of Judicial Activism: Too Much Too Soon for the WTO Dispute Settlement Body? *Journal of International Trade Law, 3 Issue 2* (RGU) (Dec 2004):21–32

Finger J.M. "Implementing the Uruguay Round Agreements: Problems for Developing Countries" *The World Economy 24 no. 9*: (2001):1097–1098

Friedman T.L. *The Lexus and the Olive Tree* Farrar, Straws and Giroux 1999

Fritz T. "Special and Differential Treatment for Developing Countries", *Global Issue Paper, No. 18*, The Heinrich Boll Foundation (May 2005)

Focus on the Global South. "Internal Transparency and Decision-making processes at the WTO Critical Issues and Recommendations" WTO NGO Symposium, 1 May 2002 [http://www.wto.org/english/tratop_e/dda_e/summary_report_intern_transp.doc]

Gabilondo J.L.P. 'Developing Countries in the WTO Dispute Settlement Procedures: Improving their Participation' *JWT 35 no. 4* (2001):483–488

George C. and Kirkpatrick C. "Putting the Doha Principles into Practice: The Role of Sustainability Impact Assessment" in Honi Katrak and Roger Strange (2004): 315–338

Glipo A., Carlsen L., Sayeed A.T., Cainglet J. and Schwentesius R., *"Agreement on Agriculture and Food Security: Perspectives from MesoAmerica and Asia"*, Americas Policy, International Relations Centre (September 2003)

Goldsmith E and Mander J. (eds) *The Case Against a Global Economy and For a Turn Towards Localisation)* Earthscan Publications Ltd (2001)

Goldstein J. & Martin L.L., "Legalisation, Trade Liberalisation, and Domestic Policies, *54 Int'l Org* (2000):603–4

Gonzalez C.G. "Institutionalising Inequality: The WTO Agreement on Agriculture, Food Security and Developing Countries" *Colombia Journal of Environmental Law* Vol. 27 No. 2 (2002):435–489

Grant C. "The WTO-ten years on: Trade and Development', *Tralac Working Paper No 5/2005* (April 2006) (TRALAC) Trade Law Centre for South Africa publications

Greenpeace, Adelphi Research and Friends of the Earth Europe; "Is the WTO the only way?-Safeguarding Multilateral Environmental Agreements from international trade rules and settling trade and environment disputes outside the WTO" *Joint NGO Briefing Paper* (2006)

Gruszynski L. "Science in the Process of Risk Regulation under the WTO Agreement on Sanitary and Phytosanitary Measures" *7 German Law Journal No. 4* (2006)

Halverson K. "China's WTO Accession: Economic, Legal and Political Implications" *Boston College International and Comparative Law Review 27 no. 2*, (2004):319–370

Hart M. and Dymond B. "Special and Differential Treatment and the Doha "Development" Round" *JWT 37 no. 2* (2003):395–415

Hertel T.W. & Winters A.L. (eds) *Poverty and the WTO: Impacts of the Doha Development Agenda* Palgrave Macmillan (2006)

Hoekman B. "Operationalising the concept of policy space in the WTO: Beyond Special and Differential Treatment" *JIEL 8 no. 2* (2005):405–424

Hoekman B., Mattoo A. & English P. *Development, Trade, and the WTO: A Handbook* World Bank Trade and Development Series (2002)

Hoekman B and Kostecki M. *The Political Economy of the World Trading System* OUP (2001)

Hoekman B., Michalopoulos C., and Winters W. "More Favourable and Differential Treatment of Developing Countries: Towards a New Approach in the World Trade Organisation" *World Bank Policy Research Working Paper No. 3107* (1 August 2003)

Holmes K.R, Feuler E.J, O'Grady M. *Index of Economic Freedom: The Link Between Economic Opportunity and Prosperity* The Heritage Foundation/Wall Street Journal (2008)

Howse R. et al; "WTO Disciplines and Biofuels: Opportunities and Constraints in the Creation of Global Marketplace" *International Food and Agricultural Trade IPC Discussion Paper* (October 2006)

Hudec Robert. E. *Developing Countries in the GATT Legal System* Gower (1987)

Hudec Robert. E. *Enforcing International Trade Law: The Evolution of the Modern GATT Legal System*, Lexis Law (1993)

Hughes H, "Policy Forum: Economic Development: Trade or Aid? Trade, Aid and Development" *Australian Economic Review 39 no. 1* (March 2006):63–68

Ikpeze N.I., Soludo C.C. and Elekwa N.N. "Nigeria: The Political Economy of the Policy Process, Policy Choice and Implementation"; (Charles Soludo, Osita Ogbu and Ha-Joon Chang eds) *The Politics of Trade and Industrial Policy in Africa; Forced Consensus?* Africa World Press/IDRC (2004) Online publication: [http://www.idrc.ca/en/ev-71263-201-1-DO_TOPIC.html]:17–18

India Express Newspapers: 'Indonesia signs revised IMF package deal' 16 January 1998 http://www.indianexpress.com/fe/daily/19980116/01655524.html

Irwin D. *Against the Tide: An Intellectual History of Free Trade* Princeton NJ: Princeton University Press (1996)

Ismail F. 'Mainstreaming Development in the World Trade Organisation', *JWT 39 no. 1* (2005):11–21

Jackson J.H. *Sovereignty, the WTO and Changing Fundamental of International Law* CUP (2006)

Jackson J.H. *The World Trading System: Law and Policy of International Economic Relations* MIT Press 2nd Ed. (1997/2000)

Jackson J.H. *The Jurisprudence of GATT and the WTO: Insights on Treaty Law and Economic Relations* CUP 2000

Jackson J.H. "Designing and Implementing Effective Dispute Settlement Procedures: WTO Dispute Settlement, Appraisal and Prospects" in Anne O. Krueger (1998) at 161,163

Jackson J.H. "Global Economics and International Economic Law", *JIEL 1 Issue 1* (1998): 1–23

Jackson J.H. "International Law Status of WTO Dispute Settlement Reports: Obligation to Comply or Option to 'Buy Out'?" (Editorial Comment), *AJIL 98* (January 2004): 109–125

Jackson J.H. "Dispute Settlement in the WTO: Policy and Jurisprudential Considerations" *Discussion Paper No. 419 Research Seminar in International Economics School of Public Policy*, University of Michigan (9 Feb 1998)

James H. (Prof, Economic History, Princeton University) "A Historical Perspective on International Monetary Arrangements" Online [http://www.bos.frb.org/economic/conf/conf43/33p.pdf]

John C. and Vaughan L. *The Settlement of Disputes in International Law– Institutions and Procedures* OUP 1999

Katrak H. and Strange R. (eds) *The WTO and Developing Countries* Palgrave Macmillan 2004

Kaneda M. "Policy Designs in a Dynamic Model of Infant Industry Protection" *Journal of Development Economics 72 no. 1* (Oct 2003): 91–115

Kennedy D.L.M and Southwick J.D. (eds) *The Political Economy of International Trade Law* Essays in Honour of Robert E. Hudec CUP 2002

Khor M. (Third World Network) "DSU process becoming an outrage of law and justice, says critic" http://www.twnside.org.sg/title/twr123i.htm

Klinck D.R. *The Word of the Law: Approaches to Legal Discourse* Carleton University Press 1992

Knirsh J. et al "Deadly Subsidies – How government funds are killing oceans and forests and why the CBD rather than the WTO should stop this perverse use of public money", *Greenpeace* (2006)

Krueger A.O. (ed) *The WTO as an International Organisation* University of Chicago Press 1998

Kundu K.K. "India's underperforming industrial sector" Asia Times Online (24 Dec 2004) Online at: [http://www.atimes.com/atimes/South_Asia/FL24Df01.html]

Kwa A. "Agriculture in Developing Countries: Which Way Forward", *T.R.A.D.E. Occasional Papers 4*, South Centre (June 2001)

Kwa A. "The a la carte undertaking: a new form of special and differential treatment?" *Global South* (2000) Online: [http://www.focusweb.org/publications/2000]

Lamy P. "The Perspectives of the Multilateral Trading System", Speech at Lima, 31 January 2006, Online: [http://www.wto/English/news_e/ppl_e/spp117_e.htm]

Lamy P. BBC 4 'Today Programme', (FM 93.90) Radio Interview, 31 January 2006

Lamy P. 'Talks Suspended. Today there are only losers', 17 July 2006, Speeches by DG; Online: [http://www.wto.org/english/news_e/sppl_e/sppl_e.htm]

Lang T. and Hines C. *THE NEW PROTECTIONISM Protecting the Future Against Free Trade* Earthscan Publications Ltd 1993

Larouer C. 'WTO Non-Violation Complaints: A Misunderstood Remedy in the WTO Dispute Settlement System', *NILR LIII* (2006): 97–126

Lee Y. *Reclaiming Development in the World Trading System* CUP 2006

Macrory P. Appleton A. & Plummer M. et al (ed) *The World Trade Organisation – Legal, Political and Economic Analysis Vol. 1* Springer 2005

Madeley J. and Barnes J. "Setting the Scene"; 'Making or Missing the links? The politics of trade reform and poverty reduction", *Panos Media Tool Kit on PRSPs* no. 3 Panos, London August 2006

Marceau G. & Trachtman J.P. 2 The TBT, SPS and GATT: A Map of the WTO Law of Domestic Regulation" *JWT* 36 no. 5 (2002): 811–881

Matsushita M., Schoenbaum T.J. and Mavroidis P.C. *The World Trade Organisation Law, Practice and Policy* OUP 2003

Matthews A. "Special and Differential Treatment in the WTO Agricultural Negotiations" *IIIS Discussion Paper No. 61* (January2005)

McGee R. "The Moral Case for Free Trade" *JWT Vol 29 No. 1* (Feb 1995):64–76

McGuire S. "Between Pragmatism and Principle: Legalisation, Political Economy, and the WTO'S Subsidy Agreement" *Int'l Trade Journal* XVI no. 3 Texas A & M International University (Fall 2002):319–343

Messerlin P. "Reforming Agricultural Policies in the Doha Round", in Evenett S. and Hoekman B. (2006)

Michalopoulos C. *Developing Countries in the WTO* Palgrave Macmillan 2001

Michalopoulos C. "The Role of Special and Differential Treatment for Developing Countries in GATT and the World Trade Organisation" *Policy Research Working Paper WPS 2388*, World Bank Development Research Group Trade (July 2000) Available online on the World Bank Documents and Reports web page: [http://www-wds.worldbank.org]

Mike J.A. "Proliferation of regulations: The challenges of doing business in Nigeria" *The Guardian Newspapers* (Nigeria) 6 September (2006):22

Morris R.K (The Global Business Dialogue), *The Global Positions Note Book* Vol 5, No. 9, The Global Business Dialogue Inc, August 11, (2006)

Mosisili P. (Prime Minister of Lesotho), "What WTO for the 21st Century?" *Keynote Address at the 2006 WTO Public Forum, Geneva, Switzerland* 25 September 2006.

Mukherjee N. "GATS and the Millennium Round of Multilateral Negotiations: Selected Issues from the Perspectives of the Developing Countries" *JWT 33 no. 4*; 1999):87–102

Murphy S. "Food Security and the WTO" *CAFOD Policy Papers* (September 2001)

Narayana M.R. "ICT Sector and regional economic development: Evidence from Karnataka State" (June 2005) *ISEC-Cornell University Revised Conference Paper September 2005*. Available online [http://www.isec.ac.in/MRN]

Narlikar A. *International Trade and Developing Countries: Bargaining Coalitions in the GATT and WTO* Routledge 2003

Nielson J. "Aid for Trade" in *Trade, Doha and Development: A Window into the Issues* World Bank Papers, World Bank (2005)

Nigeriafirst (Online) "ECOWAS Common External Tariff now effective" Online: [http://www.nigeriafirst.org/printer_4869.shtml]

Nwuche C. (Deputy Speaker Nigeria House of Representatives), "Nigeria and the World Trade Organisation" (Speech) *The Guardian Newspapers* (Nigeria) 6 March (2002):70

O'Brien John, *International Law* Cavendish Publishing Ltd (2001)

Ocheng C. 'The EU-ACP Economic Partnership Agreements and the Development Question: Constraints and Opportunities Posed' *JIEL Online:* [doi:10.1093/jiel/jgm009v1]

Odell J.S., "The Seattle Impasse and its implications for the World Trade Organisation", Kennedy D.L.M and Southwick J.D. (eds) (2002): 400–429

Ogundele "Whatever happened to SAP?" *The Guardian Newspapers* (Nigeria) 25 October (1991):13

Ogunleye B. 'Why SAP was adopted, by Sanusi', *The Guardsian Newspapers* (Nigeria) 5 September (2001):27

Okeke R. "Nigeria: Manufacturer's claim ECOWAS tariff will be damaging" *The Guardian Newspapers* (Nigeria), 20 March 2005 Online at [http://www.guardiannewsngr.com]

Okigbo P. "S.A.P and Financial Intermediaries (1)" *The Guardian Newspapers* (Nigeria), 31 August (1987):7

Olaleye Y. "Nigeria's Debt and Her Future" *ThisDay Newspapers* (Nigeria) 16 November 2004 Online at: [http://www.thisdayonline.com/archive/ 2002/12/09/20021209bus08.html]

OnlineNigeria (Nigeria Information Portal): "Oil Boom Era (1971–77)" [http://www.onlinenigeria.com/economics/?blurb=490]

Ortino F. *Basic Legal Intruments for the Liberalisation of Trade A Comparative Analysis of EU and WTO Law* Hart Publishing 2004

Ostry S. "The Uruguay Round North-South Grand Bargain: Implications for future negotiations" Kennedy D.L.M and Southwick J.D. (eds), (2002): 285–300

Oxley A. "Implications of the Decisions in the WTO Shrimp Turtle Dispute" International Trade Strategies Pty Ltd (February 2002). Online: [http://www.tradeandenvironment.com/files/PDF/shrimp-turtle.pdf]

Ozden C. and Reinhardt E. "The Perversity of Preferences: GSP and Developing Country Trade Preferences" *Journal of Developmental Economics* (El Sevier B.V) 78 Issue 1 (Oct 2005):1–21

Oyejide A., Ogunkola A. and Bankole A. "Import Prohibition as Trade Policy Instrument: The Nigerian Experience" (WTO Study) Case Study 32: *Managing the Challenges of WTO Participation.*

Patterson E. "World Trade Ruling on US Continued Dumping and Offset Act of 2000 (CDSOA)" Feb 2003 Online [http://www.asil.org/insights/insigh98.htm]

Pauwelyn J. "The Role of Public International Law in the WTO – how far can we go?" 95 *AJIL* (2001):535–578

Pepple A.S. "The New Business Investments Regulations: Implication and the Dilemmas of Compliance" *Nigerian Current Legal Problems* (Ayua 1.A ed) Vols 4 & 5 1996–98, NIALS (2000):159–181

Petersmann EU. "The Dispute Settlement System of the World Trade Organisation and the Evolution of GATT since 1948" *CMLR 31 no. 5* (1994):1157–1244

Petersmann EU (ed) *International Trade Law and the GATT/WTO Dispute Settlement System* Kluwer Academic Publishers 1997

Pomfret R. (University of Adelaide), "Trade Policy in Canada and Australia in the Twentieth Century" Online [http://www.economics.adelaide.edu.au/staff/pomfret/cda&austradepolicy.pdf]

Power P. (EU Commission trade spokesman): "Poor countries will gain from Doha" *(Reply) The Guardian* (London) 5 July (2006):33

Qureshi A.H. "Interpreting World Trade Organisation Agreements for the Development Objective" *JWT. 37 no. 5* (2003):847–882

Qureshi A.H. *The World Trade Organisation – Implementing International Trade Norms,* Manchester University Press 1996

Rao G. "The Law Applied by World Trade Organisation Panels" *Temple Int'nl & Comp L. J. 17* (Spring 2003):125–137

Raustiala K. "Form and Substance in International Agreements", *AJIL 99 no. 3,* July (2005): 581–614

Ray A. *International Business Law: Text, Cases, and Readings* Prentice Hall (3rd Ed.) 2000

Roddick A. *TAKE IT PERSONALLY How Globalisation affects you and powerful ways to challenge it* Thompson 2001

Rodrik D. "The Limits of Trade Policy Reform in Developing Countries" *Journal of Economic Perspectives 6 no. 1* (1992):87–105

Rodrik D. "Industrial Policy in the 21st Century" (UNIDO Paper) Sep 2004

Roessler F. "The Institutional Balance Between the Judicial and the Political Organs of the WTO", *Conference on "Efficiency, Equity, and Legitimacy: The Multilateral Trading System at the Millennium* June 1–2, 2000 [Online] http://www.ksg.harvard.edu/m-rcbg/Conferences/trade/roessler.htm

Roessler F. "Should Principles of Competition Policy be Incorporated into WTO Law Through Non-Violation Complaints?" *JIEL 2 no. 3* (1999):413–421

Rosen J.R. "China, Emerging Economies and the World Trade Order" 46 *Duke L. J.* No. 5 (April 1997):1519–1564

Samuelson P. *Economics* (10th Ed) 1976

Samuleson P. and Nordhaus W.D. *Economics* International Edition (16th Ed) Irwin McGraw-Hill 1998

Sauré P. "Revisiting the Infant Industry Argument" *Journal of Development Economics 84 vol 1* (Sep 2007):104–117

Sands P. & Klein P. *Bowett's Law of International Institutions* Sweet & Maxwell 5th Edition 2001

Schott J.J. and Buurman J.W. *The Uruguay Round: An Assessment* Washington Institute for International Economics 1994

Schott J.J and Watal J. "*Decision Making in the WT*" *Policy Brief 00-2 Institute of International Economics* March 2000 Online [http://www.iie.com/publications/pb/pb00-2.htm]

Schuh G.E. "Developing Country Interest in WTO agricultural policy" Kennedy D.L.M and Southwick J.D. (eds) (2002):435–449

Scott J. "European Regulation of GMOs: Thinking about Judicial Review in the WTO" *Jean Monnet Working Paper 04/04* NYU School of Law (2004).

Sen A. *Development as Freedom* OUP 1999

Singh A. "Elements for a New Paradigm on Special and Differential Treatment: Special and Differential Treatment, the Multilateral Trading System and Economic Development in the 21st Century" *A Joint publication of UNCTAD, ICTSD, UNDP* (April 2003)

Shin S.H. "Comparison of the Dispute Settlement Procedures of the World Trade Organisation for Trade Disputes and the Inter-American System for Human Rights Violations" 1, *16 New York Int'l Law Review 43* (Winter 2003)

Smaller C. "Can Aid fix trade?: Assessing the WTO's Aid for Trade Agenda", *Institute for Agriculture and Trade Policy* (IATP) *Publication*, September 2006

Smith A. *An Inquiry into the Nature and Causes of the Wealth of the Nations* (1776) Canaan E (ed) University of Chicago Press (1976) Vol 1: 478–9

Smith F. "Reconciling the Irreconcilable: Law, Politics and Non-Trade Concerns in the WTO Agreement on Agriculture" *Conference Paper: British International Studies Association (BISA) 31st* Annual Conference, University of Cork 18–20 Dec 2006

Soames C., Spooner A., and Hawker S. (eds) *The Compact Oxford Dictionary Thesaurus and Word Power Guide* OUP 2002

Sogolo G. "The Blessings of SAP", *The Guardian Newspapers* (Nigeria) 1 May 1989: 9

South Center: "Issues Regarding the Review of the WTO Dispute Settlement Mechanism" *Trade-Related Agenda, Development and Equity (T.R.A.D.E)* (*Working Papers*) Feb 1999. Online at [http://www.southcentre.org/publications/trade/dispute.pdf.]

Steger D.P *Peace through Trade: Building the World Trade Organisation* Cameron May 2004

Stewart F. and Fitzgerald V., "The IMF and global economy: Implications for Developing Countries" *QEH Working Papers Series No. 3*

Stiglitz J. "Addressing Developing Country Priorities and Needs in the Millennium Round" R.Porter & P.Sauvé (eds) *Seattle, The WTO and the Future of the Multilateral Trading System*, Havard University Press (2000):31–60

Stiglitz J.E. *Globalisation and its Discontents* Penguin 2002

Stiglitz J.E. *Making Globalisation Work* Penguin 2006

Stiglitz J.E and Charlton A. *Fair Trade for all: How Trade can Promote Development* OUP 2005

Sutherland P. (ed) "The Future of the WTO: Addressing Institutional Challenges in the New Millennium" (Report by the Consultative Board to the WTO Director-General) Chapter VI WTO, Geneva (2005):49–60

Sutherland P. "The Doha Debacle" *Wall Street Journal* (*New York*) August 2, 2006

Sykes A. "Domestic Regulation, Sovereignty and Scientific Evidence Requirements;' A Pessimistic View" *3 Chi J. Int'l Law* (2002):353

Sykes A. "Comparative Advantage and the Normative Economics of International Trade Policy" 1 *JIEL no. 49* (2002):49–56.

The Economist *Guide to Economic Indicators – Making sense of economics* Fifth Ed. 2003

This Day Newspapers (Nigeria) (Editorial) "Reviewing the WTO Treaty" 28 October 2004: 11

ThisDay Newspapers Online (Nigeria) Editorial: "The ECOWAS Common Tariff" 30 July 2006 Online Archives at [http://www.thisdayonline.com]

Thomas J.S. and Meyer M.A. *The New Rules of Global Trade: A Guide to the WTO* Caswell Publishing 1997

Todaro M.P. *Economic Development* 5th Ed Longman Group UK Ltd 1994

Trachtman J.P. "The Domain of WTO Dispute Resolution", *40 Harvard Int'l L.J.* 2 (Spring 1999): 333–377

Trebilcock M.J. & Howse R. *The Regulation of International Trade* 2nd Ed. Routledge (1999); 3rd Ed. (2005)

Van den Bossche P. *The Law and Policy of the World Trade Organisation Texts, Cases and Materials*, CUP 2005

VanGrasstek C. "The African Growth and Opportunity Act: A preliminary Assessment" (Report for UNCTAD); UNCTAD/ITCD/TSB/2003/1

VanGrasstek C & Sauvé P, "The Consistency of WTO Rules: Can the Single Undertaking be Squared with Variable Geometry?" *JIEL. 9* (2006):837–64

Wade R. "The Doha talks must fail for the sake of the world's poor", (Comment) *The Guardian* (*London*) 3 July 2006.28.

Wert E., "The International Constitutional Order", *Intl & Comp LQ, Vol 55, Part 1* (January 2006); 51–76.

Wiener J. "World Trade Organisation's Identity Crisis: Institutional legitimacy and Growth Potential in the Developing World" *MJIEL 2 Issue 2* (2005):54–71

Winsham G. *The Evolution of International Trade Agreements* University of Toronto Press 1992

WTO Economic Research and Statistics Division (Staff Working Paper) "Special and Differential Treatment in the WTO: Why, When and How?" *ERSD–2004–03*, May 2004 Online at: http://www.wto.org/english/res_e/reser_e/ersd200403_e.doc

WTO: *A Handbook on the WTO Dispute Settlement System* Cambridge (2004)

WTO: *Understanding the WTO* WTO: Geneva (2006)

Yenkong N.H. "World Trade Organisation Dispute Settlement Retaliatory Regime at the Tenth Anniversary of the Organisation: Reshaping the "Last Resort" Against Non-Compliance" *JWT 40 no. 2* (2006): 365–384

Youssef H. "Special and Differential Treatment for Developing Countries in the WTO" *South Centre T.R.A.D.E. Working Paper 2* (June 1999)

Zleptnig S. "The Standard of Review in WTO Law: An Analysis of Law, Legitimacy and the Distribution of Legal and Political Authority" *European Integration Online Papers (EIoP)* 6 no. 17 (2002) Online at http://eiop.or.at/eiop/texte/2002–017a.htm

Other

Central Bank of Nigeria: *'Twenty Years of Banking in Nigeria'* 1979

Centre for Trade Law and Policy, Carleton University, Canada: 'From the GATT to the WTO: A Chronology. *Essential Documents in Commercial Diplomacy* – (Timeline): Online [http://www.carleton.ca/ctpl/Essential/timeline.htm]

EC: *'The European Consensus for Development'*, Joint Statement by the Council and the Representatives of the Governments of the Member States Meeting Within the Council,

The European Parliament and the Commission. Doc No. 14820/05 Annex 1 and Annex 11 DGE11

Europa: 'The World Trade Organisation' *The Europa World Year Book* Vol 1 AJ 42nd Ed. (Europa Publications 2001)

Federal Government of Nigeria: National Economic Empowerment Development Strategy Development Plan (2004) 'NEEDS' Document: Nigerian National Planning Commission, 'Meeting everyone's needs', (2004). Available online: [http://www.nigerianeconomy.com/downloads/part1.pdf#search='NEEDS% 20nIGERIA']

Federal Government of Nigeria Export Prohibition List (2003)

Federal Ministry of Commerce Nigeria: 'Trade Policy Review: Report by Nigeria'; also WTO Document *WT/TPR/G/147* 13 April 2005

Federal Ministry of Industry Nigeria; 'Industrial Policy of Nigeria (2003) Available online: [http://www.fmind.gov.ng/docs/industrial_policy.doc].

GATT: 1966 Decision on Procedures under Article XXIII 5 April 1966, GATT BISD (14th Supp)

GATT: Understanding Regarding Notification, Consultation, Dispute Settlement and Surveillance, 28 November 1979, GATT BISD (26th Supp)

GATT: 1982 Decision on Dispute Settlement Procedures, 29 November 1982, GATT BISD (29th Supp)

GATT: 1984 Decision on Dispute Settlement Procedures, 30 November 1984, GATT BISD (31st Supp)

GATT: Trade Policies for a Better Future (GATT: Geneva, 1985)

GATT: 1989 Decision on Improvements to the GATT Dispute Settlement Rules and Procedures, 12 April 1989, GATT (36th Supp)

GATT/WTO: Declaration on Trade Measures Taken for Balance-of-Payments Purposes adopted on 28 November 1979 (BISD 26S/205-209)

GATT: Annex 1, Notes and Supplementary Provisions to the GATT, Additional Article XVIII

GATT/WTO: Understanding on the Balance-of-Payments Provisions of GATT 1994

Georgetown University USA: 'History and Basic Information From the GATT to the WTO', Georgetown University Law Library January 2003; Online [http://www.ll.georgetown.edu/intl/guides/gattwto/gatt_1.html]

G8: The Gleneagles Communique 2005

Government of Japan: Japan's Medium-Term Policy on Official Development Assistance [Provisional Translation] Government of Japan, Feb 4 2005 Online [http://www.mofa.go.jp/policy/oda/mid-term/policy.pdf]

Greenpeace, Adelphi Research & Friends of the Earth Europe: "Joint NGO Briefing Paper: Is the WTO the only way?-Safeguarding Multilateral Environmental Agreements from international trade rules and settling trade and environment disputes outside the WTO" [2006]

IMF: World Economic Outlook, (May 1998) Statistical Appendix

League of Nations Photo Online Archive 'Chronology 1931' [http://www.indiana.edu/~league/1931.htm]

OECD: 'The DAC Journal Development Cooperation Report 2004', *Journal of the OECD Development Assessment Committee (DAC) Vol 6. No. 1* 2005

OXFAM Report: "Rigged Rules and Double Standards: Trade Globalisation and the Fight against Poverty" (2002)

Research & Information System for Developing Countries: *World Trade and Development Report 2006–Building a Development Friendly World Trading System* (RIS) 2006

South Centre: "A Historical Note' Special and Differential Treatment: Background and Policy Issues at Stake" Online: [http://www.southcentre.org/publications/snd/snd–03.htm#P295_44724]

US Government: US Congressional Research Service Report *'Foreign Aid – An Introductory Overview of US Programs and Policy'*, Updated April 15 2004 Library of Congress Order Code 98–916 [http://usinfo.state.gov/usa/infousa/trade/files/98–916.pdf]

UN: *United Nations, Commission of the European Communities, International Monetary Fund, Organisation for Economic Cooperation and Development and World Bank System of National Accounts 1993* (SNA 1993) Series F, No. 2 Rev. 4 (UN Publication Sales No. E. 94. XVII. 4

UN: *United Nations Standard Country or Area Code for Statistical Use*; Series M, No. 49, Rev. 4 (UN Publication, Sales No. M. 98. XVII. 9)

UNCTAD: *UNCTAD Hand Book of Statistics 2005* Doc No. TD/STAT.30

UNCTAD: *New Features of Global Interdependence* 2005, UN Trade and Development Report (2005)

UN Document: *International Cooperation at a Crossroads Aid Trade and Security in an Unequal World* UN Human Development Report (2005)

UNESCOR, 29 Session. Supp No. 2 at 64, 67; UN Doc E/1994/22 (1994)

UNEP: *Sustainable Trade and Poverty Reduction-New Approaches to Integrated Policy Making at the National Level* UNEP Publication (2006)

USCC: *Testimony of Senator Robert C. Byrd* United States China Economic and Security Review Commission (3–4 February 20050. Online: [http://www.uscc.gov/testimonies_speeches/testimonies/testimonies.php]

World Bank: *World Development Indicators* World Bank (2005)

World Bank: *Equity and Development* (2005) World Bank & Oxford University Press, 2006

WTO GATT Secretariat: "Multilateral Trade Negotiations Final Act Embodying the Results of the Uruguay Round of Trade Negotiations" *33 Intn'l Legal Materials 1125–1227* (April 15, 1994)

WTO: WTO Deletion of the International Dairy Agreement from Annex 4 of the WTO Agreement' *Decision of 10 Dec 1997 WT/L/251* (17 Dec 1997)

WTO: WTO Deletion of the International Bovine Meat Agreement from Annex4 of the WTO Agreement', *Decision of 10 Dec 1997, WT/L/252, 16 Dec 1997*

WTO: *Developing Countries in the WTO System-Guide to the Uruguay Round Agreements Part Five* 235–259 Online at: [http://www.wto.org/English/docs_e/legal_e/guide_ur_devinh_country_e.pdf]

WTO*: Summary of Provisions Contained in the Uruguay Round Agreements for the Differential and More Favourable Treatment of Developing and Least Developed Countries.* Available online: [http://www.wto.org/english/tratop_e/devel_e/anexii_e.doc]

WTO: *Guidelines for Appointment of Officers to WTO Bodies* Preparatory Committee for the World Trade Organisation Subcommittee on Institutional, Procedural and Legal Matters *PC/IPL/14* of 9 December 1994; revised in *WT/L/31* of 7 February 1995

WTO: Report of DSB Meeting Held in the Centre William Rappard, Geneva, *WT/DSB/M/21*, 5 August 1996

WTO: Working Procedure for Appellate Review WTO Document WT/AB/WP/5 of 4 January 2005. (Add: WT/AB/WP/W/8; WT/AB/WP/W/9)

WTO: Annual Report 2003

WTO: Annual Report 2005

WTO: WTO International Trade Statistics 2005

WTO: WTO International Trade Statistics 2006

WTO: Annual Report 2006

WTO: Nigeria Trade Policy Report *WT/TPR/G/39*, 8 June 1998

WTO: Trade Policy Review-Belize WT/TPR/S/134 (12 and 14 July 2004)

WTO: Trade Policy Review-European Communities *WT/TPR/S/136* (25 and 27 October 2004)

WTO: Trade Policy Review Nigeria: Report by the Secretariat *WT/TPR/S/147* (13 April 2005)

WTO: Trade Policy Review-Nigeria *WT/TPR/S/147* (11 and 13 May 2005)

WTO: Trade Policy Review-Trinidad and Tobago *WT/TPR/G/151* (14 and 16 September 2005)

WTO: Trade Policy Review: Angola (Government Report) *WT/TPR/G/158* 14 & 16 February 2006

WTO: Trade Policy Review-USA WT/TPR/S/160 (22 and 24 March 2006)

WTO: Trade Policy Review United Arab Emirates *WT/TPR/G/162* (24 and 26 April 2006)

WTO: *Implementation of Special and Differential Treatment Provisions in WTO Agreements and Decisions'* (Committee on Trade and Development) Doc No. WT/COMTD/W/77 (25 October 2000)

WTO: Doha Ministerial Declaration *WT/MIN(01)/DEC/1 20* November 2001, adopted on 14 November 2001 at the Doha Ministerial Conference, Fourth Session Doha (9–14 November 2001)

WTO: Doha Declaration Implementation-Related Issues and Concerns *WT/MIN(01)/17* adopted on 14 November 2001 at the Doha Ministerial Conference, Fourth Session Doha (9–14 November 2001)

WTO: Declaration on the TRIPS agreement and Public Health *WT/MIN(01)/DEC/2*, (14 Nov 2001)

WTO: Implementation of Special and Differential Treatment Provisions in WTO Agreements and Decisions. Mandatory and Non-Mandatory Special and Differential Treatment Provisions *WT/COMTD/W/77/Rev. 1/Add.1* [WTO 2001a] (21 Dec 2001)

WTO: Implementation of Special and Differential Treatment Provisions in WTO Agreements and Decisions: A Review of Mandatory Special and Differential Treatment Provisions *WT/COMTD/W/77/Rev.1/Add.*; [WTO 2001b] (21 Dec 2001)

WTO: A Corrigendum: Implementation of Special and Differential Treatment Provisions in WTO Agreements and Decisions-Mandatory and Non-Mandatory Special and Differential Treatment Provisions *WT/COMTD/W/77/Rev. 1/Add. 1/Corr. 1*, [WTO 2002a.] (4 Feb 2002)

WTO: Non-Mandatory Special and Differential Treatment Provisions in WTO Agreements and Decisions *WT/COMTD/W/77/Rev. 1/Add. 3*, 4 February 2002, [WTO 2002b]

WTO: Information on the Utilisation of Special and Differential Treatment Provisions (Committee on Trade and Development) Note by the Secretariat, Addendum; *WT/COMTD/W/77/Rev. 1/Add. 4*, 7 February 2002.

WTO: Communication from Zambia on behalf of the LDC group *TN/DS/W/17* (9 October 2002)

WTO: Decision on Implementation of Paragraph 6 of the Doha Declaration on the TRIPS Agreement and Public Health WT/*l/540* (1 Sep 2003)

WTO: Poverty Reduction-Sectoral Initiative in Favour of Cotton' Cancun Ministerial Conference *WT/MIN(03)/2* (10–14 Sep 2003)

WTO: Special and Differential Treatment for Least Developed Countries (Committee on Trade and Development) *WT/COMTD/W/135* (5 October 2004)

WTO: Hong Kong Ministerial Declaration *WT/MIN(05)/W/3/Rev. 2* (13–18 December 2005)

WTO: Hong Kong Ministerial Conference: *Doha Work Programme WT/MIN(05)/DEC* (22 December 2005)

WTO: *Reclaiming Development in the WTO Doha Development Round* A Submission by Argentina, Brazil, India, Indonesia, Namibia, Pakistan, the Philippines, South Africa, Venezuela (Committee on Trade and Development) 28 November 2005: *WT/COMTD/W/145* (1 December 2005)

WTO: Communication from the Bolivarian Republic of Venezuela, and Cuba: *"Irregularities Identified in the Negotiation and Decision Making Process at the Sixth WTO Ministerial Conference"*, of 7 February 2006: TN/C/7 WT/GC/105 (9 February 2006)

WTO: Committee on Trade and Development (*COMTD)Work Programme for 2006, WT/COMTD/56* (10 March 2006)

WTO: Communications from Zambia on behalf of LDCs (Committee on Agriculture Negotiation Group on Market Access) *TN/CTD/W/30; TN/MA/W/74; TN/AG/GEN/20* (12 June 2006)

WTO: An Enhanced Integrated Framework; Report of the Chairman of the Task Force on an Enhanced Integrated Framework Including Recommendations *WT/IFSC/W/ 15* (29 June 2006)

WTO: Recommendations of the Task Force on Aid for Trade *WT/AFT/1* (27 July 2006)

INDEX

Lightning Source UK Ltd.
Milton Keynes UK
UKOW051722230911

179184UK00001B/25/P